THE AUDIT SOCIETY

THE AUDIT SOCIETY

Rituals of Verification

MICHAEL POWER

OXFORD UNIVERSITY PRESS

1997

Oxford University Press, Great Clarendon Street, Oxford OX2 6DP

Oxford New York
Athens Auckland Bangkok Bogota Bombay
Buenos Aires Calcutta Cape Town Dar es Salaam
Delhi Florence Hong Kong Istanbul Karachi
Kuala Lumpur Madras Madrid Melbourne
Mexico City Nairobi Paris Singapore
Taipei Tokyo Toronto
and associated companies in
Berlin Ibadan

Oxford is a trade mark of Oxford University Press

Published in the United States by
Oxford University Press Inc., New York

British Library Cataloguing in Publication Data
Data available

Library of Congress Cataloging in Publication Data
Power, Michael.
The audit society : rituals of verification / Michael Power.
Includes bibliographical references.
1. Auditing. 2. Responsibility. 3. Management.
4. Organizational effectiveness. I. Title.
HF5667.P654 1997 96-50995
657'.45—dc21
ISBN 0-19-828947-2

1 3 5 7 9 10 8 6 4 2

Typeset by Best-set Typesetter Ltd., Hong Kong
Printed in Great Britain by
Bookcraft (Bath), Midsomer Norton, Somerset

For Claire, Giles, and Oliver

CONTENTS

LIST OF FIGURES

LIST OF ABBREVIATIONS

AAA	American Accounting Association
AAU	Academic Audit Unit
ACCA	Chartered Association of Certified Accountants
AICPA	American Institute of Certified Public Accountants
APB	Auditing Practices Board
APC	Auditing Practices Committee
ASB	Accounting Standards Board
ASC	Accounting Standards Committee
BATNEEC	Best Available Techniques Not Entailing Excessive Cost
BCCI	Bank of Credit and Commerce International
BRAP	Business Review And Planning
BSI	British Standards Institute
CA	Clinical Audit
CAG	Comptroller and Auditor General
CAJEC	Chartered Accountants Joint Ethics Committee
CEC	Commission of the European Community
CICA	Canadian Institute of Chartered Accountants
CIPFA	Chartered Institute of Public Finance and Accountancy
CPA	Certified Public Accountant
CPE	Continuing Professional Education
CVCP	Committee of Vice Chancellors and Principals
CWEC	Corporate Wide Environmental Care
DAS	District Audit Service
DTI	Department of Trade and Industry
EAD	Exchequer and Audit Department
EMAS	Environmental Management and Audit Scheme
EPA	Environmental Protection Agency
ESRC	Economic and Social Research Council
EU	European Union
FDA	Food and Drug Administration (USA)
FIMBRA	Financial Intermediaries and Money Brokers Regulatory Association
FMI	Financial Management Initiative
FSA	Financial Services Act
GAAP	Generally Accepted Accounting Practice

GAO	General Accounting Office
GDP	Gross Domestic Product
HAS	Health Advisory Service
HEFC	Higher Education Funding Council
HEQC	Higher Education Quality Council
HMIP	Her Majesty's Inspectorate of Pollution
ICAEW	Institute of Chartered Accountants in England and Wales
ICAI	Institute of Chartered Accountants in Ireland
ICAS	Institute of Chartered Accountants in Scotland
ICC	International Chamber of Commerce
ISO	International Standards Organization
JDS	Joint Disciplinary Scheme
JMU	Joint Monitoring Unit
LMS	Local Management for Schools
MAAG	Medical Audit Advisory Group
NACCB	National Accreditation Council for Certification Bodies
NAO	National Audit Office
NHS	National Health Service
NPM	New Public Management
PAC	Parliamentary Accounts Committee
RAE	Research Assessment Exercise
SIB	Securities and Investment Board
SRO	Self Regulating Organisation
SSI	Social Services Inspectorate
TQM	Total Quality Management
UFC	University Funding Council
UGC	University Grants Committee
UKAS	United Kingdom Accreditation Service
UNEP	United Nations Environmental Programme
VC	Vice Chancellor
VFM	Value for money

PREFACE

Books on auditing are generally intended to help the reader either to conduct an audit or to pass a professional examination on the subject (the two tasks are only loosely related). This means that auditing texts tend to be technical and that the field as a whole is distinctly unglamorous. When I mention that I am interested in auditing, academic colleagues smile politely and wonder how it could be intellectually engaging. This image of auditing as a dull field of work scarcely worthy of research is often reinforced by audit practitioners themselves. In the large firms, financial auditing has for many years functioned as a training ground in which the brightest and most ambitious are quick to move on to other things. Indeed, to be a pure audit enthusiast in a firm of accountants is to be viewed with some suspicion, if not ridicule. And yet one should not take this inferiority complex at face value. The French thinker Michel Foucault reminds us that the most boring practices often play an unacknowleged but fundamental role in social life. This book shows how this is undoubtedly true of auditing.

I enjoyed my four years in financial auditing. At times it was great fun. I met many interesting people and gained valuable experience about how businesses work. I learned many things, not least skills in eliciting information from reluctant and suspicious client staff. This has been helpful for the conduct of subsequent research. However, if the experience was positive, there were two big problems. First, I never really knew what auditing was for, other than a means of training people like myself. To be told by senior colleagues that the whole thing was common sense did not really help. Whose sense and how common was it? Second, I always found financial auditing puzzling in terms of the knowledge it delivered; the techniques seemed crude and often messy, sampling practices rarely corresponded to the text book and the production of working papers seemed at least, if not more, important than the production of credible proof. As auditors we would huddle on winter evenings in the worst part of the client premises producing . . . what?

The official story, on which I was periodically examined, stated that the financial audit was for the benefit of shareholders. But I never met one of these people and I doubt if they ever saw what I was doing on their behalf, which was probably just as well for everyone. Before I eventually left public practice, I began to see a side of audit which had little to do with my epistemological concerns: a growing emphasis on time management and client servicing with a view to creating further fee earning opportunities. What happened to knowledge?

This book grew out of these puzzling first-hand experiences of financial auditing. When I joined the London School of Economics in 1987 it would have been easy to have left them behind; auditing remains an unfashionable research specialism. But in the late 1980s the world changed. Auditing, for all the problems of image and status, was taking on new forms and being promoted in a wide variety of areas. How and why did auditing become so attractive to so many diverse groups? Do all these audits have something in common? How do they work? How can auditing be such a robust policy tool when it often seems to fail so spectacularly? And how do we begin to understand a society which seems to invest so heavily in such an instrument of regulation? Is Britain becoming an 'audit society'?

This book is an attempt to answer these questions. It is a book about auditing which does not tell you how to do one or how to pass an examination. For this reason I hope that it may be interesting to a wider audience, an audience of newly created auditees who have begun to experience at first hand the effects of the audit explosion. If the book is critical, this is primarily in the Kantian sense of trying to understand the conditions which have made an 'audit explosion' in Britain possible, a focus on the why and how of auditing. However, I am also critical in a more common sense meaning of the term; the audit explosion contains many dangers and the concept of an audit society suggests the pathologicality of excessive checking.

A project like this is risky. I have been accused of trying to make auditing too interesting; adding the word 'society' to anything is provocative yet it leaves everything to be said. Indeed, the attempt to see in the audit explosion matters of more general social and intellectual significance may simply reflect my own need to escape from the truth that auditing *really* is boring. I leave the reader to judge this point. Another risk is that, in attempting to look beyond financial audit into other fields, such as medicine and education, systematic conclusions are bought at the price of depth. Practitioners and academics in each particular field may find the analyses superficial but I rather hope that the strengths of the synoptic view will outweigh these weaknesses and that credible markers can be established for future research.

In this book I have tried to keep explicit theorizing to a minimum. Yet this is also a theoretical book whose arguments are not necessarily confined to the UK. In saying this, I am probably condemning myself to criticism from self-styled practical men and women as well as high theorists. But I hope that the text will appeal to both groups, offering the former occasion to reflect on that which they have always regarded as most concrete and secure, and providing the latter with an example of theorizing close up. Accounting practitioners may invoke ideas of what is common sense, but that 'common sense' has a history of formation and what is accepted today as obvious was not always so. Of necessity, practices like auditing and accounting must forget these complex histories as they continually remake themselves and create stories about how they function.

There is quite a lot of talk about theory in accounting research and opinions are diverse, ranging from an anti-theoretical hard empiricism to heavily theorized and politically committed work. Anti-theorists accuse others of needless obscurantism and intellectual flashing, while theorists point to the fact that theory and normative commitments are always there, acknowledged or unacknowledged. And then there is the constant image of accounting practice lurking in the background. Do academics really identify with practitioners, in some cases the sponsors of research, or are they more removed, looking in at accounting practice from the outside?

A proper history of these antagonisms, for which there is truth on all sides, would take the discussion well beyond the field of accounting research. For my own part, I believe that theoretical commitments subsist not so much in a set of explicit propositions to which one subscribes and which must be explicitly laid at the door of the reader, but as a certain style of addressing problems, of seeing and writing. Of course this theoretical lens or template can be made an explicit object of reflection, and stories of the methodological structure of research can be told. But there are definitely not two separate things, observing the world and then theorizing about it.

What is the relation between a book like this and audit practice itself? Is it merely critical or might it be useful? My answer to such questions is evasive and no doubt irritating. First, practices are themselves littered with strictly 'useless' elements and do not operate according to their efficient blueprints. Often we do not even understand practices well enough to be sure of what is or is not useful in reforming them. Second, it is usually easier to demand relevance and use-value than to know what would count as an answer. As an accounting academic one is constantly aware that demands from practice for useful research are often simply demands for excuses which rationalize and support that practice. Professions tend to be conservative whereas the best research is not. Third, things can always be useful in surprising and unanticipated ways, just as projects conceived with a specific use in mind may turn out to fail. One should be aware of research as a 'quick fix'.

So what, after all this, is the 'relevance' or 'use-value' of this book? Notwithstanding a few remarks on policy at the end of Chapter 6, the answer is that I really do not know. And yet, I believe that this gives the book the best chance of *actually* being useful.

A book with a single author is always a collective project. I have benefited enormously from the stimulating environment at the London School of Economics and from the support and encouragement of colleagues. I am grateful that Anthony Hopwood and Michael Bromwich saw fit to recruit a strange philosopher-accountant who could not really put the two halves

of his training together. I enjoyed an exciting period when the LSE established itself as an international focus for research into the social and institutional character of accounting practices. This period also required me to
make two somewhat uncomfortable changes. First, I had to be 'de-
professionalized' in order to look at accounting and auditing practices
objectively without becoming bewitched by their own terms of reference.
Second, I had to make an intellectual switch from philosophy to the
sociology of knowledge; the latter has proved to be a more fruitful starting
point for research on auditing and accounting practice. For both of these
difficult processes, the help and encouragement of able and sympathetic
colleagues was invaluable. If this casts me in the role of outsider to all but
the most reflective practitioner, it is also worth pointing out that the ideas
in this book emerged from discussions with practitioners themselves. To
repeat, a book is a collective project.

The book was written in the wonderful research environment of the
Wissenschaftskolleg zu Berlin, the Institute of Advanced Study in Berlin,
where I was fortunate to be a fellow during the 1995/6 academic year. It
was a rich and stimulating experience and there were many intellectual and
cultural temptations to deviate from my planned course of work. An enjoy-
able irony was that the *Kolleg* itself was audited during the year by the
Berlin authorities, the *Landesrechnungshof*, an event which gave my
research an added local relevance. I am grateful for the interest and encouragement of Wolf Lepenies, Joachim Nettelbeck and Reinhart Meyer-Kalkus
and for the administrative support provided by Christine von Arnim,
Barbara Sanders, Andrea Friedrich, Gesine Bottomley and many others
during my year in Berlin. A number of people have also provided invaluable detailed advice on the substance of this book. I would like to thank
Mary Morgan, Peter Miller, Christopher Napier, Christopher Pollitt, Claire
Sinnott and Liisa Uusitalo for their help and I hope that they may remain
pleased to be associated with the result.

Finally, it must be emphasized that books are not simply written, they are
imposed on the world. I would like to thank my family for tolerating the
intolerable. There is perhaps no better illustration of the economists'
concept of a 'free rider' than a father and husband who has decided to write
a book.

1

The Audit Explosion

People are constantly checking up on each other, constantly monitoring the ongoing stream of communicative exchanges and accounts that make up daily life. Normally, this process is unconscious and we do not feel that we are really doing it. But accountability and account giving are part of what it is to be a rational individual (Douglas, 1992a:132). It is through the giving and monitoring of the accounts that we and others provide of ourselves, and of our actions, that the fabric of normal human exchange is sustained. These accounts only become objects of explicit checking in situations of doubt, conflict, mistrust, and danger. Only then do we check restaurant bills carefully, make sure that the children have put on their car seat belts, see whether the ball was over the line on the action replay, go to the reference library, seek a second medical opinion, ask independent witnesses what really happened, take up references for a prospective employee, and even hire private detectives.

Methods of checking and verification are diverse, sometimes perverse, sometimes burdensome, and always costly. We normally reserve these actions for extreme cases. While it costs me little to check that my children have fastened their seat belts in the car, the use of a private detective to check up on a lover can lead to obsession, despair, and even financial ruin, regardless of whether doubts and suspicions are verified. And there are circumstances where checking and demands for proof are just not appropriate. A dinner party guest who constantly demands explanations and justifications for the manner in which the food was prepared will probably not be invited again. And when we ask a partner to prove the depth of their feelings for us we do not usually expect a detailed written account of all the favours and kindnesses that they have shown in the past.

Trust releases us from the need for checking. When I lend a friend five pounds I do not normally require a written agreement specifying interest payable, default conditions, and a due date for repayment. Nor do I usually make her formally accountable to me for what she does with the money. Nevertheless, a certain kind of accounting goes on between us, albeit implicitly and in the background. One can imagine a deterioration in the friendship if the money were not repaid. The financial loss is small but perhaps this behaviour regarding a small amount of money is a signal for other difficulties in the friendship.

Could one imagine a society, or even a group of people, where *nothing* was trusted and where explicit checking and monitoring were more or less constant? Even Popper's ideal community of scientists engaged in daily conjectures and refutation could not carry such attitudes back to their family lives or even to the cashier at the laboratory canteen. Pockets of doubt and checking may be created and institutionalized but surely not as an entire principle of social organization? The more one thinks about it, the more apparent it is that the imperative 'never trust, always check' could not be a universalizable principle of social order: constant vigilance is somehow autodestructive. Nothing could be produced collectively, human relations would be intolerable, individuals would need personally to check the capital adequacy of their banks on a daily basis. If we start hiring a private detective to follow the private detective who is following a lover, when does the need for checking stop? Of course, some societies have tried to institutionalize checking on a grand scale. These systems have slowly crumbled because of the weight of their information demands, the senseless allocation of scarce resources to surveillance activities and the sheer human exhaustion of existing under such conditions, both for those who check and those who are checked. In the end checking itself requires trust; the two concepts are not mutually exclusive.

Having said this, could one imagine a society without any checking at all, a society of pure trust where all accounts are taken at face value? This is equally difficult to conceptualize. Where expectations are disappointed is it not simply naive to carry on as before? When my trading partner does not pay, my bank collapses, the restaurant makes a 'mistake' with the bill, or an employee has falsified educational qualifications, is it not just silly to carry on trusting? Should we positively encourage our children to accept lifts from strangers? An unfaithful lover who is forgiven may come to be trusted once more but should a bank do the same for a defaulting debtor? In short, there are clearly many circumstances where we think that some checking and monitoring is justified and where it would be unreasonable not to learn from the experience of disappointed expectations. What we need to decide, as individuals, organizations, and societies, is how to combine checking and trusting. What kinds of activities should be checked? How much explicit checking is enough? How does checking affect those who are checked and when does the demand for monitoring become pathological? Can the benefits of checking be clearly demonstrated?

The difficulty with answering these questions is that checking up on each other is not simply a matter of technical expediency. It is also a cultural issue, a product of the communities in which we live and the forms of accountability, approval, and blame that constitute our normative environment. Different societies have developed patterns of institutionalized checking and trust to deal with activities where resources are exchanged or entrusted. For example, for companies which are financed by shareholders, a form of accounting has evolved which allows a check, or what is called an 'audit', to be made of the activities of the company. But the idea of audit need not be restricted to financial matters alone. I may be required to account for a particular activity not just in terms of money spent but also in terms of the activity itself. Someone may wish to check that the activity was carried out efficiently and whether it achieved its goals. Even though accountability in a general sense is built in to the very structure of human interaction and account giving is fundamental to everyday structures of reciprocity, concrete practices of checking or auditing can vary considerably. Much depends on what the community or society demands and this in turn is often a function of what it is prepared to trust and the types of risk to which it feels vulnerable.

During the late 1980s and early 1990s, the word 'audit' began to be used in Britain with growing frequency in a wide variety of contexts. In addition to the regulation of private company accounting by financial audit, practices of environmental audit, value for money audit, management audit, forensic audit, data audit, intellectual property audit, medical audit, teaching audit, and technology audit emerged and, to varying degrees, acquired a degree of institutional stability and acceptance. Increasing numbers of individuals and organizations found themselves subject to new or more intensive accounting and audit requirements. In short, a growing population of 'auditees' began to experience a wave of formalized and detailed checking up on what they do. It is the meaning, nature, and effects of this explosion of checking which are the subjects of this book.

In the United Kingdom the rate of growth of state audit bodies, for example the National Audit Office and the Audit Commission, has been striking since they were established in the early 1980s. At the same time, the rise of auditing in the medical field and the emergence of markets for environmental auditing and quality assurance have been prominent subjects of discussion. New schemes to realize accountability, such as Citizen's Charters, have been created and existing entities, such as charities, have been subjected to accounting and audit reform. Formal audit and evaluation mechanisms have been installed in universities and schools and within financial auditing itself the relaxation of audit requirements for small companies has been offset by the growth of assurance related services on the back of the basic audit product. Very few people have been left untouched by these developments; the need to give more and better accounts and to have these accounts checked by auditors has become widespread. New career opportunities in checking have emerged for individuals prepared to 'change sides'.

What does this 'audit explosion' (Power, 1994*b*) in the UK mean? Is there a systematic trend towards the extreme case described above—a society engaged in constant checking and verification, an audit society in which a particular style of formalized accountability is the ruling principle? One way to answer such a question would be to count the proportion of auditee income absorbed by monitoring activity or to count how many people are working in the industries of checking. This task would be complex, not least because of difficulties in defining the boundaries of audit work, but it would be feasible for a number of areas. However, useful as this data might be, such an exercise would only conceptualize the rise of auditing in quantitative terms. Relative to national income, this is probably not spectacular.[1] A quantitative approach like this would not capture the sense in which the growth of auditing is the explosion of an idea, an idea that has become central to a certain style of controlling individuals and which has permeated organizational life.

I suggest that the audit explosion in the UK refers to a certain set of attitudes or cultural commitments to problem solving. And the 'audit society' refers to the tendencies revealed by these commitments rather than an objectively identifiable state of affairs. In short, audit is an idea as much as it is a concrete technical practice and there is no communal investment in the practice without a commitment to this idea and the social norms and hopes which it embodies. Before turning to the substantive arguments of the book, it is necessary to clarify this a little further by making a short theoretical detour.

THE IDEA OF AUDIT: PROGRAMME AND TECHNOLOGY

It seems logical to start a study like this with a definition of auditing. In this way the field of inquiry can be delimited and made manageable from the start. But this is not easy or even desirable for two reasons. First, despite the general references to account giving and checking above, there is no precise agreement about what auditing really is, as compared with other types of evaluative practice, such as inspection or assessment.[2] It is wiser to speak of a cluster of definitions which overlap but are not identical. Second, one must in any case understand that the production of *official* definitions of a practice like auditing, in legislation or promotional documents, is an idealized, normative projection of the hopes invested in the practice, a statement of potential rather than a description of actual operational capability. Defining auditing is largely an attempt to say what it *could* be.

Having said this, it is necessary to start somewhere, even if only provisionally. The example of corporate account giving and checking was mentioned above. Companies produce accounts, otherwise known as financial statements, and these are audited by financial auditors. This type of financial auditing has been defined broadly as an 'independent examination of, and expression of opinion on, the financial statements of an enterprise'. Here are the most general conceptual ingredients of an audit practice: *independence* from the matter being audited; technical work in the form of *evidence* gathering and the examination of documentation; the expression of a *view* based on this evidence; a clearly defined *object* of the audit process, in this case the financial statements.

Systematic attempts have been made to explicate these presuppositions of audit practice. For example, Flint (1988) focuses on the conditions under which auditing is demanded. First, there must be a relation of accountability, i.e. the requirement for one party (the agent) to give an account of his actions to another party (the principal). Second, the relation of accountability must be complex such that principals are distant from the actions of agents and are unable personally to verify them. On this view audit is a form of checking which is demanded when agents expose principals to 'moral hazards', because they may act against the principals' interests, and to 'information asymmetries', because they know more than the principals. Audit is a risk reduction practice which benefits the principal because it inhibits the value reducing actions by agents. Audit will be undertaken by principals up to the point where its marginal benefits equal its marginal cost. Interesting economic models have also been developed which demonstrate that, under certain conditions, *agents* will rationally demand auditing and will voluntarily contract to be checked (Jensen and Meckling, 1976).

The economic approach to audit as a form of costly monitoring suggests that 'four people performing a cooperative task, say loading trucks, find that the risk of any one of them slacking is such that they hire a fifth to monitor their work' (Perrow, 1990:123). However, Perrow is critical of the way in which such models abstract from institutional context and argues that they assume a capitalist form of production which 'started because four workers could not trust each other'. The point is that different communities will institutionalize different forms of accountability; the categories of principal and agent can be filled out in a variety of ways. Who are the relevant principals: shareholders, local residents, taxpayers, future generations?

Such a relativization of the idea of audit is important and provides a reminder that definitions are attempts to fix a practice within a particular set of norms or ideals. Even practitioners in the same field argue about what auditing really is as compared with, say, investigation or assessment. For example, it has been suggested that auditing only exists where there is a clear 'verifiable assertion' i.e. a statement whose veracity can be objectively checked, and this distinguishes it from other forms of inquiry. Many attempts have also been made to break down the idea of auditing into its constitutive parts in order to outline different preoccupations. For example, distinctions can be formulated between *ex post* and *ex ante* auditing, between verification and review, between the audit of transaction regularity and value for money, between private and public sector audits, between financial and non-financial audits, between auditing, evaluation, assessment, and inspection, between big and small audits, between auditing and other forms of assurance services, between financial and environmental audits, between internal and external audits.

In later chapters I shall elaborate further on these distinctions. For the moment it is necessary to ask whether the 'idea' of audit can withstand such diversity. The concept of the 'audit explosion' suggests a systematic development which is common to a wide variety of functional areas but it is harder to characterize precisely and simply what this is. It could be said that this so-called 'audit explosion' is in fact a myth and that the widespread use of the word 'audit' is a trivial and accidental feature of the situation. Sceptics could point to the historical, conceptual, and technical diversity of monitoring practices mentioned above; many so-called 'audits' are really research, evaluation, or data gathering. However, the problem for such a sceptical view is to explain the power of the word.

At this point I can understand if the reader is a little puzzled. This study of auditing is actually unable to be precise about what it is talking about. However, and this is the point, it is precisely this fuzziness in the idea of auditing that enables its migration and importation into a wide variety of organizational contexts. The ambiguity of auditing is not a *methodological* problem but a *substantive* fact. Of course, not just any practice can be called an audit. Many of the examples of checking given above, such as hiring a private detective, would not ordinarily merit the title because a relation of accountability of some kind is lacking. But equally, the limits of the term are not always clear. And the reason that they are not always clear is that the word is not used simply *descriptively* to refer to particular practices, but *normatively* in the context of demands and aspirations for accountability and control. Some light can be shed on this issue by appealing to Rose and Miller's (1992) distinction between programmes and technologies, a distinction which will reappear throughout this book.[3]

Any practice can be characterized by *programmatic* (normative) and *technological* (operational) elements. The former relate to the ideas and concepts which shape the mission of the practice and which, crucially, attach the practice to the broader policy objectives which exist in the political sphere. At the level of programmes broad goals are formulated and it is more or less assumed that the practice is capable of serving these goals. This is the level at which audit practices are demanded by regulatory systems. It is the level at which a certain abstract ideal of what auditing is intended to achieve subsists in policy discourse, a vagueness which allows the idea to percolate into different policy arenas and to become attached to different goals.

Technologies or operations are the more or less concrete tasks and routines which make up the world of practitioners. Samples, checklists, analytical methods, and so on constitute an operational bedrock for audit practices, a body of knowledge which over the years has become codified and formalized, thereby allowing the audit process to be written up and recorded in a certain way. At the level of these technologies, practitioners constantly debate the efficiency of different methods and seek to elaborate cost-efficient solutions to the problem of providing assurance. Accordingly, even audit techniques are surrounded by sub-programmes and meta-discourses about their potential. Technical practice cannot be disentangled from the stories which are told of its capability and possibility.

The distinction between programmes and technologies is helpful in understanding that the audit explosion is the explosion of an idea which has become embodied in a wide range of programmes for accountability and control. The idea of audit has become an essential condition for talking about the prospective realization of a regulatory programme. In Chapter 2 it will be argued that this level of programmatic appeal to the idea of audit and the level of audit technology are only loosely coupled. The auditing field is characterized by a gap between the explosion of programmatic demands and expectations of auditing and the more 'local' stories which are told of its underlying operational capability.

The power of auditing is the vagueness of the idea and to comprehend the audit explosion it matters less what different audit practices 'really are', the endless agony of definitions, than how the idea of audit has assumed such a central role in both public and private sector policy: 'Affixing the right labels to activities can change them into valuable services and mobilize the commitment of internal participants and external constituents' (Meyer and Rowan, 1991:51). The label 'audit' has played an important role in many different organizational settings, such as hospitals, schools, water companies, laboratories, and industrial processes. In this sense, audit is much more than a natural and self-evident response to problems of principal–agent accountability. The idea of audit shapes public conceptions of the problems for which it is the solution; it is constitutive of a certain regulatory or control style which reflects deeply held commitments to checking and trust.

To focus on the programmatic dimension of auditing is to distance the analysis from a narrow technocratic and functional concern with operational matters. Auditing may be a collection of tests and an evidence gathering task, but it is also a system of values and goals which are inscribed in the official programmes which demand it. From this point of view auditing is always for something, an ill-defined goal which it may serve only imperfectly but through which its daily routines make sense and have value. However, it must also be recognized that the technological basis of auditing at the level of practice has its own sub-programmatic discourse which develops and affirms the efficacy of specific practices. This needs clarification.

All practices give accounts of themselves which are aspirational rather than descriptive. These accounts exist at the collective, or what can be called the 'official', level and for many years sociologists and others have been interested in digging into these accounts, showing what they leave out and demonstrating how a certain ideal and institutionally acceptable 'front stage' account of a practice is only produced after much 'back stage' work, which is rendered invisible. Many studies of science, medicine, and the law show how scientific, medical, and legal knowledge is produced and how the official accounts which these fields and their, often academic, representatives give are deficient in some way. What has been left out must be brought back in, even at the expense of the official account itself. The obviousness of practitioner common sense must be questioned by revealing the processes by which that common sense was formed.

This is an intellectually attractive programme at the same time as it is a source of irritation to practitioners. It is particularly attractive to apply some of these ideas to financial accounting and auditing since they are institutionalized forms of account giving in general. Like every other institutionalized field they produce official accounts of their account giving, rationalized meta-accounts of themselves and their potential. This meta-accounting is not simply a cynical public relations exercise but an intermediate and necessary aspect of the programmatic side of practice which connects concrete technical routines to the ideals which give them value. However, meta-accounting for the technical dimensions of a practice is not necessarily a neat and consistent matter.[4] It is often loosely coupled to programmatic ideals on the one hand and technical operations on the other.

Change and reform may be articulated at the level of meta-accounting or sub-programmes without any real change at the level of operations: 'Practices are carried out for reasons quite different from their accompanying stories. Incompatible stories are used to justify the same practice' (Cohen, 1985:157). Technical routines are loosely coupled to the purposes which they are intended to serve and rarely function according to the official blueprint. For example, in the case of accounting as a resource for improved decision making it has been shown that its production is often more important than its use and that it often frames decisions which have already been made. In contrast to official stories, accounting is constitutive of a certain style of communication and a key element of the myth structure of rationalized societies (Miller, 1994:9). Like the accounts for which it provides a check, auditing is also implicated in the framing of organizational life, in contributing to a style of evaluation from which organizations emerge as legitimate, safe, efficient, cost-effective, and so on.

This book provides a critical challenge to the audit explosion.[5] The underlying theoretical emphasis is to understand how official accounts of practices endure and constitute auditing as an institutionalized field of knowledge. Numerous strategies exist to connect the daily technical operations of practitioners to the different meta-accounts of their potential, thereby constructing and supporting the unities which we call practices. From this point of view, the meta-accounting of different auditing practices in technical terms is not simply descriptive but also performative, projecting and enacting ideals of their capability which legitimate the field of knowledge as a whole. But the auditing field of knowledge also operates in an environment which is constantly producing shocks, disturbances, and new programmatic demands. With this theoretical detour in mind, it is now time to introduce the main arguments of the book. They address the preconditions, causes, consequences, and prospects of the audit society.

PRECONDITIONS: FINANCIAL AUDITING

The audit explosion represents a certain kind of rupture in organizational life but it also draws from long standing practices of financial auditing. Ideal accounts of the financial audit described above function as a kind of paradigm and exert an influence over developments in other areas, even when this paradigm is modified. This ideal of financial auditing survives at a time when the practice itself has undergone a crisis in the last ten years. Large scale corporate collapses constantly generate inquiry and concern about the financial audit function and, increasingly, auditors are subject to litigation on the grounds that they have performed their task negligently. An extensive literature is developing on the subject of auditor liability and on the problems of auditor independence. In Chapter 2 I dig beneath these discussions and expose some of the assumptions which are common to both critics and supporters of financial auditing. In particular, a certain way of problematizing audit activity allows the regulatory mission of auditing to remain relatively untouched by particular examples of failure. This is the great puzzle of financial audit practice; it has never been a more powerful and influential model of administrative control than now, at a time when many commentators talk of an auditing crisis. It is paradoxically but necessarily both a success and a failure story.

Chapter 2 briefly considers the history of financial auditing and draws attention to the uneasy and shifting relationship between audit practice and the programmatic goal of detecting fraud. If official meta-accounts of auditing overemphasize the goal of detecting fraud, then programmatic expectations may be created in excess of those that it can really satisfy. Practitioners refer to this as an 'expectations gap'. On the other hand, if these stories of financial auditing reject the goal of detecting fraud, then it will be asked whether auditing has any value at all. This dilemma provides an illustration of an issue which is generally instructive: a loose coupling in the auditing field between accounts of potential and operational capability. Furthermore, this loose coupling supports a certain ambiguity about the audit process and its objectives which in turn supports practitioner discretion. In this way the 'expectations gap' is a resource for the auditing field and not merely a problem. The history of financial auditing, and of the development of official guidance on the auditors' responsibility for the detection of fraud, reveals a complex process of constructing a credible, if fragile, role for the auditor between high and low expectations.

It is also argued that some kind of expectations gap is, in any event, a constitutive feature of practices like auditing whose criteria of effectiveness are opaque and which therefore invest heavily in due process. I refer to this somewhat polemically as 'the essential obscurity' of auditing and illustrate its implications in the context of financial services auditing. The power of the idea of audit and its ready exportability from the financial auditing context depends on a certain vagueness about its scope and meaning. Financial auditing is not simply a practice which is applied in new contexts, although this has been part of the audit explosion. There is rather a spillover effect at the programmatic level which takes place through general ideas about the audit process as well as through the transfer and adaptive reception of specific routines and procedures. In sum, Chapter 2 sets the scene for a broader consideration of the audit explosion by introducing the supply side features of the auditing field which are developed further in Chapters 4 and 5.

CAUSES: DEMANDS FOR GOVERNANCE
AND ACCOUNTABILITY

Chapter 3 argues that the audit explosion has its conditions of emergence in transformations in conceptions of administration and organization which straddle or, better, dismantle the public–private divide. The so-called New Public Management, related shifts in regulatory style and initiatives in quality management have all, in overlapping ways, provided the conditions under which very similar forms of monitoring practice have been demanded. By virtue of pushing control further into organizations, relying on the cognitive and economic resources of self-control, markets for internal and external auditing have been created to satisfy the need to connect internal organizational arrangements to public ideals.

The forms in which these markets have developed are different but they all have something to do with making individuals and organizations accountable, that is, they require the giving of 'auditable accounts'. The audit explosion has its roots in a programmatic restructuring of organizational life and a new 'rationality of governance' (Rose and Miller, 1992). Audit has become a benchmark for securing the legitimacy of organizational action in which auditable standards of performance have been created not merely to provide for substantive internal improvements to the quality of service but to make these improvements externally verifiable via acts of certification. As the state has become increasingly and explicitly committed to an indirect supervisory role, audit and accounting practices have assumed a decisive function. The state cannot play this indirect role without assuming the efficacy of these practices at the foot of a regulatory hierarchy. Audit is not simply a solution to a technical problem; it also makes possible ways of redesigning the practice of government.

Value for money (VFM) audits play an important role in this process but, like financial audits, they too are constituted by a certain vagueness which makes for considerable discretion in their implementation. VFM auditing is more than just a neutral monitoring technique. It is bound up with programmes to shape the performance of the auditee in terms of economy, efficiency, and effectiveness. As a consequence, organizations such as the UK National Audit Office and the Audit Commission have acquired an important role, not merely in the implementation of official policy but also in its interpretation. Chapter 3 also addresses the extension of the quality assurance model into the environmental auditing field and draws attention to the crucial role played by management control systems in making a certain style of regulation and control possible which is common to auditing in many areas. Overall, audit is a practice whose effectiveness is demanded and presupposed by regulatory systems and Chapter 3 discusses the various programmes through which this demand is articulated.

MEANS: THE AUDIT PROCESS

Although Chapter 2 emphasizes the essentially elusive epistemological character of auditing, this is not to say that the procedures and routines through which audits are operationalized are in any way vague. Indeed, they are often very precise. The issue is how technical routines like the sampling of purchase invoices, the circularization of debtors, the assessment of inherent risks and so on actually come to be regarded as constituting 'reasonable' practice. Most practitioners do not have the luxury of asking such questions; techniques constitute the 'common sense' of practice. They may be applied well or badly and they may not be ideal, but they contribute to the production of assurance. The question which is addressed in this chapter is how such routines can be regarded as *systemically* effective. This is a question which points to the social support for 'best practice'. Auditing is a practice which must work because it is demanded. Therefore official meta-accounts of its efficacy must be given which suggest that this demand can be met.

Whereas Chapter 3 dealt with the programmes which demand auditing, Chapter 4 deals with the sub-programmes or meta-accounts of the technical efficacy of auditing. Three key areas for auditing knowledge are analysed; sampling, reliance on external expertise, and the assessment of internal control systems. It is argued that sampling in its general sense is an essential component of auditing. Audits have value because they seek to draw general conclusions from a limited examination of the domain under investigation. But despite statistically credible foundations for sampling, audit practice is driven by economic pressures to derive more, or at least as much, assurance from fewer inputs. Financial auditing has surrounded itself with stories of efficiency gains, the most recent example of which has been the development of approaches which focus on high risk areas.

Reliance on other experts enables the unauditable to be auditable by creating a chain of opinions in which the auditor distances himself from the first order judgements of the expert. The knowledge of, say, chartered surveyors, actuaries, and management can be 'black boxed' and subject to various tests for reliability. In this way reliance on others substitutes for directly checking the thing itself. This indirect relation between auditing and its object also applies in the case of internal management control systems. For many years auditors have focused upon control systems rather than directly examining large quantities of transactions; they have checked the systems which allow direct checking. In the 1980s this 'control of control' systems became generalized within quality assurance programmes. Detailed conceptions of service quality may be very different if a supermarket is compared to a hospital. But the general principles of quality control systems for these organizations can be made to look similar and enable them to be compared at an abstract level. In this way, the systems audit approach which underlies quality assurance programmes is not just a technical innovation. Abstraction has facilitated portability into different organizational contexts at the same time as it has enabled audits in complex fields.

What emerges from these three cases is a view of auditing as a collection of pragmatic and humble routines which may add to confidence about the veracity of statements made by the auditee but not in a way that can be easily quantified. Verification emerges as a more negotiated and interactive practice than is commonly imagined. The three cases demonstrate how auditing in general has to be made to look as if it works, as if it implements the programmes which demand it. Hence the need for an official self-accounting process which binds the atomistic operational components of auditing into a whole. And, where this is successful, a certain paradigm of knowledge is created which can become taken for granted, adapted, and exported to new arenas.

EFFECTS: THE CONSEQUENCES OF AUDITING

While Chapter 4 concerns the construction of an audit knowledge base which constitutes 'best practice', Chapter 5 analyses the manner in which auditing works by virtue of actively *creating* the external organizational environment in which it operates. It is here that a number of the most important themes of the audit explosion are visible. Audit is never purely neutral in its operations; it will operationalize accountability relations in distinctive ways, not all of which may be desired or intended. New motivational structures emerge as auditees develop strategies to cope with being audited; it is important to be seen to comply with performance measurement systems while retaining as much autonomy as possible.

Chapter 5 argues that the consequences of auditing can be analysed schematically in terms of *decoupling*, where audits are rendered ineffective, and *colonization*, where they are effective in unintended ways. Three cases are examined in which these consequences are visible: higher education, medicine, and financial audit itself. These three examples suggest the growing role of systems-based approaches to auditing which support abstract managerial values at the expense of other cultures of performance evaluation. Nowhere is this issue more apparent than in the audit of 'effectiveness' or performance. It is well known that in many service sectors the notion of effectiveness is not easily calibrated and may be relative to different bodies of knowledge. Here there is a problem of combining financial and non-financial logics of evaluation. There is some evidence that VFM audits tend to prioritize that which can be measured and audited in economic terms—efficiency and economy—over that which is perhaps more ambiguous from this point of view—effectiveness or performance. In the end auditing in general, and the auditing of performance in particular, may have dysfunctional side-effects and there is a need for a greater empirical understanding of the consequences of audit. In short, auditing needs to be evaluated.

PROSPECTS: THE AUDIT SOCIETY

Chapter 6 moves the argument into the territory of social theory more generally and the themes of democracy, trust, and risk. It is argued that the audit explosion, driven by programmatic commitments to greater accountability is far from contributing to transparency and democracy. Many audit reports communicate little more than the fact that an audit has been done and the reader is left to decode specialized and cautious expressions of opinion. The essential epistemological obscurity of audits described in Chapter 2 is reflected and reproduced in the varied forms of reporting which it generates. Rather than providing a basis for informed dialogue and discussion, audits demand that their efficacy is trusted. Furthermore, audits themselves are necessarily trusting practices because they co-opt management systems into the monitoring process. This style of control can be contrasted with forms of inspection and, although the distinction is not always sharp, the audit society is certainly not the surveillance society (Dandeker, 1990).

Chapter 6 argues that the fashion for auditing signifies a distinctive, if unevenly distributed, phase in the development of advanced economic systems as they grapple with the production of risks, the erosion of social trust, fiscal crisis and the need for control—all under the umbrella of accountability. The 'audit society' motif refers to a collection of systematic tendencies and dramatizes the extreme case of checking gone wild, of ritualized practices of verification whose technical efficacy is less significant than their role in the production of organizational legitimacy. Does institutionalized checking trust, and make use of, order which is 'there and which is constantly being recreated' (Van Gunsterten, 1976) or do its own imperatives of auditability create dysfunctionalities? Are stories of quality a cover for increasing mediocrity? The answer to these questions is ultimately a matter for further empirical inquiry; this book seeks only to place them on the agenda.

2

Fraud, Expectations, and the Rise of Financial Audit

INTRODUCTION

An analysis of tendencies towards an audit society must begin with a consideration of financial auditing. Financial auditing practice has a much longer history than many of the other developments considered in this book and the large firms of accountants, in which many financial auditors work, have become influential advisory institutions throughout the world.[1] Thus financial auditing has provided the model which has influenced the design of auditing practice in many other fields. Although environmental, medical, or value for money audits are conceived as distinct from financial auditing, the latter continues to exert its normative influence as a centre of gravity for debate and discussion. And it is in the context of financial auditing that the dependency of acts of verification on judgement and negotiation is most apparent.

The power of the financial auditing model lies in its benchmarking potential for other audit practices. In part this potential is realized indirectly through the work of accountant advisors, for whom the financial auditing model is a fundamental component of their expertise and whose advice in areas of control is shaped by it. But the influence can also be direct as entities such as hospital trusts, privatized industries, charities, and many other organizations become subject to an intensification of financial control and reporting requirements. This is an expanding domain, not just of neutral checking but also of judgement and of an evaluation of the fundamental purposes of organizations.

Paradoxically, given the influential role of the financial auditing model suggested above, its status as a practice is unclear. What do audits produce and how are they effective? In this chapter it will be argued that, below the wealth of technical procedure, the epistemic foundation of financial auditing, i.e. the relation between its inputs and the production of assurance, is essentially obscure. Ultimately financial auditing requires that the judgements of auditing experts are trusted. In the first instance the historical development of auditing, and its origins in response to problems of control and trust, must be considered. Secondly, the argument focuses on the close association between financial auditing and the objective of preventing and detecting fraud. Financial auditing is subject to expectations and demands which are, justifiably or otherwise, often disappointed. Nevertheless, the official procedural knowledge base of auditing has evolved in response to scandals and corporate failures in such a way that the essential puzzle of what audits produce—their effectiveness—remains hidden from view as an article of faith.

Finally despite, and probably because of, this puzzle it is argued that financial auditing maintains itself as an institutionally credible system of knowledge. Notwithstanding crisis and scandal it satisfies the aspirations and demands of a variety of regulatory programmes. Particular audits may fail but the system as such cannot. The possibility of effective auditing is necessarily presupposed by regulatory intentions.

A BRIEF HISTORY OF CORPORATE
FINANCIAL AUDITING

Auditing in one form or another has existed as long as commercial life itself; even the earliest forms of writing seem to have been accounting documents. In Chapter 1 an ahistorical model of the demand for auditing was considered: when the economic resources of one party are entrusted to another, human nature is assumed to be weak, untrustworthy and in need of some kind of check. In short, the need for principals to monitor agents gives rise to auditing. Because of the remoteness and complexity of the subject matter of auditing, principals are unable to do this monitoring themselves and require the services of an auditor (AAA, 1973; Flint, 1988).

There is much historical variation around this basic model. The earliest financial audits seem to have been oral in form and judicial in structure. The auditor would stand in judgement over a party giving the account; hence the original 'aural' meaning of auditing in which the aim was to establish the trustworthiness of agents.[2] Over time, no doubt as the volume and complexity of transactions increased, audit practice co-evolved with the development of accounting records and statements which acquired evidential status as a supplement to oral traditions of proof. This reflects a more general shift in the idea of evidence and proof from testimony to documentation (Hacking, 1975): '[I]n preindustrial society, probative and other legal requirements may have been as influential as the needs of business decision making in determining the form, content and treatment of accounting records' (Mills, 1987:108). As far as thirteenth-century manorial accounting was concerned, the audit process emerged as a legal remedy in which the disputed liability of the accountor could be determined. It has been suggested that 'this power of committal is testimony to the status of the thirteenth century auditor' (Noke, 1981:150).

There is general agreement that modern financial auditing, as a discrete practice distinguishable from accounting, began to take shape from the middle of the nineteenth century. The emergence of corporate entities in which ownership and control were separated provided a natural stimulus for financial auditing and the development of increasingly detailed disclosure requirements for financial statements provided the 'product' whose quality the audit process was concerned to attest. But beyond these generalities the story is complex. In the nineteenth century, statutory requirements for auditing were introduced and repealed following much debate and discussion about 'public interest' organizations, such as banks and railways (Parker, 1990). Furthermore, in the second half of this century, professional accounting associations were taking shape in response to state demands for corporate control. From a base in insolvency work, the accounting profession grew through the increased demand for its audit services.

By the time of the Companies Act 1948, the statutory shape of auditing requirements in the UK was clear; an audit process for every limited company was to culminate in an opinion on whether the financial statements of an enterprise gave a 'true and fair' view. The auditor was also required to be a member of one of the professional bodies recognized for this purpose and was given a number of rights and duties which would support his independence and enable the discharge of the audit function. Where auditors had once been drawn from the ranks of shareholders themselves (Napier, forthcoming) independence emerged as a dominant and controversial value for the integrity of the audit process.

The modern external audit has been described as an independent examination of, and expression of opinion on, the financial statements of an enterprise by a qualified auditor. Over time, this general definition has been filled out and adjusted in various ways, but the core idea of independent examination remains. Guidance from associational bodies in many countries on matters of independence, on technical aspects of examination, on the form of the audit report to the principal and on many other aspects of the auditors' work has been developed. Many of these official documents have evolved as a codification of 'best practice' or, in the case of the UK, have been borrowed from the USA. Only in recent years in the UK has the statutory requirement for all companies to undergo an audit been relaxed, although this has been offset by the reform and intensification of existing statutory audit functions, particularly in specialized and highly regulated areas such as banking and insurance.

This brief history of auditing is somewhat sanitized. Auditing was a practice long before it was able to give an 'account' of itself in anything approaching a conceptual fashion. When feudal lords and shareholders conducted their own audits, matters were sufficiently simple to them as insiders that the audit simply corresponded to their own 'common sense' judgement. However, as the judgements of the amateur auditor became displaced by those of the professional, justificatory discourses and technical innovations have emerged—often in the wake of crisis and scandal. Furthermore, when one looks more closely at the history of auditing and compares it with present day discussions, it is striking that many of the problems and preoccupations are the same.[3] It is as if certain difficulties are endemic to auditing, not least in terms of programmatic expectations about its scope and whether this includes the requirement to detect fraud. Before considering this problem in detail, it is necessary to address the evolving technical base of audit.

VERIFICATION AND INTERNAL CONTROL[4]

Most contemporary guidance on the audit evidence process contains a general requirement that the auditor obtain relevant and reliable audit evidence sufficient to enable an opinion to be formed on the financial statements. This concept of *sufficiency* can be further broken down into two components:

(1) *Operational scope* i.e. how many transactions need to be tested?
(2) *Operational depth* i.e. what kinds of tests must be performed on the transactions selected?

These two operational issues must be addressed either explicitly or implicitly and relate in part to the economic base of audit practice. For any given resource allocated to auditing activity, fewer transactions can be tested if the testing process is more detailed. In short, operational scope and depth must usually be traded off against one another.

Throughout the second half of the nineteenth century discussion about the audit process in professional journals focused largely on point (2) above and on the question of the extent to which the auditor must go 'beyond the books', beyond an essentially arithmetical process, to determine the correspondence between financial statement items and events with an economic and legal basis. To the voice of leading practitioners was added judicial criticism of the methodology of auditing for being 'mechanical' and for involving no comparison of accounts with an underlying reality. An example is the case of the *Leeds Estate Building and Investment Company* in 1887 in which the auditor had certified that the accounts were 'a true copy' of the books, but had not undertaken a detailed examination as required by the company's articles of association. The judgement was that it was the auditor's duty to enquire into the substantial accuracy of the balance sheet provided by management, not merely its arithmetical correctness (Chatfield, 1977:116).

The case of the *London and General Bank* a few years later reinforced this view despite the fact that the legislature continued to define the audit role in terms of showing that the accounts corresponded with the books (Chandler *et al.*, 1993:449–50). So whereas many early audits may have been thorough in terms of operational scope, they were regarded as increasingly inadequate during the nineteenth century as regards operational depth. The testing performed was simply internal to the bookkeeping system and was regarded as being of insufficient quality. Over time, further judicial author-ity was given to a variety of procedures which, in essence, served to define evolving forms of 'reasonable practice', such as the requirement to attend company stocktakes (see Chandler *et al.*, 1993:454).[5]

Towards the end of the nineteenth century, financial auditing began to emerge as a codified body of operational doctrine and Dicksee's *Auditing* assumed the status of a practice manual in Britain. This is Dicksee on oper-ational matters:

Before dealing with the various methods to be adopted to ensure the detection of errors it will perhaps be not out of place to enquire what is the extent to which an Auditor is expected to carry out his research. This will naturally vary according to the circumstances of each individual case; but, even allowing for this, the greatest diversity of opinion obtains, some claiming that an auditor's duty is confined to a comparison of the Balance Sheet with the books while others assert that it is the Auditor's duty to trace every transaction back to its first source. Between these two extremes every shade of opinion may be found; and among others, the opinion of most practical men: for—were the Auditor's functions limited to a certification that the Balance Sheet submitted to him was in accordance with the books, it would be difficult to conceive why the old-world amateur Auditor should have been found so lamentably wanting. On the other hand, it cannot be denied that (except in con-cerns of comparative insignificance) a minute scrutiny of every item would be quite impossible to the Auditor although it is in the highest degree desirable that every undertaking should possess the means of making such an examination for itself (Dicksee, 1892:7).

This complex and extensive statement by one of the founding fathers of modern financial auditing is revealing in a number of respects and contains the seeds of modern audit practice. First, despite the judgement in the *Leeds* case a few years earlier, it seems that practitioners were by no means unanimous about the technical basis of their craft and, like all practitioners, probably resistant to externally imposed change in the form of codified practice. Second, the problem of the operational scope or extent of audit testing in terms of (1) above is conceived largely as a problem of what it is practically (and economically) feasible to do. There is no rationalization of the scope of audit work in terms of formalized 'sampling' at least until the 1930s (see Chapter 4 for a more extended discussion of sampling).

It is also in this first edition of Dicksee that an important dimension of modern auditing comes into view: reliance on the self-imposed control environment of the auditee as a basis for limiting testing. Internal checking and accounting system design have a long administrative history, particularly in the railway industry. However, it is only in the late nineteenth century that the idea is developed that these arrangements may be useful for the audit process. Thus, 'to the intelligent auditor . . . who has grasped his system thoroughly it is generally practicable to dispense with some portion of the mechanical means of checking . . . a proper system of internal check frequently obviates the necessity for a detailed audit' (Dicksee, 1892:8).

This is the origin of the modern selective audit, premissed on the control systems of the auditee (although perhaps Dicksee's ideas were ahead of the practitioners of the day, his primary audience in this text). According to Lee, during the period 1881–1941, financial auditing consisted in the verification of financial accounting records' accuracy. He argues that selective testing only begins to emerge in the 1930s—forced upon the auditor by virtue of an expansion in the volume of business by companies: 'The auditor was finding that instead of checking the arithmetical accuracy of every transaction, document or entry, he could verify these factors on a test basis if he first evaluated the strength of internal control' (Lee, 1986:162). It is therefore suggested that from the 1930s, large companies which had established systems of internal control became operational partners in the financial audit process.

The 'systems audit' approach, in which the auditor would attend to the quality of the company internal controls by conducting tests of control compliance, became conventional practitioner wisdom.[6] However, it is also at this point that the audit process begins to disengage itself from the transactional realities which underly these control systems; the system becomes the primary auditable object. This is an important theme which will be taken up in succeeding chapters. The systems approach also introduces the problem of defining the scope of the internal control system relevant to the financial audit. Hay (1993) shows how official definitions of internal control have varied over time and recent debates in the UK, about how to interpret the Cadbury Code requirement that directors maintain an effective system of internal control, suggest that such definitions are always controversial (see Chapter 3 for more detail).

To conclude, the history of audit practice, insofar as this can be inferred from text books and commentaries,[7] is a history of attempts to grapple with operational problems of inference subject to economic constraint. This history also reflects a tension between increasingly precise codification of the operational dimensions of the audit task and persistent demands for expert judgement and discretion to be preserved. Perhaps nowhere is this tension more pronounced than in questions about the very purpose of auditing itself.

AUDITING, FRAUD, AND EXPECTATIONS

The Problem of Objectives

There has always been widespread debate about what the financial audit process is for. One view is that early forms of the audit process involved looking at every transaction with the objective of proving primarily that assets had not been misappropriated (fraud) and only secondarily, if at all, forming some view of the management representations of performance in using those assets. Such a story points to the close association between financial auditing and the detection of fraud and error. This is an association which has generated an almost continual politics of financial auditing on the question of objectives.

If one inspects the many editions of Dicksee's *Auditing*, the detection of fraud seems to have been a primary objective of auditing until well into the twentieth century when it became a derived or secondary objective. This is consistent with Lee's (1986) view that it is not until after 1941 that the provision of an opinion on the financial statements finally becomes the primary role of the audit. As company management gradually became aware of its responsibility for preventing fraud and error, the primacy of fraud detection for the external financial audit began to shift. However, this version of events is contested by Chandler *et al.* (1993) who point to the existence of financial statement verification as early as 1840. According to their interpretation, the detection of fraud subsequently became important as an issue, and was registered in texts such as Dicksee's, as a consequence of the wave of corporate collapses in the late nineteenth century and was then never fully revised out of these texts to correspond to changes in practitioner sentiment. In the USA, there is a similar issue: the 1912 edition of Montgomery's (1905) *Auditing*, the first 'home' edition, stated that the primary objective of auditing is to ascertain 'the financial condition and earnings of an enterprise for various parties'. Only after 1940 is the confusion over audit objectives finally resolved and fraud detection is generally agreed not to be a primary objective (Brown, 1962).

If the world were a tidy place, one might expect that this change in primary audit objectives, whenever it occurred, would map on to underlying changes in the audit process itself, such as the switch from 100 per cent testing towards some kind of selective sampling. In other words, the normative objectives of auditing would somehow match its operational self-understanding. But despite attempts to run these two issues in parallel, and there is a certain logic in doing so, one is always struck by the extent to which technical discussion and debates on objectives are decoupled from each other. There are good reasons for this. One set of issues is orientated towards the level of practice, the other concerns the level of programmatic intentions. In Chapter 1 it was suggested that there is a looseness of fit between these two levels: the role that is shaped for and demanded of auditing may have only a slender relation to its technical capabilities. As long as the latter are not too precisely specified, it can always be assumed by governments, regulators, and members of the public that auditing can just do what it wishes.

Historical studies which attempt to specify when the explicit objectives of financial auditing changed necessarily attend to a small portion of the social reality of auditing. What is stated in textbooks and commentaries by auditors themselves is one thing. What a society, or parts of it, may demand and expect from audit practice is another. One can trace in the texts of Dicksee, Montgomery and other commentators a certain kind of transformation *within* auditing about its objectives and one can argue about when this really happened. But this is not to say that this transformation is well understood by those whom the audit process is intended to serve. Today it remains true that most people, when asked about auditing, will tend to associate it with the search for fraud. And when auditors fail to uncover fraud which subsequently comes to light, these same people will assume that the audit process has failed in some way.

This issue of the objectives of audit has been described in terms of an 'expectations gap'. The gap is between what the public expects—the detection of fraud—and what auditors claim to be delivering—an opinion on the financial statements which appeals to notions such as 'fairness' or 'true and fair' (e.g. see KPMG Peat Marwick McLintock, 1990; Humphrey, 1991; Humphrey *et al.*, 1992). Audit practitioners have mostly, until very recently, claimed that the problem lies with the misunderstanding of the public. They also argue that, on grounds of cost and technical feasibility, the primary responsibility for the detection and prevention of fraud lies with management and its systems. Attempts to build this view into official audit guidance are revealing.

Developing Audit Guidance on Fraud

The late 1980s and early 1990s will be remembered as a crucial period for financial auditing in the UK. The Bank of Credit and Commerce International (BCCI) was closed by the Bank of England and the Maxwell business empire collapsed. Both events, which were prominent but by no means isolated, fuelled the ongoing debate about what financial auditing is really for. Research into the 'expectations gap' was commissioned which culminated, as an initial measure, in a new form of words for the auditor's report (APB, 1993). This was devised to educate readers on the difference between the directors' and the auditors' duties under company law and to draw attention to the test basis of auditing. However, for some years prior to this efforts were underway to develop technical guidance on the question of the auditors' responsibility for the detection of fraud. These efforts provide a useful case study in the politics of financial auditing and the problem of objectives.[8]

Fraud, which has no definition in UK law, generally involves the theft of assets coupled to a falsification of the books of account. Furthermore, it is important to distinguish between employee and senior management fraud. There is some agreement that responsibility for the former may be reasonably delegated to management control systems. The fundamental operational issues for external auditors arise in the context of senior management fraud and deliberate mis-statement.

In 1985 a working party of the Institute of Chartered Accountants in England and Wales (ICAEW) was established to address the whole issue of auditors' responsibilities regarding fraud. The pressures for this initiative arose in part from criticisms of the audit function following the collapse of the Johnson Matthey Bank (Moran, 1986:163–77). The ICAEW working party reported to the Department of Trade and Industry (DTI) in late 1985 and resisted any explicit extension of the auditor's role, largely on the grounds of cost and practicality. The working party proposed instead that large companies should be required by statute to maintain adequate systems of internal control. The proposal was rejected at the time but the concept has influenced financial services legislation and the recommendations of the Committee on the Financial Aspects of Corporate Governance (Cadbury Committee, 1992). Financial auditors have always pleaded for an effective sharing of liability between management and auditor, although without wishing to push this so far as to devalue the external audit.

It took a further three years for the professions' self-regulatory body to issue draft guidance on the auditor's responsibility for detecting fraud and other irregularities. This document was subsequently modified and published as a full operational guideline in February 1990, five years after the working party had reported to the DTI (APC, 1990a). Needless to say, management responsibility for establishing adequate systems of internal control is emphasized, but it is acknowledged that the auditor must plan the audit to provide a 'reasonable expectation' of detecting material mis-statements. 'Materiality' has been interpreted qualitatively in professional guidance as the degree of tolerable or acceptable error in financial statements but, like the term 'reasonable expectation', is not precisely specified beyond this. In short, the general question as to whether auditors have a responsibility to detect fraud hangs on particular interpretations of these terms. The guidance document is significant because it does not deny that the auditor has a duty to detect fraud. But this duty is qualified by the concept of a 'reasonable expectation' of detection.

Throughout the development of this guidance on fraud, it is hard to believe that audit practitioners were anxiously waiting for clearer operational instructions on how to do their work. For the purposes of internal consumption it was 'business as usual', the new guidance simply codified what had always been common knowledge. The significance of the process lay rather in the external visibility of these deliberations and in the production of a legitimate text which could be regarded by all parties as a solution to a problem. In short, the problem was *programmatic* rather than *technical* and the document which was developed needed to balance competing demands. On the one hand, the history of the development of formal guidance shows clearly that it is generally resisted by practitioners. On the other hand, external pressures lead to greater demands for clarity and precision in the standards by which it can be judged whether audit practice works.

For good philosophical reasons, no rule or system of rules can entirely control the conditions of its own applicability. Every rule requires a second-order rule which says when it applies and so on. So there is always discretion, even in very precisely specified instructions, where one might still ask 'does this set of instructions apply here?' But aside from this issue it is possible to see in the development of audit guidance in general, and that on fraud in particular, a certain emergent style in which judgement is reserved for the interpretation of key terms. In this way, self-developed guidance documents reconcile the programmatic demands for rational control, which are often triggered by crisis and scandal, with the conservative demands of practitioners. The guidance on fraud is an example of a 'technical text' which both formalizes and simultaneously maintains zones of discretion at critical junctures. And while auditors may formally lose control of a concept such as 'reasonable expectations' in a court of law, it should also be remembered that what accountants in general do will often be invoked as a standard.

It is beginning to sound as if audit were mere illusion, a game of writing. This is not the case. At the operational level, auditors do indeed have an array of techniques which have some capacity for detecting large mis-statements in financial statements. Audit procedures are generally intended to demonstrate the completeness, accuracy and validity of transactions which, when aggregated, make up the financial statements. Audit firms have always concerned themselves with the development of in-house procedures for detecting fraud over and above the normal ones. Attempts have been made to develop red flags, risk analyses and other techniques (Sorensen *et al.*, 1980). For example, in the financial services sector and other similarly highly regulated domains, regulatory compliance is often regarded as a proxy for management integrity. Non-compliance, fines, irregularly filed returns are all 'red flags' and should put the auditor on alert. Operational issues relating to management fraud are on the agenda of the ICAEW audit faculty and there is considerable interest in the need to audit the 'integrity' of senior management, a partial return to the medieval auditing process which focused on the trustworthiness of people.

So much for technique. At the programmatic level, the official front stage of financial auditing is effectively decoupled from all these efforts. Here one encounters a more cautious style, especially on matters relating to audit scope. Much of what goes on here is not guidance for practitioners at all but a certain kind of institutionalized presentation of the knowledge base of financial auditing. It must be 'practical' enough to look like guidance to outsiders but not so practical that these outsiders could replicate or judge it without the help of insiders. In this way disturbances to the system, in the form of new demands, or old demands with a new rhetoric, can be managed by transforming the unfamiliar and intractable into the familiar and possible. Furthermore, there is no clearly defined notion of what is 'reasonably expected' of the auditor in relation to any particular act of fraud and its impact on the financial statements. Accordingly, the objectives of financial auditing in the UK are expressed in general terms of an opinion on truth and fairness whose relation to fraud detection always remains negotiable. The detection of management fraud is neither ruled out of the audit process, because this would lower expectations to the point where audit might lose its value, nor clearly ruled in, since this would unfairly burden the auditor and would make audits much more expensive.

This strategy of keeping objectives stated generally and in terms which do not mention fraud (material mis-statement) is part of the ongoing competition for interpretive control in which technical guidance is both a basis for, and a product of, negotiation with regulators (Baldwin, 1990:322). These negotiations, whose exact form can only be presumed but whose effects are often clear, are set in motion by claims about 'audit failure'. Large scale frauds make headline news and regulatory structures are always under pressure to react, particularly to prevent perceptions of systemic failure. Inevitably the creation of new regulatory organizations, like the Serious Fraud Office, follows. While there is nothing new about fraud, particularly in the financial services sector where the collpase of Barlow Clowes and the Levitt Group in the UK demonstrated the temptations of poorly controlled access to client money, there are heightened expectations that this should not happen. But as these programmatic demands on the financial auditing function increase, the criteria of success or failure of the audit process are increasingly unclear. This must now be considered.

AUDITING AND THE DIALECTIC OF FAILURE

The problem of audit failure encompasses the discussion of fraud above. The problem exists because, in the absence of clear criteria of what audits can and cannot do, the question of failure is often highly contested (Power, 1993*b*). When companies collapse, for whatever reason, and have previously received a 'clean' opinion from the auditors, public reaction focuses first on those auditors and the possibility of their failure. However, it is difficult to disentangle particular facts about an audit process from particular facts about the company collapse. It is always logically possible that a 'good' audit was performed even though the company failed; auditor defences usually take this form. Not all these defences are successful but the phenomenon of audit failure (and success) remains elusive: 'audit failures are almost impossible to judge because the activities of accounting and auditing are so vaguely defined' (Keasey and Wright, 1993:299).

The history of auditing reads, like the history of regulation more generally, as a history of failure. Efforts at social control, it seems, always fail and failure is always the condition for further attempts at control. Audit failure is a particular form of 'gatekeeper failure' (Grabosky, 1995*b*:539) which sets in motion reactions in the form of litigation, congressional inquiry, special investigations by the DTI, adverse media comment and so on.[9] These various criticisms have been instrumental in creating new institutional structures. For example, the Auditing Practices Committee (APC) had its origins in publicly perceived audit failure (see Taylor and Turley, 1986:139) and similar pressures for reform led to its replacement by the Auditing Practices Board (APB) in 1991. Auditing standards have been rewritten, largely to conform to the style and content of US standards, and the APB initiated fundamental discussion into the future of auditing (APB, 1994). Coupled with these domestic pressures for reform, self-regulatory arrangements for the monitoring of audit quality have been introduced as a consequence of the European Union Eighth Directive and professional institutes have been wrestling uneasily with their dual role as regulator and trade association. More will be said on these arrangements for the 'audit of auditing' in Chapter 5.

The development of financial auditing seems to be caught up in a dialectic of failure whereby each crisis leads to a further round of institutional change. Indeed, the development of auditing guidance on fraud discussed above exhibits the traits of a 'regulatory dialectic' (Kane, 1993:182–3) in which auditors respond creatively to each new programmatic attempt at reform. In the face of criticism, accountants have been determined to defend their interpretative control over financial auditing (Sikka and Willmott, 1995). Much of the defensive character of these reactions can be explained by reference to increased litigation against auditors in the late 1980s and early 1990s.

Financial auditors in the UK have responded individually and collectively on a number of different fronts: by contesting the litigation in the first place (although there remains a reluctance to take proceedings to court); by campaigning for some kind of limited liability; by leading a campaign to establish a clearer understanding of the audit role and thereby to close the expectations gap; and by establishing limited companies for part (like the firm KPMG) or all of their audit practice, thereby providing partners with a shield of limited liability. Ironically, many of these defensive efforts seem to be occurring at a time when one of the leading cases, *Caparo v Dickman and others*, suggests that auditors have very little legal responsibility to third parties who may place trust in their work.

There is much more that could be said about institutional developments in financial auditing and more will be said about technique in Chapter 4. But beneath all this there is something that remains puzzling, constantly elusive and yet also fundamental to the power, not just of financial auditing, but of auditing as such. The puzzle is that auditing lacks clear output based criteria of performance, despite the fact, as Chapters 3 and 5 suggest, it is a practice which has itself been instrumental in helping to define performance for many organizations. In demanding financial audits to serve programmatic goals, like shareholder control of directors or corporate compliance, it is also necessary to ask how it is possible to tell whether they are successful or not. This requires a knowledge of what audits produce.

THE ESSENTIAL OBSCURITY OF AUDITING

It may be argued that financial auditors have deliberately obfuscated the issue of what audits really do and that this lies at the heart of the expectations gap. But there is also the interesting analytic problem which was mentioned above: it is difficult to disentangle the success of auditing from the success of the auditee. Crime rates may fall because of improved policing *or* because of other changes in society. Equally, corporate financial statements may be generally reliable because of good auditing *or* because of good internal company accounting policy. Furthermore, the concept of a 'dialectic of failure' is appealing because of a certain asymmetry. Corporate failure will often give rise to public questions about financial audit failure, as noted above. However, corporate success will not usually yield public acclaim for the role of audit. The reasons for this go to the heart of the matter; there is an essential obscurity about what auditing produces which lies beneath its various routines and procedures.

Although official definitions of financial auditing do not mention the fact, it is of course a practice bounded by economic constraints. Regardless of whether one thinks that audit partners are paid too much, the fact remains that infinite resources are not available for auditing or for any other form of monitoring. From the point of view of the individual auditor, there are costly inputs into the audit process in the form of various grades of staff time spent performing procedures, making inquiries, taking samples, inspecting assets, producing working papers and so on. These input costs are known and the careful budgeting and control of staff time is an increasingly important dimension of professional advancement (Hanlon, 1994).

However, it is the relation between these inputs and the assurance produced that gives an audit its so-called added economic value. In simple terms, the output of the audit process is an opinion. The presumed effect of this opinion is to enhance the credibility of the audited object. In the case of financial auditing that object is the financial statements of an enterprise and the opinion is expressed in the statutory terms of the 'true and fair' view.

At this point the deep epistemological obscurity of auditing becomes evident, despite the mass of technical procedures available to the auditor. What is the nature of the assurance given by audits? Can it be observed? Can it be measured other than in broad qualitative terms or in terms of a consensus among auditors themselves? It may not be possible to know what audits really produce but can one at least ascertain whether auditors come to similar conclusions in similar circumstances? And is it simply the case that more staff time will yield more assurance? These questions relate in essence to the shape of a cost–assurance function for auditing. Fig. 2.1 describes an often assumed cost–assurance function, a function which also describes audit quality. First, there are diminishing returns to audit expenditure such that 100 per cent assurance or certainty is never possible.[10] Second, in the shift from function A to B, efficiency gains over a certain range can be suggested but the question as to whether B is superior quality auditing depends where on the function one is. Third, only in the case of function C, which dominates A and B, can one talk unequivocally of higher quality audit.

Notwithstanding the didactic usefulness of modelling the audit function in the form suggested by Fig. 2.1, it remains difficult, if not impossible, to specify it empirically other than in broad terms. Of course, statistics allow us to quantify levels of assurance, and auditing practice continues to be informed by statistical sampling procedures. However, theoretical quantitative sampling schemes and risk assessment models are often translated into qualitatively based tasks for practitioners, while official histories of auditing tend to paint a picture of the efficiency gains described in Fig. 2.1 (see Chapter 4). This cost–assurance relation is ultimately inscrutable. Not only do practitioners not know the shape of the function, they do not know where they are on it or how to calibrate the assurance axis. In short they do not know how to demonstrate publicly what they produce; they appeal instead to their expert judgement.

It is in this sense that auditing has a 'weak' knowledge base; there is no way of specifying the assurance production function independently of a practitioner's own qualitative opinion process. Financial auditing constantly asserts the value which it adds, and this may be true in broad terms, but there is something fundamentally unspecifiable about its output. In the end, auditors must be trusted about what it is they produce, a theme which will be taken up again in Chapter 6.

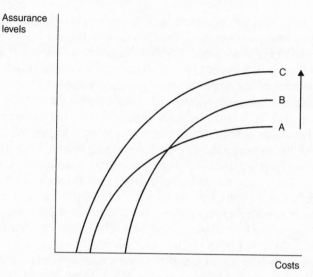

Fig. 2.1 The cost–assurance function for financial auditing

If the cost–assurance relation of auditing is obscure then so too are the consequences of any attempt to intervene in and reform the auditing process. For example, it is not obvious that making financial auditors more independent, whatever that means, will maintain or enhance the existing cost–assurance relation. One can imagine circumstances in which that relation could deteriorate and the values of independence and competence might involve trade-offs. This leaves financial auditing with an apparently enormous problem. Not only is it unclear what auditing is for but, even if this could be agreed, it would still be very unclear how well auditing serves the purposes for which it is intended and whether, in particular circumstances, it really succeeds or fails. There is no robust conception of 'good' auditing independent either of auditor judgements or of the system of knowledge in which those judgements are embedded and against which particular audits could be judged. Good auditing ends up as conformity to agreed procedures which have stood the test of time.

I can begin to imagine practitioners' reaction to this argument. Understandably, they would point to an extensive body of audit guidance which provides the benchmarks for best practice. And the professional bodies in the UK now police the quality of financial auditing by registered auditors (Chapter 5). In short a whole apparatus of quality control for the financial audit process exists. But the existence of all these things is not denied. The problem is that they do nothing to illuminate the underlying cost–assurance function of the audit process. Official and semi-official techniques define good auditing in terms of a series of procedural inputs which can be more or less programmed into the audit process and which leave room for practitioner judgement. But they do not touch, other than by mere assertion and in the most general terms, the relation between these procedures and the production of levels of assurance. The assurance axis in Fig. 2.1 is therefore the site of negotiation and judgement.

To repeat: the knowledge base of the financial audit process is fundamentally obscure. It is this obscurity which sustains the expectations gap, an obscurity which practitioners overcome by appealing in the end to the authority of their own judgement in determining what is reasonable practice. However, it must also be emphasized that to draw attention to this obscurity is not to regard auditing entirely as a fiction or myth. In very simple terms it is clear that if one person adds up a column of figures and another, with no interest in those figures, does the same thing with the same result, then one can have some feeling of added assurance that the total is correct. And if another person does the same, it is not wild to presume that the assurance is even greater. But the cost–assurance relation cannot be specified in more precise terms than this. Auditing remains at the level of a folk craft or art.

To say all this is to suggest that audits operate in 'inscrutable markets' (Gambetta, 1994) where reputation and image management acquire a distinctive role. The problem is more radical than the agency issues of information asymmetry or moral hazard encountered in Chapter 1. Even audit practitioners themselves cannot define the good audit epistemically other than in terms of their own judgement, so the much discussed role of liability as a control over the quality of auditing leaves intact the problem of knowing what this quality really is. Gambetta (1994:218) suggests that 'moral codes and conventions are likely to emerge and stand as signs for hard-to-test products'. This is very clearly the case in auditing. The essential obscurity of the audit product is offset by massive investment in formal procedural audit knowledge and in the development of professional codes of ethics, rules on independence and so on (Preston *et al.*, 1995). If it is impossible to know what financial auditing really produces, then it becomes important to trust practitioners to do their best. And if one does not know what audits are for or what they produce, one does not really know whether they fail either.

Theorists of professional practice would not be at all surprised by any of this. A certain obscurity in the professional craft gives the practice its aura and sustains its monopoly privilege. So a professional task like auditing must be 'abstract enough to survive objective task change but not so abstract as to render jurisdiction indefensible' (Abbott, 1988:239). In other words, the legitimacy of the practice requires some publicity of the operational process but not so much that it could be readily replicated by outsiders. One could extend this thesis to the problem of audit objectives too. The objectives must be sufficiently concrete to be perceived as usefully satisfying programmatic needs, but not so clear that outsiders can readily judge the success or failure of the process in meeting its objectives. From this point of view the expectations gap, far from being a disadvantage to auditors, is in fact a condition of their economic success. Without an expectations gap there would be full transparency of the audit process, both in terms of its objectives and its production of assurance in relation to those objectives. The market for audit services would be dangerously 'scrutable'.

This is the great institutional strength of financial auditing and the idea of audit which it promotes. Auditing responds to pressures for reform in a manner which constitutes a legitimate response but at the same time also preserves its essential obscurity, an obscurity which is overcome by trust in auditor judgement. As a result the success or failure of auditing is never a public fact but is always an object of persistent dispute, an adversarial process in which questions of blame are at stake. Furthermore, the abiding paradox of the audit society becomes apparent at this point: the expansion of auditing and its assumption of new roles is conditioned by its failure and by an essential obscurity in what it can deliver. This can be illustrated by auditing developments in the UK financial services sector, an example which also provides a useful link to the themes of Chapter 3.

THE AUDITOR IN THE FINANCIAL SERVICES SECTOR[11]

The history of financial services regulation suggests a dialectic of regulatory failure. Control strategies have been developed in the wake of successive scandals and the residues of crises remain inscribed in regulatory systems and regulations long after the original events (Moran, 1991:17). But a financial crisis also provides opportunities as well as threats, often being 'an occasion for specialist problem-solvers to advertise their wares in front of a wider-than-usual audience.'[12] Crisis stimulates the 'search for new and more rigorous standards of surveillance and control' (Moran, 1986:96), a search which has given rise to auditing reforms and the demand for better standards.

It is often suggested that 'gentlemanly' patterns of motivation and self-control in financial markets have recently given way to profit motivated expert advisors. But it is doubtful whether human nature has really changed that much.[13] The changes have been more structural in form as traditional self-regulatory practices in financial markets have given way to an intensification and codification of financial regulation (Moran, 1991). The so-called deregulation of financial markets in the 1980s has been accompanied by a style of regulation in which the authority for principles is centralized, but enforcement is delegated to agents, such as auditors.

In part, these developments represent an increasing formalization and institutionalization of local control structures, effectively giving a new public status to interest groups and associations.[14] For example, in the UK financial services industry, the Financial Services Act 1986 (FSA) led to the creation of the Securities and Investments Board (SIB), essentially a private body with quasi-state functions, which oversees another level of Self Regulatory Organizations (SROs) with a mixture of associational and regulatory roles. Similar patterns of hierarchically-ordered state-recognized institutions are visible in other areas. Increased formalization and new 'proto-professionals' (e.g. compliance officers) are elements of a style of control in which regulation is a professional stake, an opportunity in the market for advice and mediation.

Investor protection lies at the heart of the FSA. The SIB and the SROs are required to determine whether a person registered with them is 'fit and proper' to carry on investment business and whether they comply with rules for the prudent conduct of that business. These arrangements and their counterparts for banking, insurance and building societies have increased the demand for attestation services and new reporting duties for financial auditors have evolved as a consequence (Tattersall, 1991).[15] In general, the auditor must now report on the adequacy of accounting systems and internal controls more explicitly than for a normal statutory audit. This is a regulatory pattern which is becoming more prominent in many different areas, as the chapters that follow will show. The external audit function is becoming more orientated towards control systems and the self-assessment capability of all organizations. Consequently the public significance of internal auditors has also grown (Russell, 1996).

As described above, the practice of assessing internal control systems as a basis for determining the necessary amount of detailed auditing work reaches back to the beginning of the century. Only recently has there been an explicit reporting requirement for certain aspects of these controls in financial institutions.[16] This is not simply a matter of making public what was previously private. Internal control systems are emerging as public objects of regulatory attention in a way that they were not before. Concepts of internal control have been debated and defined and, as the example of the Cadbury Code shows, are often controversial (Chapter 3). So the changes in the financial services sector are more complex than merely requiring auditors to be explicit about what they have always done anyway. The external auditor is located in a new space of programmatic expectations (investor protection) with the risks and rewards that this entails.

The various pieces of legislation which have restructured the regulatory landscape for banks and other financial institutions are heavily dependent on the audit function. One may argue that an organization like the Bank of England has distinctive in-house supervisory and inspection capabilities. However, there is still a dependence on audit based assurance. For example,

SIB regulations specify the responsibilities of SROs to ensure that they have effective arrangements for the monitoring and enforcement of principles. In turn, SROs depend on auditing to reach inside member organizations. Audit provides a primary signal that the financial sector is in control.

The problem is that regulatory expectations of control are not always satisfied and the fraud related collapse of Dunsdale Securities demonstrates how a network of layered control structures can quickly turn into a network of blame allocation involving SIB, FIMBRA, the APC (who quickly produced a guidance note on the audit of client money (APC, 1991)) and the financial auditors involved (one of whom was eventually disbarred by the ICAEW). A similar politics of intra-regulatory blame is visible in the aftermath of BCCI, Maxwell, and Barings Bank. In all these cases, and despite a variety of investigative reports, the question of audit failure is difficult to disentangle from failures elsewhere in the regulatory system (SROs, the Bank of England, Boards of Directors).

Despite this dramatology of scandal and crisis (Moran, 1991:138) in which the media play a large role, programmatic confidence in regulation must be maintained and the general expectations of the efficacy of financial auditing must be preserved. Accordingly systemic doubt about the capabilities of audit, such as a radical questioning of what it really produces, is not a regulatory option. Audit sits near the bottom of a regulatory structure which attempts to reach into the internal workings of organizations. Particular audits may go wrong but not audit as such. Consequently, a certain cosmetic reform is visible in the wake of crisis. Auditors are censured, conferences are organized, articles are published and, very often, new audit guidance is issued. Things settle down until the next time. As in the case of the development of guidance on auditors' responsibilities for the detection of fraud and material errors, this reform process may intensify the textual basis of auditing practice but continues to obscure questions on the scope and objectives of financial auditing.

One example of this cosmetic reform process is the attempt to formalize the communicative relationship between auditors and regulators further up the control hierarchy. The design of a communicative relationship which in effect supports 'blowing the whistle' on clients is far from being a technical question of reporting requirements. It relates once again to a new 'regulatory rationality' (Miller and Rose, 1990) by which the auditor is linked to the state in a hierarchy of control. The collapse of Johnson Matthey Bank and related criticisms of banking supervision gave rise to the legal arrangements under the Banking Act 1987 for improved communication and consultation between auditors and banking regulators (Clarke, 1986:48; Moran, 1986:163–77).[17] The legislation enables *ad hoc* reporting between regulator and auditor, initially as a *right* to communicate then, following BCCI, as a *duty*. It was left to the relevant associational body, in this case the APC, to spell out the operational detail (APC, 1989*a*; 1989*b*; 1990b).

More is at stake here than is initially apparent. A formalized communicative relationship to a third party challenges the traditional relationship of confidentiality between auditor and company management (Tattersall, 1991). As with the guidance on fraud, the operational documents developed by the APC are primarily defensive, concerned with maintaining interpretative control of the scope of audit work. The guidance explicitly states that the auditor is not required 'to change the scope of his audit or other work for the authorised business' and is not 'placed under an obligation to conduct his work in such a way that there is a reasonable certainty that he will discover a notifiable matter'. In effect the APC sought to design a form of words around the imprecisely specified legal right to communicate with regulators which avoided taking on an explicit duty to find reportable matters while also satisfying regulatory expectation.

The guidance document admits that the auditor may be put on alert that client money may be at risk. In such a case reasonable expectations of what he or she should do will change. But the new reporting possibilities are expressed in such a way as to leave the operational dimensions of the audit process as they were while leaving open the possibility of reporting to regulators. A certain impression of operational guidance is given which preserves the obscurity of objectives. In effect, external programmatic demands on auditors are translated into the range of practices which are already familiar and which preserve practitioner discretion.[18]

It should not be assumed that the process of developing guidance is without internal conflict. Towards the end of its life the APC issued draft guidance to auditors in relation to illegal acts in general (APC, 1990c) which mirrored similar guidance in the USA.[19] As with the guidance on fraud, there was an implied acceptance that, subject to reasonable expectation, the auditor has a responsibility to detect illegal acts which may be remote from the financial statements or from his/her normal range of competence. Modelled on the language of earlier guidance, this document recommends that the auditor must plan his audit to understand the legal environment in which the auditee operates and there are possibilities for reporting breaches of regulations to third party regulators, such as the Serious Fraud Office. However, unlike earlier guidance, practitioner resistance to the Trojan horse of new responsibilities meant that the draft has not progressed.

Much more could be said about the development of particular forms of audit guidance. Some, like the procedures for testing debtor balances by circularization are focused and detailed and could indeed be used by practitioners in the field to guide operations. These forms of guidance really do consolidate best practice in terms of operational depth described above. In contrast, I have considered some of the forms of guidance (on fraud and reporting to regulators) which have their origins in response to crisis and where fundamental issues of objectives and operational scope are at stake.

Given that wholesale condemnation of the monitoring function would undermine the structure of financial regulation itself, there are pressures to *particularize* audit failure even where systemic issues seem to be at stake. Investigative discussion is dominated by finding out what particular auditors did or did not do. There are also pressures to intensify the procedural nature of the audit process, to be more prescriptive on operational matters, but to manage this in such a way that practitioner discretion is preserved. In this way systemic issues about the purpose of audit and the cost–assurance function can be avoided and replaced by essentially procedural questions of quality control for existing responsibilities, such as improved licensing arrangements and revised codes of ethics. Fundamental operational problems of scope and of the cost–assurance function are resolved into arrangements for securing trust in practitioners. As Wolnizer (1987) has argued, preoccupation with the ethical independence of auditors has deflected attention from the issue of what they really know.

The various forms of proceduralization of the knowledge base of auditing are responses to demands and expectations made upon it in the name of various programmes for control. It has already been said that there is no *a priori* reason why these demands should be congruent with the operational capability of auditing to provide assurance and the very possibility and nature of enforcement is often misconceived by delegating authorities (Marx, 1981). There is a 'looseness of fit' between different layers of the regulatory process, 'expectation gaps', with each layer making demands of the other. The financial audit guidance discussed above represents the diverse interests of the Secretary of State, regulators like the SIB, auditing practitioners, the APC, and an often-invoked investing public. The linking of these multiple constituencies is essentially a political act in a competitive market for the allocation of responsibility. New scandals disturb the consensus supporting this network of expectations and new reforming reactions are set in motion to preserve faith in the audit function. But the nature of the enforcement product provided by auditing is, despite many pages of technical procedure, persistently elusive.

To conclude, the obscurity of auditing is a deliberately polemical idea. I use it to dramatize a point which may not be readily apparent and is often overlooked in the climate of enthusiasm which characterizes the audit explosion. Of course, to say all this is to say only that auditing, like teaching, policing, social work and many other practices in which a society must invest, has problematic criteria of effectiveness which are often contested. It is frequently said that these practices are arts rather than sciences but this is unhelpful, especially since philosophers of science would question such a stark distinction. The problem is really to do with a certain

indeterminacy of effectiveness which is compensated for by heavy investment in the process and by trusting individual practitioners to act in good
faith. When audit practitioners talk of common sense and judgement, they
know very well that the nature of the assurance provided by the audit
process is elusive and problematic. Audit is rather a craft whose central concepts, such as materiality, resist precise codification (Hanlon, 1994:85) and
it is no accident that practitioners talk of providing 'comfort' (Pentland,
1993) rather than 'proof'.

THE FINANCIAL AUDITING SYSTEM[20]

There is more to financial auditing practice than the politics of developing
professional guidance described in previous sections. This is one part, albeit
importantly illustrative for my purposes, of a wider field of interacting elements. Indeed, it is the institutionalized strength of these different elements
which protects auditing from systemic doubt and which constitutes a robust
'system' of knowledge.[21] This system has four principal levels or points as
shown in Fig. 2.2.

The first level concerns the official knowledge structures of audit practice as discussed in previous sections. This is the public face of financial
auditing practice, its codified rules and regulations on appropriate procedure and behaviour which have evolved over time. Such practical routines are often developed *ad hoc* at the level of practice and, due to
environmental demands, gradually percolate upwards and become codified,

FIG. 2.2 The system of financial auditing knowledge

first at the level of in-house documentation, then sometimes more abstractly at the level of professional institutes and regulatory bodies.[22] Professional institutes and the large firms lead a process of self-presentation (Stevens, 1981) in developing this knowledge base and constantly work to reconcile the competitive realities of audit work with periodic demands for reform. Practitioners complain of regulatory overload and of incursions into professional judgement while regulators and politicians demand that something must be done.

All these procedures, with varying degrees of formal authority, constitute what is often called 'generally accepted' practice. Previous sections have dealt a little with the circumstances under which guidance documents relevant to audit scope have been developed and there is evidence that this process of rationalization of auditing knowledge affects the production of audit working papers for particular audits. Practical auditing must be written up to conform to the public face of auditing since there is always a possibility that auditors will need to justify themselves to legal audiences (Cushing and Loebbekke, 1986; Francis, 1994:260; Van Maanen and Pentland, 1994). So audit documentation is only partly descriptive: 'the audit working papers "do not tell the real story" of why decisions are made, and [processes of] . . . selecting, or excluding, information from any explanations so as to create a desired portrayal of what happened' (Gibbins, 1984:117). The process of writing up makes the audit process conform, more or less well, to its institutionalized knowledge base.

The second level of the system concerns the diverse mechanisms by which all this procedural knowledge is disseminated to practitioners. These mechanisms involve varying degrees of formal and informal, on and off-site, education (Power, 1991), training, and socialization (Harper, 1988; Coffey, 1994). At this level styles of behaviour and speech—the tacit rules of self-presentation—are learned, as well as practical skills. The 'need to look busy' and to aquire a 'reputation for industriousness' (Roslender, 1992:189) are not unique to auditing practice but provide a reminder that financial auditing is perfomed by people doing a job like any other. In addition formal examination systems, which arguably function more as barriers to entry than as education, support the institutionalization of audit knowledge by connecting idiosyncratic procedures to legitimate forms of abstract knowledge (Abbott, 1988; Carpenter and Dirsmith, 1993). Of equal significance are the wealth of in-house courses, technical updates, conferences, seminars and other schemes which contribute to the ideal of continuing professional education (CPE).

The third level of the system does not feature greatly in this book but must be mentioned. This is the level of financial audit practice itself where particular audit judgements are made and written, although not always in that order. At the level of practice the public production of statements of assurance ('the financial statements give a true and fair view') emerges from underresearched but elaborate internal interactions between auditor and auditee. Auditing and accounting 'facts' are negotiated (Roslender, 1992:194; Pentland and Carlile, 1996) in contexts where local discretion is often high and where the form of the interaction with the client may threaten to become too collusive (Grabosky, 1990). Audit opinions also emerge from the 'lonely monotony of backroom adding and subtracting' (Stevens, 1981:11) and a prevailing image of the financial auditing field is one of boredom, of waiting to move on to higher things, of 'ticking and bashing', of daily conflict with clients who resent the intrusion, and of long hours to finish the job. Career orientated pressures exist to produce management letter points, to beat last year's budget (which means reducing inputs or, at least, recording reduced inputs) and, for more senior colleagues, to win clients (Hanlon, 1994).

The economics of financial audit practice is a crucial constraint, as the cost–assurance function in Fig. 2.1 suggests. Practitioner intuitions about assurance levels must be written up to connect to legitimate myths of official knowledge (Boland, 1982; Humphrey and Moizer, 1990), a process in which feelings of comfort must be represented as cognitive in form, even though audit operates in an 'essentially unknowable situation' (Pentland, 1993). At the same time economic pressures exist to restructure the audit process itself and to make it more efficient without any dilution of cognitive capacity. The large firms are investing heavily in information technology and increasing the analytical responsibilities of junior members of staff in an attempt to shift the cost–assurance function 'upwards' (Fig. 2.1). But the problem of reconciling economic pressures to trim and prune the audit process with programmatic demands for assurance is a fundamental issue: 'The problem is that audits are supposed to be planned and performed on the basis of accuracy and thoroughness, not the accounting firm's profit goals' (Stevens, 1981:86). Economic pressures may lead to what has been called 'premature sign-off' and, worse still perhaps, a psychological desire to avoid finding mistakes (Grabosky, 1990).

It was suggested above that the audit process is also not without conflict between practitioner values and the institutional demand for acceptable representations of practice. This is essentially a tension between the third and the first levels of the system of audit knowledge. There is an eternal dialectic between institutionalized demands for formal structure and practitioner desires for preserving situated judgement and discretion, an essentially craft based expertise resistant to rationalization (Francis, 1994:251–7). It was noted above how auditing authorities like the APC needed to negotiate a balance between these demands in producing written guidance under pressures for reform.

The fourth element of the system of audit knowledge concerns the various feedback mechanisms by which practice (level 3), official knowledge structures (level 1), and training (level 2) are connected to broader issues of quality control. To a large extent this is not a discrete level of the system but is built into all the others, usually in response to external pressures for reform. Thus, institutionalized mechanisms of peer review which essentially exist to provide comfort about comfort production, emerged from critcisms of auditing and a recognition of the need to regulate firms rather than individuals (Stevens, 1981:217; Fogarty, 1996). The UK monitors audit quality through the Joint Monitoring Unit (JMU) (see Chapter 5).

These four basic elements, which could no doubt be further refined and analysed, provide the essential structures which support and reproduce the knowledge base of financial auditing practice. It was seen that corporate failure supplies a jolt to this system, registered initially at level 1, which reacts conservatively to proceduralize the official audit process and defensively in lobbying for reformed liability rules. But although the essential epistemological puzzle of financial auditing remains intact, these exogenous disturbances may also lead to some more general forms of internal inquiry and reflection (APB, 1994). There are concerns that the financial audit will become an ever more proceduralized 'regulatory compliance' product, as each new crisis pushes it in this direction, at the expense of a credible space for 'professional' judgement. For example, Hatherley (1995*b*) argues that existing educational and regulatory structures (levels 2 and 3) in the UK tend to overvalue an audit approach based on the defendable objectivity of formal process. Senior financial auditors have also begun to debate the future of the financial auditing product, locating it within a broader portfolio of assurance services (Elliott, 1995).

These four levels of knowledge elaboration and dissemination are highly institutionalized in the case of financial auditing, in the UK and elsewhere. Other forms of audit practice have attempted to replicate this structure. In particular, there are pressures in a number of different cases to shift emerging auditing practices from private, local, *ad hoc* and informal contexts of self-learning towards public, general, routinized and formal practice serving public accountability (see Chapter 4). The financial auditing system remains a powerful model of how this can be done and how a legitimate field of auditing practice must organize itself. It is a system which is at once rich in formal rules and technical procedures and which also preserves the discretionary space of the community of audit practitioners.

CONCLUSION

In this chapter, I have tried to suggest that the production of assurance within financial auditing is problematic and that the expectations gap is endemic to auditing. What audits really produce, other than working papers, is more opaque than is commonly admitted. One hears much about what financial audit is not; it is not insurance or certification. But it is much harder to know what it really is deep down and opinions are produced which may have value only because they are unclear. The audit process shrouds itself in a network of procedural routines and chains of 'unverified assurance' (Grabosky, 1990:84) which express certain rituals of evidence gathering but which leave the basic epistemic problem intact. The production of 'letters of comfort' in the securities industry presupposes a 'weaker' form of assurance that can be readily compared with the statutory audit. But without any calibration of assurance, this claim can only be made in terms of inputs and negatively in terms of work *not* done. In this sense audit is a craft and society must trust in the judgement of the individual auditor.

Despite these difficulties, financial auditing as a system remains strong. History suggests that it satisfies and operationalizes regulatory hopes and aspirations. Despite crisis and scandal the lid stays on the black box of auditing practice because it has become essential to programmes for control and public accountability. The operational procedures of auditing express a particular manner of making things auditable and of securing acceptance that the system of auditing works. In particular, the management control system as a primary auditable object assumes a central operational role for all forms of audit and inspection. This will be taken up in Chapter 4.

Finally, an important lesson to carry forward from this chapter is that the audit process, for all its density of operational procedure, is interactive and judgemental. The production of comfort is negotiated, both in the case of particular audits and in the development of official technical guidance. To some extent the ambiguity of forms of accounting and performance measurement necessitate negotiation about what constitutes compliance, performance, and so on. But one is struck by the emergence of the auditor not just as one who exercises expert judgement but also as one who is in the role of judge. This return to the medieval function suggests an expanding institutional domain for auditor judgement, beyond mere verification towards questions of propriety and effectiveness. Why has this happened? Why has auditing, financial and otherwise, constructed new roles on the back of verification? Partly this is because verification itself demands the exercise of judgement. However, a more comprehensive answer lies in the varied programmatic aspirations which require auditing for their realization. The context of financial services regulation was considered above, but it is now necessary to examine the demand side of the audit explosion in a broader context.

3

Auditing and the Reinvention of Governance

INTRODUCTION

In the previous chapter it was suggested that transformations in the supervisory environment of financial services, stimulated largely by particular corporate failures, intensified the demand for financial auditing and related forms of assurance. It was argued that financial audit responded to the need for better corporate governance by elaborating an official knowledge base in which fundamental issues of scope and output remain imprecise. However, it is not only in the financial sector that auditing has found itself in demand by programmes for enhancing and transforming organizational governance. This chapter explores the diverse pressures and demands which have contributed to the growth of auditing practices in other areas.

There has been extensive discussion of governance during the 1990s but views differ on what it is and how it might be improved. Governance concerns the effectiveness of market based controls, in the sense of the ability of an active takeover market to 'discipline' managers into maximizing a firm's value. Equally it relates to the effectiveness of regulatory initiatives to penetrate the organization and ensure compliance with rules via specifically designated officers, audit committees, and other internal representatives. Governance is also an intra-organizational issue of control and motivation in which working practices must be made more sensitive to customers, more outward looking in orientation and in which systems of control require constant vigilance and improvement. And governance may also relate to the democratization of organizational life and more radical senses of empowerment which include the labour force and other stakeholders with a legitimate interest in the workings of the organization. Here there is a focus on the ethics of organizations and their relationships with natural and social environments.

Despite this apparent diversity of approach and emphasis there is nevertheless something in the concept of governance that is not quite captured by related and equally negotiable notions of government or control or management or accountability. The diverse nuances of governance are linked by a common thread which is important for understanding the programmatic demand for auditing: the increasingly prominent role of internal control systems. It has been argued that 'Governance is not a choice between centralisation and decentralisation. It is about regulating relationships in complex systems' (Rhodes, 1994:151). This idea is at the heart of reformist programmes both in public sector service provision and in regulatory systems; in both cases there is a commitment to push control further into organizational structures, inscribing it within systems which can then be audited. In this respect governance is not to do with policing or surveillance in the normal sense of external observation, although elements of this may exist; it has more to do with attempts to re-order the collective and individual selves that make up organizational life.

In this chapter three overlapping programmes for enhanced governance and control are considered. The first programme is the so called 'new public management' (NPM), a label which has been used to characterize observable changes in the style of public administration. Auditing institutions have assumed an increasingly important role in the implementation of these changes and 'value for money' (VFM) auditing has become a prominent and constantly evolving instrument of financial control. The second programme parallels these transformations in public sector administration and reflects a shift in regulatory style. Regulatory initiatives are increasingly and explicitly seeking to utilize the cognitive and economic resources of regulated entities to ensure compliance. In particular the internal and external audit of control systems, which were mentioned in Chapter 2, have begun to assume a central role in operationalizing these intentions. The Cadbury Code for corporate governance is considered as an illustrative example. The NPM and changes in regulatory style also overlap with the third programmatic factor which drives the audit explosion: the rise of quality management initiatives and the development of new markets and professional opportunities in assurance services. By way of illustration, the example of environmental auditing is considered in some detail.

These three programmatic developments, the rise of New Public Management, a shift in regulatory style and the rise of quality assurance, constitute a demand for a particular style of control in many different fields. They share a managerial transformation of organizational governance which must assume *a priori* the efficacy of different forms of auditing. A new public role is being forged as much for internal auditing activities as for the external audit and the boundary between these different sources of monitoring activity is constantly moving. Auditing practices continually reassemble themselves and adjust their mostly vague accounts of their potential to meet the expectations of these three programmes. As in the case of financial auditing, a certain gap between what is demanded of VFM and quality audits and their capabilities enables rather than inhibits the audit explosion.

INTERNALIZING GOVERNANCE: THE NEW PUBLIC MANAGEMENT
AND VALUE FOR MONEY AUDITING

Over the past ten years or so there have been profound changes in the
nature of public administration. These changes have proceeded in different
ways in different countries.[1] But there has been enough commonality for
commentators to talk of the 'new public management' (Hood, 1991). The
NPM is constituted not by a single practice but by a variety of overlapping
elements which are programmatic in Rose and Miller's (1992) sense (discussed in Chapter 1). Broadly speaking the NPM consists of a cluster of
ideas borrowed from the conceptual framework of private sector administrative practice. It emphasizes cost control, financial transparency, the
autonomization of organizational sub-units, the decentralization of management authority, the creation of market and quasi-market mechanisms
separating purchasing and providing functions and their linkage via contracts, and the enhancement of accountability to customers for the quality
of service via the creation of performance indicators. Osborne and
Gaebler's (1992) *Reinventing Government*, which effectively translates
private sector managerial ideas about quality into the context of public
administration, has become something of a NPM bible, especially in North
America.[2]

One might put the NPM ideal very simply as a desire to replace the presumed inefficiency of hierarchical bureaucracy with the presumed efficiency
of markets. Although links between government and business have a long
history through contracting (Kettl, 1993), the NPM represents a more
radical programme to make the state more entrepreneurial. For example,
elements of the new institutional economics are clearly visible as doctrine
(Hood, 1991:5; Ezzamel and Willmott, 1993) and have been disseminated
through various think tanks.[3]

The NPM has become prominent for a number of related reasons.
First, the need for fiscal restraint is a theme which seems to cut across
old political divisions as the equation linking public sector borrowing,
taxation, and expenditure on public services begins to look increasingly
unsustainable for demographic and other reasons. Second—and this is
often difficult to disentangle from the first reason—one can identify
ideological commitments to the reduction of state service provision.
Neoliberal values of small government drive much of the commitment
to the NPM, in particular the creation of quasi-markets and the introduction of contracting between newly separated service providers and purchasers. As Rose and Miller (1992) have noted, neoliberalism embodies a
commitment to forms of intervention and control which are more indirect
and distant, seeking to act on and through the interests and motivations of
subjects and organizations. This gives practices of accounting and auditing

a central role in operationalizing the administrative ideals that constitute the NPM.[4]

A third reason for the rise of the NPM has been the success of political discourses which have demanded improved accountability of public service, not simply in terms of their conformity to legally acceptable process but also in terms of performance.[5] It has been argued that taxpayers have rights to know that their money is being spent economically, efficiently, and effectively—the three Es—and that citizens as consumers of public services are entitled to monitor and demand certain minimum standards of performance, as embodied in Citizens' Charters (Lewis, 1993). Whatever the reality of popular pressure for these changes, the NPM claims to speak on behalf of taxpayers and consumers and against cosy cultures of professional self-regulation. Taxpayers and citizens, rather like shareholders, are the mythical reference points which give the NPM its whole purpose.

The three Es, in conjunction with these populist appeals to notions of empowerment and service quality, make up what is commonly referred to as 'value for money' (VFM). VFM is a vague normative space in which an ensemble of operational routines and auditable performance can be harnessed to broader political ideals. Tensions exist within the very concept of VFM. Most notable in the eyes of many commentators (e.g. Pollitt, 1995) is the tension between the theme of fiscal crisis, questions of economy, efficiency and cost control, and the theme of service quality enhancement or effectiveness. This tension, which is managed if not resolved in a variety of ways, will be addressed below and again in Chapter 5. Of importance for the present discussion is that each element of the NPM identified above demands an intensification of financial and non-financial information flows. The 'hollowing out of the state' by the NPM generates a demand for audit and other forms of evaluation and inspection to fill the hole. According to Rhodes (1994:151), this is a deliberate erosion of central capability in favour of the long distant mechanics of auditing and accounting. Auditing has the qualities of 'portability and diffusion' and apparent 'political neutrality' (Hood, 1991:8) which serve the programmatic elements of the NPM. The disaggregation and devolution of public service provision require the specific technologies of reaggregation and recentralization which accounting and auditing promise. In its simplest form the NPM demands newly autonomous entities with financial reporting and audit requirements. However, these operational demands require an organization base for their realization. Accordingly, it is necessary to discuss UK public sector auditing institutions.

The Rise of Public Sector Audit Institutions[6]

Most developed states have a supreme audit body. For example, in the USA, there is the General Accounting Office (GAO); in Germany the

Bundesrechnungshof; in Canada the Office of the Auditor General. In the UK, there are currently two prominent institutions, the National Audit Office (NAO) and the Audit Commission. In addition, there is the European Court of Auditors, a supra-national body which interacts with the national bodies in the European Union (EU). Not all of these bodies are recent in origin and those that are have developed out of pre-existing arrangements for state auditing. Accordingly, it must be borne in mind that the institutional landscape of public sector auditing has a long and diverse history in different countries, as long as preoccupations with political accountability itself. Indeed, it is this admixture of administrative and political themes which makes the conception and the practice of public sector audit so varied and which locates the construction of an agreed language of performance for auditing within distinctive national contexts. Public sector auditing implicates questions about the distribution of authority and control in a way that financial auditing does not. In mediating the tensions between the legislative and executive organs of government, supreme audit bodies are unique and distinctive institutions of constitutional significance (White *et al.*, 1994).

The modern welfare state in many countries is a professional state in which specialist skills in fields such as health and education have been charged with the implementation of programmes. Under a pure form of representative democracy, these experts would perform well defined tasks for well defined objectives according to clear rules. However, as the history of public administration shows, this ideal is problematic. Links in the chain of public accountability connecting executive functions to the legislature, and hence to the populace, are weakened, if not broken, by pockets of self-regulating expertise. Expert professionals and public accountability often express competing values.

Public sector audit institutions have evolved in this changing legal and political environment by moving beyond narrow legalistic concerns with the regularity of transactions, i.e. the legitimate authority of state expenditure (Normanton, 1966). For example, the history of the GAO, established in 1921, is a microcosm of the tensions that have pervaded American public life and demonstrates how the separation of accounting and audit, and the question of auditor independence, can be constitutional issues (Mosher, 1979:233–8). Originally consituted as a low level *ex post* authorization facility for federal transactions, the GAO underwent a number of important transformations in the post-war period. Preoccupations with financial management, internal control and the improvement of government accounting brought it into conflict with an executive which often wished it to retain its original independent post-audit function and was often embarrassed by some of its judgements relating to military procurement. Relations between the auditor general and the attorney general were often adversarial and brought to a head the problem of the status of the GAO as an arm of congress.

After the war the GAO sought to embrace modern auditing techniques, such as sampling, and it employed an increasing number of professional accountants. The CPA was a line qualification, although the GAO tradition has always been to encourage its staff to broaden skills. The private sector knowledge base was constantly adapted and extended as the GAO developed its 'comprehensive audit' approach, a precursor to what is now called value for money auditing. Its work was not purely the financial inspection of books and records and in 1952 the manual of the day made explicit reference to the evaluation of effectiveness (Mosher, 1979:176). Efficiency and economy audits were regarded as distinct from financial and legal on the one hand and effectiveness auditing on the other. The latter rose to prominence in the mid-1960s, what Mosher has called the 'third GAO', with the development of programme evaluation. At this time the GAO recruited many different forms of expertise, in particular economists for cost–benefit analysis and *ad hoc* studies. The balance between accounting and non-accounting expertise is a continuing issue for supreme audit bodies in different countries.

Developments in the UK have taken a different course. The 1780 Statutory Commission for Examining the Public Accounts was a notable innovation and replaced what had hitherto been a largely *ad hoc* approach. In 1866 Gladstone created the Exchequer and Audit Department (EAD) headed by the Comptroller and Auditor General. The EAD was constitutionally a tool of parliament and controlled the financial regularity of executive functions.[7] Pressures for change in the audit function emerged from concerns about the maladministration and accountability of state agencies. A number of constitutionally significant reforms took place, mainly in the form of creating specialist committees and reaffirming ministerial responsibility. There were also calls to expand the role of Comptroller and Auditor General (CAG). These reformist pressures culminated in 1983 with the transformation of the Exchequer and Audit Department into the National Audit Office (NAO), a change which, not without some resistance (Garrett, 1986:423–6), coincided with increasing political and administrative preoccupations with efficiency and financial management. Furthermore there was pressure to raise the status of public sector auditing and to reinforce the parliamentary reporting role of the CAG. These changes demanded an investment in accounting and control systems with the aim of re-shaping central control capability and of dividing policy and management oversight from operational autonomy (Harden, 1993:34).

In the UK the enhanced role and status of the supreme state audit body rendered political conceptions of accountability increasingly dependent upon effective managerial accountability, a development which created problems. The constitutional myth of ministerial responsibility requires that the policy neutrality of auditing expertise is constantly reaffirmed; the NAO must be a neutral relay which enables parliament to monitor the executive. Accordingly, state audit is intended only to evaluate the means and not the ends of government programmes; formally the CAG may not question the merits of policy objectives.

As long as supreme audit bodies concerned themselves solely with the legal regularity of state transactions myths of neutrality had some prima facie plausibility. With the emergence of VFM auditing they have become more problematic. In reality there is a complex alliance between the Treasury, the Parliamentary Accounts Committee (PAC), and CAG which oversees autonomous units and relies on internal controls and performance indicators (Harden, 1993:33–4). Within this alliance, the boundaries of state audit and the role of CAG are constantly moving (Dewar, 1991).[8]

These complex developments are mirrored at the level of local government where the faith in the reforming and revelatory power of audit is also evident.[9] In 1982 the Audit Commission was established (although first proposed in 1970) to oversee local government[10] and to appoint local government auditors for a wide range of audit tasks, mixing up special studies with more traditional audit work (Kimmance, 1984). The constitutional position of the Audit Commission is even less clear cut than that of the NAO: it is effectively a body established by, but independent of, the executive and is accountable to the secretary of state. In the mid-1990s it was responsible for the audit of £90bn of expenditure, almost 15 per cent of GDP (gross domestic product); 'Its growth is a staggering success given that it has only been in existence for 13 years.'[11]

Although the Audit Commission operates explicitly as an agent of NPM based changes by encouraging and developing performance measures for local authorities and other service providers, it has also been critical of central government, often for not pursuing its reformist programme vigorously enough. In part the Audit Commission was created to act as a brake on profligate local government and as an instrument of central executive control it is much more than a monitoring institution. In this respect its title may be misleading; 'it provides an example of a policeman constantly tempted to turn consultant' (Day and Klein, 1990:13). Indeed, as audit guidance is developed on the back of national investigations and analyses, both roles are combined. Organizations must be changed to make them auditable, a theme which runs throughout this book.

The Audit Commission has been instrumental in introducing private sector firms into the audit process. In the mid-1980s almost 26 per cent of local authority audits were performed by the private sector firms and the maximum permitted 30 per cent was the subject of constant discussion. The remaining work was conducted by the District Audit Service (DAS), an organization which was made autonomous in order to introduce greater competition and which has needed to adjust its role accordingly (Henkel, 1991:30). It is consistent with NPM philosophy that the Audit Commission has become a purchaser of audit services and that District Audit, the successor to the DAS, is one of the providers. And it is understandable that the private firms, as competitors to DAS in providing audit services, have been instrumental in introducing many of the private sector financial disciplines which characterize the NPM. The financial audit has provided a skills base on which to build and sub-contract expertise. The boundary between the familiar regularity audit work and the less familiar VFM type work—a boundary which involves different expertise bases—was initially vague, leaving considerable room for discretion (Tomkins, 1986; Greenough, 1991:244). Importantly, the effectiveness element of VFM was not so much audited in a traditional manner, as *installed* within local government with a view to creating a capability for self-evaluation.

In areas where the work of the NAO and the Audit Commission overlap one would expect some cooperation but, as Bowerman (1994a) has shown, differences in cultures, working patterns, and reporting constituencies have tended to separate them. The Audit Commission is rich in comparative data across local authorities whereas the NAO deals with one-off institutions; the Audit Commission acts as consultant on a variety of matters whereas the NAO is more distant from operational issues affecting audited entities. Roberts and Pollitt (1994:546–7) also suggest that the Audit Commission can be more 'up front' in its recommendations largely because it is not a servant of parliament. The NAO tends to pull back from open-ended evaluations which would divide the Parliamentary Accounts Committee on party lines and undermine its credibility.

The European Court of Auditors should also be mentioned. Established in 1977, the Court had a staff of nearly 500 in the mid-1990s. Over time its work evolved from a rolling programme of systems audits towards a more comprehensive mission culminating in a 'statement of assurance' on the financial reliability and regularity of the EU accounts as a whole (Harden *et al.*, 1995; Middelhoek, 1995). In Chapter 4 I consider the mechanics of auditing the EU budget in more detail since the Court faces a considerable operational task. Notwithstanding its elevation into a full EU institution following the Maastricht Treaty in 1993, the Court has constitutional and operational difficulties which correspond to those of programmatic and operational scope dealt with in Chapter 2.

The lack of a common Euro-audit community, imperfect links with national audit bodies, ambivalent relations with the budgeting arm of the European Parliament, European Commission hostility to criticism of internal controls in its implementation of the EU budget, an uneasy operational mixture of regularity and value for money auditing, the absence of an internal audit function in the Commission, at least until recently (Pratley, 1995:252–3), and a spending culture in conflict with constraint values have all rendered the Court's functioning problematic (Harden *et al.*, 1995). Its work has expanded as the EU budget has increased and the politics of failure, described in Chapter 2, is clearly visible in the context of Euro-fraud. As with private sector financial auditors, the NAO and the Audit Commission, the Court has an expectations gap problem. As the EU grows and as a financial management culture takes hold in the Commission one can expect the Court to assume an ever higher profile role. Its imperative is that the EU be made auditable.

To conclude: the executive arm of modern states raises funds through the legislature for mandated programmes. As supreme audit bodies have grown in significance, political accountability to the electorate has been more explicitly supplemented, if not displaced, by managerial conceptions of accountability embracing the need to deliver value for money. Expenditure programmes (welfare, policing, etc.) have specific objectives and manager-ial accountability through the state audit function is intended to be achieved in a neutral manner, i.e. without making any judgement about the pro-gramme objectives themselves. However, the realization of managerial accountability through value for money auditing suggests that this neutral-ity is problematic.

Value for Money Auditing and the Construction of Effectiveness

VFM auditing did not arrive out of the blue in the UK in the early 1980s. Concerns with waste and extravagance and with the effectiveness of state programmes have a long history in the UK (see Henley, 1989:256–7) and in the USA. Programmatic commitments to VFM are internationally wide-spread, coinciding with the development of NPM in many different coun-tries.[12] However, there are interesting variations in the extent to which the supreme audit body operationalizes VFM.[13] As far as the NAO is con-cerned, there is statutory authority to carry out examinations into economy, efficiency, and effectiveness—the law does not mention VFM as such. The NAO has a rolling programme of VFM studies in addition to more tradi-tional forms of financial auditing. Some studies will be of an investigative nature following evidence of weaknesses, others are based on issues deemed to be important. At the level of local authorities, the auditor appointed by the Audit Commission is required not only to provide an opinion much like the financial audit process but also to satisfy himself that proper arrangements exist for securing economy, efficiency, and effective-ness. Beyond this there is no standardized prescribed form of reporting for value for money studies.

To understand the operational characteristics of value for money auditing, it is necessary to distinguish four possible auditing orientations and, thereby, four possible operationalizations of the concept of accountability:

(1) *Fiscal regularity* in the sense of accountability for the properly legal stewardship of inputs.
(2) *Economy* as accountability for obtaining the best possible terms under which resources are acquired.
(3) *Efficiency* as accountability for ensuring that maximum output is obtained from the resources employed or that minimum resources are used to achieve a given level of output/service.
(4) *Effectiveness* as accountability for ensuring that outcomes conform to intentions, as defined in programmes.

Value for money auditing addresses (2), (3), and (4) and today it is usually distinguished from regularity auditing under (1), although it has evolved out of this role. Philosophies of audit state that the subject matter of audit must be verifiable in the sense of the existence of clear standards of accountable performance which can be compared to observed performance (Flint, 1988). At first glance, the three Es lend themselves to the relatively clear definitions given above. However, these definitions describe a pro-grammatic intention which can by operationalized in many different ways. So, despite attempts at definition, it is argued that VFM auditing has a 'wide and often ambiguous meaning' and that considerable discretion exists in the interpretation of the enabling statutes (Fielden, 1984:223; Glynn, 1985a:27).

In the previous chapter it was argued that a certain obscurity in the financial audit process supports its appeal as a technology demanded by programmes for regulating the corporate economy. Much the same can be said of public sector auditing where different objectives co-exist and where the rhetoric of VFM is often invoked to justify expenditure cuts (Glynn, 1985a:27). Furthermore, even at the level of definitions, there is a fundamental tension between the effectiveness and the economy/efficiency components of VFM. They seem to depend on fundamentally different evaluative logics, the one standing in a tradition of social scientific inquiry into policy outcomes, most notable in the work of the GAO, the other stand-ing more firmly within the ambit of accountancy and business disciplines. These different logics will be considered further in Chapter 5.

In Chapter 2 it was suggested that the conventional financial audit is a coalition of different types of procedures and routines only loosely coupled to objectives. The development of VFM auditing has also been an incre-mental repackaging and extension of existing audit capabilities. At the time when 'comprehensive auditing', the precursor to VFM, was being developed in the USA and Canada, formal guidance was built on the financial audit model base. VFM is in this sense an assembly in which new conceptions of audit have been grafted on to existing routines and in which political programmes forced audit to be certain about a new range of ideals, such as efficiency (Hopwood, 1984; Radcliffe, 1995).

In this respect VFM audit practice is a constantly evolving construct shaped by an available repertoire of technologies and by the programmatic demands and assumptions which are made about its capabilities. VFM audits do not follow a common pattern and reflect different emphases and values. In general, the mix of emphasis on the three Es varies almost by assignment, a function of the specific programmatic demands made of the audit and of the routines and experts which can be assembled in its name. The US experience is instructive. As an arm of the legislature, the GAO responds to congressional requests and the fluctuating balance of account-ants/non-accountants has shaped its responses and methodological emphases in determining whether programmes satisfactorily achieve their results. Since 1980 the GAO has consolidated its expertise into a distinctive evaluation division which draws upon a wider range of social scientific knowledge in the programme evaluation process, providing research syn-theses of existing relevant literature for evaluation purposes. However, ignorance and prejudice against the social sciences and the inherently politi-cal nature of policy issues are continuous problems (Chelimsky, 1995). In contrast to this concept of programme evaluation, effectiveness reviews can be reviews of management systems for monitoring effectiveness. This will be an important general theme in the next two chapters but it is important to note now that ideas of effectiveness emerge from within, and are con-structed and installed by, an evolving audit process.[14]

In reviewing effectiveness the VFM auditor encounters problems in maintaining the myth of neutrality and runs the risk of questioning politi-cal values (Garrett, 1986:426) for two main reasons. First, political processes tend not to generate clear objectives against which effectiveness can be judged (Day and Klein, 1987:28). This means that the effectiveness of the means to achieve a particular policy goal and the question as to whether the policy is worthwhile as an end are difficult to distinguish. In such cir-cumstances auditors also stray into policy issues in order to assert their credibility. Second, when organizations do not have clear measures of pro-ductivity which relate their inputs to their outputs, the *audit* of efficiency and effectiveness is in fact a process of *defining* and operationalizing mea-sures of performance for the audited entity. In short the efficiency and effec-tiveness of organizations is not so much verified as constructed around the audit process itself.[15]

In the UK VFM auditing has been operationalized historically by a skills base which is grounded in (private sector) accounting. In their study of one NAO audit, Roberts and Pollit (1994:545) suggest that auditors gravitate towards certain evaluation designs. Auditors claim to be looking at effec-tiveness but they are really emphasizing economy and efficiency. In this way the audit of effectiveness gets constructed and shaped to suit a par-ticular skills base, even though there have been various demands for this base to be extended (Garrett, 1986:433). Accountability for effectiveness is therefore a vague ideal and can be operationalized in a number of different ways with very different emphases and related bodies of knowledge. Making effectiveness auditable is closely bound up with defining performance and installing a management system to measure that performance. In this way changes in information systems are a prerequisite for new forms of audit (Fielden, 1984:226), as the work of the Audit Commission demonstrates.

To conclude, this section has argued that while state auditing and concerns with value for money have a long history, they have received a decisive stimulus since the mid-1980s as programmatic commitments to the reform of public sector administration have taken hold. The NPM has given rise to an audit explosion in the form of new financial audits where none had existed before together with a rapidly evolving agenda for value for money auditing. The NPM necessarily presupposes that these audits are themselves instrumentally effective and neutral in their operation despite evidence that this is not the case. VFM auditing functions not only verify what is already there but also *install* an internal control system which embodies auditable performance measures. However, this is not only a feature of VFM auditing. It also reflects a broader shift in regulatory style as control responsibility is passed down into organizations.

INTERNALIZING GOVERNANCE: REGULATION AND
THE RISE OF INTERNAL CONTROL

Among other things the NPM represents a programmatic commitment to state withdrawal as a direct service provider in favour of a more regulatory role through accounting, audit, and other instruments. Although this commitment has only been partially realized, there has been enough change to talk of a shift from the welfare state to the regulatory (Day and Klein, 1990) or evaluative (Neave, 1988) state. This shift has been complemented by longer standing ideas about the 'limits of government'. For many years legal and administrative scholars have recognized and analysed the operational difficulties of so-called traditional styles of regulatory control in many different areas; there has been talk of overload and of the regressive effects of direct intervention (Sieber, 1981:17–19). For example, the operational limits of hierarchical command and control philosophies have been exposed in the face of creative resistance, lagging developments in the domain to be controlled and excessive knowledge and expertise requirements. Accordingly, attempts have been made to articulate a role for government in a sceptical age and a new regulatory mood has begun to emerge from these critiques.

The concept of deregulation is widely regarded as too simple a label for these changes. It would be more accurate to speak of regulatory experimentation with mechanisms of self-regulation. Notions of 'holistic regulation' (Dunsire, 1990; 1993),[16] 'mutual regulation' (Simmons and Wynne, 1994), 'self-organization' (Teubner *et al.*, 1994), 'responsive regulation' (Ayres and Braithwaite, 1992), 'organizational leverage' (Grabosky, 1994*b*), 'reflexive adaptation' (Kane, 1993), and 'governmentality' (Rose and Miller, 1992) have been suggested both descriptively and prescriptively. In particular, there are calls for regulation to be redesigned around the need to understand the incentive structures of regulatees and for effective structures of voluntary self-regulation. It has been said that 'in the post-industrial world there is a continuing and even growing need for the state not only to monitor what is happening, in absolutely every corner of life, but also to take a hand in it . . . ; not by the enforcement-heavy methods of regulation . . . but, just as a child at the fulcrum of a see-saw' (Dunsire, 1990:17–18).

These developments do not merely reflect a failure in and abandonment of central state control, but rather its transformation from direct to 'liberal' technologies of indirect influence (Rose and Miller, 1992) such as market-based instruments. Ayres and Braithwaite's (1992) notion of 'responsive regulation' demands an appropriate 'mix' of regulatory instruments which combines the advantages of delegating regulatory competence down into organizations, where it has the greatest chance of success, while retaining credible options for escalating enforcement. Grabosky (1994*b*) alludes to a new self-ordering potential in which the regulatory system consists of 'layered webs of regulatory influence'. The structure of financial services regulation discussed in Chapter 2 conforms to this model.

The distinction between state and self-regulation is too simple to capture what is at stake in the idea of regulatory layers. There is rather increasing formalization of existing structures of state sponsored regulation (Baggott, 1989) or what Teubner (1990:69) has called the legal stabilization of 'micro-corporatist' arrangements. The state begins to assume an overall monitoring role which emphasizes procedural values and which permits and encourages private interests to police each other. Centres maintain strategic control, exercised through policy levers of evaluation, audit, and inspection. In this way the state is able to withdraw from the 'murky plain of overwhelming detail' (Neave, 1988:12).

The growing formalization of regulatory layers has generated interest in the internalization of control mechanisms and the validation of their integrity by internal and external audits. New roles have been created, such as financial services compliance officers (Weait, 1993) and environmental managers (Rehbinder, 1992), and new institutional stages have been provided for old roles, such as internal auditors who are an increasingly credible point of reference in public debate. Furthermore there has also been a reworking of inspectorial institutions. With enhanced managerial capability has come greater attention to systems of self-inspection. Neave (1988:15) describes this as 'the development of bottom up, though top-down initiated, institutional self-assessment contained in the various "strategic plans" put forward by each establishment'. In Chapter 5 the consequences of institutionalizing these self-auditing arrangements will be considered further.

Generally, an audit explosion has been driven directly by this formalization of regulatory layers. Gatekeeping mechanisms like auditing (Kraakman, 1986) and record keeping and disclosure requirements become important as ways of connecting the different layers and of encouraging a certain kind of organizational introspection (Grabosky, 1995b:531). Audits offer the promise that effective regulation is still possible, still capable of reaching into the inner motives of target organizations. Auditing, whether internal or external, regularity or VFM, mediates different elements of regulatory strata. It looks into and out of organizations simultaneously; it is close to internal control structures while also fulfilling the expectations of distant regulators. The development of the Cadbury Code and of risk management systems for derivatives provide an example of these programmatic hopes for a form of voluntary regulation which can be legitimated by an external audit process.

The Cadbury Code and the Regulation of Risk

Corporate failure and scandal inevitably lead to demands for reform and for 'better' regulation, particularly in the field of corporate governance. In the UK a number of issues in the early 1990s, most notably the collapse of the Maxwell business empire, stimulated discussion and debate about structures for controlling executive power. Conferences were organized, papers were written, newsletters and journals were formed. Concerns about ethics in public life and excessive senior management remuneration added further fuel to the debates. There was, and continues to be, much discussion of optimal governance structures and, until the problems experienced at Metallgesellschaft AG in 1994, a constant fascination with the merits of the German two tier board system. Rather like the uncritical western fascination for Japanese manufacturing methods, the German corporate governance system has often been held up as an ideal as compared with US style audit committees.

Regulatory reaction and deliberation led to the development of a voluntaristic approach to corporate governance shaped by the London Stock Exchange, the DTI, the Bank of England and the accountancy profession. A code of best practice was developed by a committee chaired by Sir Adrian Cadbury, the 'Cadbury Code'. Although it is clear that the Code was a preemptive strike by the accounting profession to maintain control of regulation in this area (Freedman, 1993), it is equally clear that this initiative was state supported and therefore reflected the mood of regulatory experimentation described above. The original Code was published in December 1992 and included recommendations for companies to establish formally non-executive directors within internally independent audit committees. As sub-organizations independent from executive management such committees would provide the natural reporting constituency for internal and external auditors. The Code was later adopted by the UK Stock Exchange as a condition of registration and the public sector implications have been widely debated (CIPFA, 1994*a*).

There has been much criticism of the Code and its detailed requirements. At the time of writing it is undergoing a process of revision with greater formal input from the pensions and insurance industries. To some commentators it appears as a short term political fix, typical of an a prioristic policy style. Certainly, corporate pluralists who support conceptions of the stakeholder which are wider than shareholders have been disappointed by the conservative nature of the Code. There is little sense of companies as public institutions in the new arrangements.[17] It could also be argued that the Code demonstrates an excessive faith in the audit committee structure and in the resulting market for non-executive directors which has been created. Not only is the essential obscurity of financial auditing undisturbed but there is a presumed relation between disclosure and corporate activity which is highly problematic: 'Audit committees might be a means not of more effective reporting but of avoiding scrutiny' (Keasey and Wright, 1993:301).

One of the problematic features of the Code is that companies do not have to comply with *any* elements of it; they need only disclose non-compliance. The idea is that this soft approach will encourage compliance and that isomorphic pressures will lead recalcitrant companies to copy leaders of best practice. This is in keeping with the regulatory mood and there is much talk of adhering to the spirit of the guidance (Chambers, 1996). The Code requires an external auditor to review the statement of compliance, a new role which is easily grafted on to existing work offered in other areas but which has given rise to wide variations in reporting style. The exact form of reporting is not prescribed.

Perhaps one of the most controversial elements of the Code, which is likely to be repealed in the revised arrangements, is the requirement under paragraph 4.5 that the 'directors should report on the effectiveness of the company's system of internal control.' This is a requirement that reflects a general tendency for internal control systems to play a key role in regulatory policy. The controversy about paragraph 4.5 says much about the mood of caution within financial auditing. The requirement, though innocent in appearance, has generated fundamental problems about what internal controls really are and what one is saying in describing them as effective. For example, directors have been unwilling to make such statements in the absence of clear guidance. It has also been suggested that the auditor's work should consist of a review to establish *that* the directors have reported on effectiveness. This is a simple factual issue, with no implication for whether the controls *are* effective or not. In Chapter 2 it was suggested that the operational evolution of external audit was dependent on forming an opinion on the effectiveness of internal controls. In a climate of litigation the auditors, with the apparent exception of Deloitte & Touche in 1996, are unwilling to go public on what has always been a normal part of their operations. Directors in turn have taken the opportunity to interpret the Cadbury Code requirements weakly, requiring them only to state that they have reviewed internal controls, without any public assertion about effectiveness.

There have been attempts to overcome the absurdly cautious nature of reporting by defining what internal controls really are (ICAEW, 1994). Much hangs on the difference between narrow financial and broad non-financial definitions. The APB (1995) published a discussion document on the theme of internal control and advised financial auditors *against* issuing opinions on the Cadbury Code statement. Here the problems of an indirect regulatory style are apparent; a certain chain of empty opinions substitutes for information and can be created by auditors forming an opinion about the opinion of the Directors. Internal control threatens to remain a private and obscure matter (Upson, 1995) and Chambers (1996:115) is critical of definitions of internal control effectiveness which emphasize process, design, and structure, rather than outcomes. He argues that mechanisms for achieving effectiveness are not themselves part of the effectiveness of the system. This criticism can also be levelled against quality assurance initiatives (see below) and reflects the general tendency for audit processes to gravitate towards formal systems elements.

Although the Cadbury Code was developed under specific conditions and has many operational difficulties, it resembles other regulatory initiatives which give a new public role to the internal control system and which create new expectations of the audit role. For example, the collapse of Barings Bank in 1995, due to exposures under derivatives contracts, gave renewed prominence to the issue of internal control. There is a standard form of general organization control which requires a separation of duties between operational and administrative matters. In the absence of collusion this ensures that those who have access to assets do not also have access to records. In reality this is a difficult separation to maintain, particularly in small businesses and where other values, such as trust, prevail. In the case of Barings it seems clear that this segregation of duties was poor although the precise contribution of this defect to the actual problem is less clear.

To this problem of the general control environment for managing derivatives is added one which is more technical in nature and concerns the knowledge and management of the financial risks inherent in derivatives trading itself. Risk management, as a dimension of internal application control, has become an object of regulatory interest which has stimulated a market for advice (e.g. Touche Ross, 1994). During 1995, many conferences were organized on the subject of derivatives controls, J. P. Morgan published their own 'riskmetrics' model, banking regulators began to recognize the validity of in-house models for capital adequacy purposes and in the UK a derivatives control panel was established, whose members offer a risk 'healthcheck'. A survey by Price Waterhouse suggested that only 40 per cent of companies had adopted formal control parameters. Such surveys stimulate a growing market for advice as regulators demand healthchecks, remedial action and some form of assurance statement by auditors. So, once again, audit functions are likely to expand.

To conclude, the subject of internal control, once a guaranteed remedy for sleeplessness, has made a spectacular entry onto regulatory and political agendas. This in turn is moving auditing in new directions as it takes on quasi-supervisory roles by providing a public assurance function. In the case of both Cadbury and derivatives management, programmatic concerns sparked by scandals have reshaped the public role of audit to make internal organizational arrangements visible through an audit process. Concepts of 'mutual regulation' and the like are being operationalized in terms of a new regulatory role for internal mechanisms of self-assessment (Russell, 1996). The example of the Cadbury Code showed some of the difficulties and dangers of this trend but the tendency is clear: there is a visible regulatory style which seeks to internalize control at the bottom of a layered regulatory system, with oversight and ultimate sanction at the top. This is a style which compliments the demands of NPM and which also seeks to reconcile regulatory objectives with agendas for quality assurance.

INTERNALIZING GOVERNANCE: QUALITY ASSURANCE AND
ENVIRONMENTAL AUDITING

Concerns with product quality, particularly in agriculture, have a long history. In mass production industries these concerns have focused on controlling the 'fitness for use' of products (Wolnizer, 1987; Bowbrick, 1992:7; Tuckman, 1995:59–60). Forms of statistically based assurance practice with relatively well defined measurement parameters, such as defect rates,[18] were developed in the 1930s and grew during the Second World War. More recently quality has been extracted from the specificities of production processes and has been expressed in abstract and generalizable terms.[19] In short, quality has been transformed from an engineering to a management concept, a 'managerial turn' (Power, 1994*b*) which has provided advisory opportunities for a new generation of quality experts and an organizational shift in the location of these experts, up and away from the shop floor. Quality assurance has moved from its so-called 'hard' technical base towards the 'cultural' emphasis that one finds in the idea of Total Quality Management (TQM) (Tuckman,1995:64–5). Inspection at the shop floor level is giving way to standardized monitoring products.

There is a long history of programmatic interventions in the workplace, such as Taylorism and Fordism. There is also much critical debate about the extent to which TQM really differs from these earlier labour process initiatives and how serious it is in placing notions of worker empowerment at its centre. It is argued that TQM preserves hierarchies and that ideals of flexibility reproduce the subordination of labour. But TQM is also interesting in the context of regulatory style because it represents a particular project of attempting to create and regulate an internal order. A certain 'Japanization' of management process has become embedded in TQM in reaction to real and perceived problems of industrial competitiveness in North America. Concepts of quality chains and quasi-market relations within the organization are intended to make the boundaries of the organization more porous to its environment. In this sense TQM represents both the internalization of previously external relations, i.e. making the remote customer local, and also the externalization of previously internal relations, i.e. by creating chains of suppliers and customers within the production process itself. At the level of programmatic intention TQM emphasizes self-organization, responsibility and the structuring of internal sensitivities to networks of customers. From this point of view regulators can be customers as much as traditional purchasers of goods and services.

Miller and O'Leary's (1993; 1994) studies of Caterpillar Inc. show how preoccupations with competitiveness, registered both in broad industrial and political discourses and in the specific position of the company, led to attempts to 'hardwire' governance structures into the design of the factory floor. Internalization in this context may appear to be misleading since Miller and O'Leary argue for a more fluid conception of the inside and outside of an organization. However, internalization can also be understood as a reworking of boundaries. In the reforms at Caterpillar, the idea was to saturate the company with the voice of the customer. Furthermore, Caterpillar's main Japanese competitor was internalized as a persistent point of reference via benchmarking within the production process. In this case, the transformation in governance was accomplished in a number of different but complementary ways. Product quality was operationalized in conjunction with a set of controls which turned the organization inside out and which reorganized the physical space of production to achieve this.

TQM is less a set of discrete operational practices and more a programmatic umbrella for a number of different changes, not least as a stimulus to self-auditing (Munro and Hatherly, 1993). The appeal of TQM and notions of quality lies in their ambiguity, their 'diverse and fluid meanings' (Wilkinson and Willmott, 1995a:1) which do not necessarily correspond to common sense: quality is not about high standards but those which are uniform, predictable, and verifiable. Quality assurance, as an element of TQM, has more to do with a certain style of management process: '[BS 5750] is not, it must be noted, an evaluation of the quality of the product or service, but of the practices and procedures of manufacture and provision' (Tuckman, 1995:56, 71).

Tuckman also argues that the British Standards Institute, the promoter of quality assurance in the British context, emerged as a state sponsored external assessor in the field of military procurement. Over time, quality assurance has, through documents such as BS 5750, become a general product with intangible benefits which can be sold and certificated.[20] The model has also been extended and adapted in many particular directions, such as environmental management (see below), and the external audit functions to validate and communicate internal conformity to quality management dictates. Quality has become an explicit organizing concept for a wide variety of institutions and there has been an explosion of conferences and publications on the subject geared to industry specific audiences. New institutions, such as the Higher Education Quality Council, and new institutional roles, such as Quality Assessors and Directors of Quality Enhancement, have been created with the explicit aim of defining, encouraging, managing, and monitoring quality (see Chapter 5). And on the back of these developments there has even been a reflexive application of quality ideas to the quality assurance process itself.[21]

The meaning of quality in public service relates directly to concepts of effectiveness and performance auditing discussed above. The development of performance measures for teachers and doctors and of new forms of budgeting and control have generated markets for quality assurance and inspection in public service (Chapter 5). For example, the British Quality Assurance standard BS 5750 has become a condition of many contracts and, as in the private sector, can be imposed on suppliers. By 1992 70 local government authorities had been awarded a total of 106 quality management certificates and, to anticipate the arguments of Chapter 4, 'since performance cannot be demonstrated, the nature of the management system becomes, itself, the mark of effectiveness' (Walsh, 1995:94). In turn, this may have more to do with cost reduction than quality in its common sense term (Pollitt, 1993a:186).[22]

Another example of the quality revolution in public service concerns citizen's charter initiatives and the role of the Audit Commission in designing performance measures for a wide range of services. The audits of performance for charter purposes are to be done by local authority auditors appointed by the Audit Commission, a development which 'constitutes an expanded role for UK public sector auditors: that of attesting non-financial information. They are required to certify the information as genuine by reviewing the systems in place to collect the data. This does not involve verification of the data itself' (Bowerman, 1995:181). Here is the inherent tendency of auditing in a nutshell; the systems focus makes auditing possible but also more remote. It also represents a distinctive concept of evaluation (Henkel, 1991) in which the audit process and the development of indicators are inextricably linked (Bowerman, 1995:178). This idea of 'auditable performance' will be an important theme in Chapter 5.

To summarize, quality assurance initiatives show how the control system is becoming the principal focus of audit practice. Audit can provide assurance that the system works well even when substantive performance is poor. Bowerman suggests that inspectorates are used typically where quality is technically difficult to measure but one can turn the point on its head. Quality audits are used because quality *must* be made measurable. As systems become the primary focus for inspectors and auditors, technical difficulties of performance measurement become invisible. A new market for assurance services has emerged which demands a tight coupling between quality performance, however that is to be defined, and processes to ensure that this performance is visible to a wider audience, whether this is the customer, the regulator, or even the customer *as* a regulator. 'Making quality auditable' is therefore a form of impression management in which the object of audit has shifted from operations to systems of control over operations. Without audit and the certification that follows from audit, quality remains too private an affair. One might conclude that there is no quality without quality *assurance*. Perhaps nowhere is this more evident than in the rise of environmental auditing which provides a case study of the conjunction between regulatory programmes and quality assurance.

The Rise of Environmental Auditing

Gunningham and Prest (1993:495) identify the origins of environmental auditing in transactions related needs for assurance. Lenders and insurers impose such audits in order for the purchasers of land or businesses to obtain additional comfort that there are no hidden liabilities. Environmental compliance audits have become a completely standard feature of this kind of 'due diligence' work, driven largely by environmental regulations but also shaping them (Herz, 1991). As penalties have grown, so too has the market for these audits. However, in the late 1980s environmental auditing began to adapt this pure compliance based approach and to develop a management based style of self-assessment, emphasizing systems and self-informing.

The incentives for conducting voluntary environmental audits beyond a compliance framework are unclear. In the USA the Environmental Protection Agency has been reluctant to mandate or give incentives, in the form of less inspection, for voluntary audits (Van Cleve, 1991:1223) preferring a basic policy where an audit is part of an enforcement settlement with probationary conditions. Hence a compliance based approach to regulation may be more difficult where adversarial inspectorates are unwilling to cede their role to audit (Vogel, 1986:191).[23] However, business itself began to react to demands for a more integrated approach to environmental management and related audit practices. The Valdez principles, formulated in the wake of the Exxon Valdez oil spill and sponsored by a complex coalition of pension groups and public bodies (Minow and Deal, 1991:1365), included as principle number 10 the commitment to self-evaluation, 'independent environmental auditing procedures' and to making audit findings public.

In the UK there have been various pressures for change in the field of environmental regulation. The HMIP was formed in 1987 to provide a more unified and improved response to pollution control. Unlike Germany and the USA, the UK was able to build on older traditions of discretionary operations and the HMIP adapted the standard operating features inherited from its predecessor (O'Riordan and Weale, 1989) to the concept of *integrated* pollution control. In this way pollution could be programmed as a high level strategic management issue rather than in terms of 'end-of-pipe' clean up. This typifies a regulatory shift towards a more self-consciously 'responsive' style of regulation which provides for a regulatory mix of statutory and voluntary arrangements. Accordingly, environmental law is becoming more explicitly reflexive, meaning that it seeks to act indirectly on organizations (Farmer and Teubner, 1994). The shift in regulatory mood in the environmental field was further legitimized by Margaret Thatcher's address to the Royal Society in September 1988. Environmental issues were normalized and agendas for change could be shifted away from protest groups toward management consultancies and bodies representing industry. This made possible the intersection of regulatory and quality assurance initiatives.

This intersection and the related change in regulatory style is exemplified by concepts such as BATNEEC (Best Available Techniques Not Entailing Excessive Cost). BATNEEC expresses the unity of specialized, quasi-scientific bodies of knowledge and managerial disciplines with profit and cost-containment as their objectives: 'the use of the reasonably practicable means approach permits the introduction of economic considerations in a semi-formal and commonsense manner'(Manning, 1987:313). Not only do BATNEEC and its variants legitimize cost arguments in relation to environmental problems, thereby normalizing a new politics of the environmental field, but they also express a realignment of expertise. Practices of soil sampling, emissions testing and other such 'dirty' technologies have become subsumed within programmes which emphasize management *systems* of control. In this respect the transformation of 'waste disposal' into 'waste management' is more than merely linguistic, a change of labels; it seeks to reorient the symbolic field in which such practices operate and to change their visibility and location within corporate decision making structures.[24]

These developments are not just a function of the UK's so-called fragmented institutional structures for dealing with environmental or financial regulation (Vogel, 1986; O'Riordan and Weale, 1989). Even in countries with an established tradition of coherent environmental policy, experimentation is under way.[25] For example, in the Netherlands government inspection is shifting from direct control of compliance with regulations towards testing the performance of a Corporate Wide Environmental Care system (CWEC). This is a move from a deterrence to a compliance based style of control and reflects a transfer of regulatory resources from direct inspection of compliance to the indirect inspection of systems for self-checking (Aalders, 1993:88). As in other areas, the internal control system assumes a central regulatory role. Regulatory agendas for control are being pushed down into organizations and reconceived as a strategic management opportunity rather than as a regulatory sanction. The Dutch motif of *Verinnerlijking* symbolizes this new partnership between 'feasibility and ecological responsibility' (Hajer, 1994) and an 'internalisation of environmental responsibility'.

All of this amounts to a 'managerial turn' in environmental regulation which parallels very similar changes in other areas, such as financial markets. This managerial turn, albeit unevenly distributed throughout Europe and North America, is the common link between the three driving elements of the audit explosion discussed in this chapter. A regulatory space has been created for environmental auditing as a 'bottom up' self-inspecting activity which connects the inner workings of organizations to regulatory programmes. Thus, instead of regulation seeking to penetrate organizational culture from the outside, the image proffered is more that of a form of self-control embodied in the quality assurance system extending its visibility beyond the organization. The externalization of internal control and the internalization of external controls are no longer clearly distinguishable.

The International Chamber of Commerce (ICC) has taken a leading role in articulating a programmatic agenda for voluntary environmental auditing. Environmental auditing is defined as a 'management tool' (ICC, 1991) and this became an important motif in the 1990s. The new regulatory spirit of internalization has displaced and reformulated an older tradition of potentially critical social auditing conducted by groups external to targeted organizations. Rather than a 'holy grail' (Elkington, 1988), in which all issues of social responsibility can be addressed, the concept of environmental audit has been reconceptualized in a narrower pragmatic space in which the very management processes which were perceived as responsible for the production of environmental damage have been re-fashioned as its guardians.[26]

The programmatic image of financial audit has been an influential reference point, if only as a basis for articulating a distinction between it and environmental audit. Whereas the financial audit is statutory, annual, verificatory, external, and based on Generally Accepted Accounting Principles (GAAP), environmental audits are voluntary, of variable frequency, managerially oriented, internal, relative to varied standards of performance, and focused on environmental issues (ICC, 1991). This of course is an ideal typical and programmatic contrast; it has more to do with an intended mission for environmental auditing rather than its substantive practice. However, these contrasting starting points for financial and environmental audits are important and have shaped thinking about the respective fields, the one as a regulatory practice which may, secondarily, be a management tool, the other primarily as a management tool which may play a regulatory role. Whereas the financial audit has needed to 'grow inwards' and embrace internal systems of control, concerns about independent validation and reporting are relatively recent in an environmental auditing field which has 'grown outward' to attach itself to regulatory programmes and aspirations. Extracted from its 'dirty' technical origins, environmental auditing is being re-shaped and reorientated as part of efforts to internalize regulatory compliance while at the same time stimulating internal cultural change in an organization. In this respect regulatory programmes can be harnessed to quality management.

There has been much voluntary experimentation with environmental disclosures in corporate annual reports and some companies have contracted auditors to verify these disclosures (Gray, 1993:252). However, in the early 1990s two similar environmental auditing schemes were developed. The 'Eco-Management and Audit Scheme' (EMAS), modelled in part on the Dutch experience, was issued as an EU regulation in June 1993. BS 7750 was developed by the British Standards Institute and has been absorbed into the ISO 14000 series, which is to develop guidance in the whole area of environmental assurance, including standards of performance.[27] Chapter 4 will provide further discussion of the operational detail of these schemes, especially the centrality of the environmental management system to both of them. For the moment it is important to draw attention to the 'private government' dimensions of these initiatives.

In the UK, a state agency, the National Accreditation Council for Certification Bodies (NACCB), the British Standards Institute, large management consulting firms and a whole host of associational bodies constitute a network for policy development for environmental auditing which interacts closely with other national and transnational organizations.[28] Consultancies such as PA Consulting and Coopers & Lybrand have developed close links with the Directorate responsible for environmental issues at the European Commission, DG XI. These links are strengthened by the administration of regulatory pilot schemes, the secondment of staff in both directions, the production of research reports and by the development of practitioner guidance. In this way regulatory knowledge production is increasingly sub-contracted to networks of interdependent expertise.

Environmental auditing has emerged programmatically as a practice which regulatory systems demand. The practice has become an article of regulatory faith before clear conceptions of its precise role and scope have become institutionalized. This suggests that the very idea of audit is valued almost regardless of what is done in its name. Auditing is set in motion before it is understood and, as the discussion of financial auditing in Chapter 2 demonstrates, a certain 'expectations gap' between what is demanded of it and what it might produce is essential to its wide appeal. Furthermore the theme of obscurity is equally relevant in this case. There is an indeterminacy about what environmental audits produce in the way of assurance and the operational scope of their procedures is unclear. For example, on the question of accounting for environmental liabilities (AICPA, 1995; ICAEW, 1994) the relation between financial audits of environmental liabilities and environmental audits of environmental management systems is negotiable and questions of professional turf are at stake.

Practical texts and guidance documents in the environmental field serve as much to obfuscate the normative scope of the audit process and to present the field in an institutionally legitimate way as they do to provide concrete operational guidance (Power, 1995b). Like financial auditing, the essential unknowability of the cost–assurance function for environmental auditing means that it must invest heavily in procedural knowledge and in the language of professional judgement, a strategy which requires the construction of social trust in practitioners. This explains why considerable regulatory attention has been paid to accreditation schemes for environmental auditing practitioners.

On this last point it is important to recall that the sociology of regulation and of professions can no longer be separate domains (Dezalay, 1995a:6) and that the operational specification of regulatory programmes define potentials for professional advice. In addition, new collective mobility projects and claims to new forms of a profession can be articulated as practitioners see opportunities to move up, or even challenge, existing hierarchies of management knowledge (Dezalay, 1995b). All this is visible in the environmental auditing field where consulting markets thrive in the margins of regulatory initiatives. Where central agencies wish to effect management changes in target organizations management consultants take on the role of mediating regulatory compliance and economic strategy (Henkel, 1991). The emergence of environmental consulting around concepts like BATNEEC has realigned general management within the environmental field and stimulated professionalization initiatives. In the UK there have also been a number of associational initiatives, seeking the legitimacy of state accreditation under EMAS and BS 7750.

Environmental auditing provides both threats and opportunities to self-styled 'technical and scientific' consultancies, such as Arthur D. Little. At the operational level of auditable environmental systems there are problems of 'turf'. Friedman (1991:1321–2) argues that the basic review of documentation can be done by financial auditors, leaving more important tasks for specialist personnel. There is some evidence that accountants in the UK would see the hierarchical relation the other way round. General acceptance that environmental auditing must be a multidisciplinary practice has raised the stakes for those who would orchestrate such work, such as accountants and engineers (Power, forthcoming). Certainly, the managerial turn in environmental regulation, which has generated the market for environmental auditing, has also made possible accountants' claims in this area (Huizing and Dekker, 1992; CICA, 1992). Such claims are highly debated and often depend on the negotiation of similarities between environmental and financial audits. Where management control systems are specified in the high level language of TQM the claims of accountants look more plausible. It follows that the less abstract the representation of environmental auditing practice, the more that managerial disciplines like accounting lose their orchestrating foothold and hierarchical position in the field.

In this section, the third influence on the audit explosion has been addressed: programmes for quality assurance. Regulatory and quality management programmes coincide in a management system which serves both compliance and economic functions. Environmental auditing schemes which have been more or less explicitly modelled on quality assurance programmes illustrate the commitment to the internalization of control which is common to regulator and regulated. Problems of the legitimacy and effectiveness of environmental regulation have motivated experimentation in new styles and new instruments which seek to influence the internal control mechanisms of an organization. Diverse business associations have been drawn into policy processes as environmental issues have become normalized. These changes have driven an environmental audit explosion which has moved from the private ground of specific transactions to become a regulatory instrument with a public role, serviced by an aspiring class of professionals. As in the case of financial auditing, environmental auditing promises to connect the inner workings of companies to wider public demands for control inscribed in regulatory programmes. This much is the programmatic mission of an environmental audit concept whose objectives and operational scope are still widely debated. In Chapter 4, the question of what environmental audits really provide will be addressed.

CONCLUSIONS

It has been said that 'In every policy making environment there is a culture that affects the style of discussion and intervention' (Beneviste, 1973:137). This chapter has explored three overlapping programmes which share a certain culture and which have driven the audit explosion: New Public Management; 'responsive' regulation; and quality assurance. These initiatives can be regarded in part as reactions against the burden of knowledge generated by the growth of the welfare state and the increased public role of the social sciences.[29] They share a programmatic optimism about the potential for reflexive approaches to regulation and organizational control which intervene in the self-governing structure of sub-systems (Mayntz, 1993). Even though the need to govern 'in accordance with the grain of things' has long been recognized (Burchell *et al.*, 1991; Rose and Miller, 1992), there is a new enthusiasm, influenced heavily by cost considerations, for the enlistment of third parties and their related expert technologies into regulatory structures.

Emergent political rationalities are instrumentalizing the 'self-governing properties of subjects of the government themselves in a whole variety of locales and localities' (Rose, 1996:352). This implies that 'top down' transformations in regulatory style compliment 'bottom up' styles of control inherent in quality assurance. Programmatic agendas for quality management suggest that distinctions between employees, suppliers, customers, regulators, etc. are increasingly blurred. The growth of on-line information structures also means that it is no longer possible to draw a line between the inside and outside of organization. Grabosky (1995*b*:543) argues that 'The challenge facing governments in the new century is one of "meta-monitoring".' As the regulatory state (Day and Klein, 1990; Pildes and Sunstein, 1995) shrinks to the role of monitor of last resort, new forms of managerial capacity are being stimulated and hitherto private practices, like internal control, are being governmentalized and formalized.[30] From this perspective audit, internal or external, tends towards a 'control of control' (Kelly, 1995:123) as part of ever deeper loops of reflexive self-ordering.

The delegation of regulatory control to associative orders such as professional audit bodies is also intended to solve problems of legitimation for the state and to enhance possibilities for compliance (Streeck and Schmitter, 1985*a*).[31] This is not to say that state influence is absent. As the examples of the Cadbury Code and environmental auditing have shown, the state is an important sponsor of private interest regulation. And the devolution of state functions in this way must be accompanied by the 'simultaneous acquisition by the state of a capacity to design, monitor and keep in check the new self-regulating systems' (Streeck and Schmitter, 1985:26). Hence there has been a reassembly of inspectorial capacity (Henkel, 1991) to accompany the audit explosion.

Between the extremes of the compliance and deterrence styles of enforcement (Reiss, 1984), a mix is being worked out which presupposes the development of internal systems of control. The unit of regulatory attention is now the organization and its system of control rather than the individual, and in a wide variety of areas it is this shift in regulatory style which has necessitated mediating auditing activities.[32] The audit explosion is to do with the need to install a publicly auditable self-inspecting capacity which attempts to link ideals of accountability to those of self-learning. The rise of internal control as the auditable object has also made the role of internal auditors more visible and has re-opened debates about optimal balances between internal and external arrangements for assurance which may trade off competence and proximity against independence. Only time will tell as to whether there is a long term shift from external to internal self-auditing capacity.[33]

Finally, the audit explosion represents a decision to shift evaluative cultures away from social scientific towards managerial knowledge bases: 'The definition of the character of a regulatory issue is itself an important part of the process by which it is allocated to the domain of certain organizations and removed from the domain of others' (Hancher and Moran, 1989:293). And yet in allocating problems to auditing institutions not only are the boundaries between instrumental assurance and policy evaluation constantly breached but audit and inspection are also seen to constitute the conduct of politics by other means, a characteristic they share with war.

It is important not to overstate the case. Audit is not all pervasive and market mechanisms are a significant countermodel of control. Furthermore, the programmatic confidence in auditing, a confidence which of necessity must be rebuilt in the wake of failure, must work with a practice whose benefits are often difficult to demonstrate and whose cost–assurance function remains obscure. There has been debate as never before within professional ranks about the nature and scope of audit itself (APB, 1994; CIPFA, 1994b). But, for all the talk of a crisis of confidence and identity, auditing has nevertheless become increasingly essential to the operationalization of organizational governance in different programmatic fields. We may not know exactly what audits are and how they work, but institutional changes and regulatory responses are being accomplished by relying on them. Even though auditing threatens to become a negative product, constantly asserting what it is not, expectations necessarily remain high. The three overlapping programmes discussed in this chapter presuppose and demand that auditing in its different forms can deliver assurance, contribute to compliance and stimulate best practice. Furthermore, the three programmes pass costs down to regulatees who develop a self-monitoring capacity.

The reinvention of governance around audit processes described in this chapter necessarily treats the audit process as a black box. Its ambiguity enables it to satisfy different aspects of the mood of the times: it is a basis for curtailing waste and inefficiency, for reprogramming regulation, for providing a new transparency of organizational and individual performance and for reducing the risks of operating in different fields. To account and to be audited is, almost tautologically, to be accountable. And yet, as Chapter 2 demonstrates, failures can make visible the gap between the rhetorics of accountability and empowerment which set auditing in motion and the actual means for its achievement (Hopwood, 1984). Accordingly, auditing technology must constantly assert its claims to 'make things auditable'. It does this in two ways: by adapting the environment to its objectives through the creation of auditable performance measures (to be considered in Chapter 5), and by making its own operational knowledge base institutionally credible, a process which must now be addressed.

4
Making Audits Work: Samples, Specialists, and Systems

INTRODUCTION

The previous two chapters have concentrated on the programmes for control and accountability which drive the demand for auditing in its various forms. It was suggested that the programmatic demands made upon auditing are only loosely coupled to its technical capabilities; this gives rise to expectations gaps. In Chapter 2 it was also argued that the production of incremental assurance which audits promise is essentially obscure. Instead of a clear conception of output, auditing is constituted by a range of procedures backed by experience and judgement. To say this is to say that auditing is a form of craft knowledge. Auditing practices may be demanded by broader regulatory programmes but they are operationalized in the form of a series of routines which are economically constrained on the one hand and must have a certain institutional credibility as technique on the other.

The concept of evidence is at the heart of contemporary thinking about the operational dimensions of auditing practice (Flint, 1988). As has already been argued, auditing is essentially an inferential practice and auditors must collect and analyse evidential material in order to form their conclusions. Accordingly, official guidance statements in both the UK and the USA require financial auditors to obtain relevant and reliable evidence which is sufficient to enable an opinion to be formed upon the financial statements. This suggests that assertions or events can be verified by the appropriate collection and interpretation of evidence. Furthermore, the audited domain must be auditable by leaving 'a trail of evidence and procedures that can be verified' (AAA, 1966:10). So verification and evidence are complementary concepts; auditors verify on the basis of evidence.

However, verification and related processes of evidence gathering are not as simple as they first appear in official texts. Evidence is not just out there and what counts as verification or testing requires a background consensus to support the use of the technique. Latour (1987) suggests that there is nothing natural about forms of evidence. Evidence is always relative to the rules of acceptance for particular communities. Furthermore, 'auditability', which is often regarded as an intrinsic property of the elements of financial statements, is often constructed in the interaction between auditor, auditee and official knowledge in an active process of 'rendering auditable'. Indeed, even accounting and auditing theorists, who could never be described as social constructivists, point to the close conceptual relation between verification and agreement among a community of observers (Solomons, 1986; Wolnizer, 1987).

In this chapter three general operational dimensions of the audit process are considered where the social support for the authority of technical practices comes into view: sampling and risk analysis, reliance on other forms of expertise, the evaluation of internal control systems. The argument below concentrates on the *systemic* significance of these three dimensions and the manner in which ideas of effective auditing are constituted through them. Whether audits work from the individual practitioner's point of view depends on the careful application of techniques: debtors are circularized, stock is checked, post balance sheet payments are reviewed, purchases are checked against valid invoices, inquiries are made about business trends, important accounting ratios are analysed and so on. And auditors will always be looking for evidence which lies outside the audited organization to support the verification of accounting numbers. But whether audits work *systemically* depends on this network of procedures constituting a taken for granted whole, a knowledge resource which can be drawn upon in specific circumstances. Audit must make itself work and the construction of this systemic imperative is visible in the examples of sampling, specialists, and systems.

SAMPLING, RISK, AND THE ECONOMICS OF AUDITING[1]

In Chapter 2 the fundamental question for auditing was identified: how much testing is necessary? The conventional answer is that more work takes more time, costs more and provides incrementally more assurance, although possibly at a diminishing rate. It was also argued that the precise nature of the relation between inputs of work and outputs of assurance in auditing is elusive and is largely obscured by constituting the knowledge base of auditing in procedural terms. However, there is one important exception to this claim: the attempt to develop statistically based audit sampling techniques.

Auditing and sampling, in the general sense of selective testing, seem so closely related as to require no further explanation: the auditor examines a small number of transactions as a basis for drawing conclusions about the transactions as a whole. For example, for a sample of purchases the auditor wishes to establish whether the recorded transactions were authorized, correctly recorded and classified, and, importantly, actually took place. The auditor may also be interested in establishing whether the transactions were at arms length or on special terms between related parties. These and other issues have nothing to do with the sample itself; they are a question of the type of tests to be done on the sampled items. The auditor must also define what counts as an error for the sample and be prepared to extrapolate, formally or informally, from the error characteristics of the sample to the population of transactions as a whole. This is the point of a sample, to be able to learn something about whole populations. Accordingly, the sample must be constructed so as to be 'representative' of the population of transactions under examination.

The development of sampling procedures for auditing seems on the surface to be unproblematic. To recap the official story, as businesses grew in size so did the number of transactions they conducted. Auditors quickly realized that they could not audit, except in the most superficial manner, every transaction. The audit would simply be too expensive. Furthermore, there was no need to look at all transactions if the company itself was engaged in a process of self-checking through its own internal control system. So the idea developed that one could move along and up the cost–assurance function (Fig. 2.1) by sampling. In this way, sampling made the audit more efficient while giving it a basis for making 'hard' quantitative statements of assurance. Nevertheless, this story is too neat and it is necessary to consider another which reveals much about the principal theme in this chapter: how audits are made to work.

The Rise of Sampling

The concept of sampling is normally associated with forms of inference which, typically, can be formalized in statistical terms, e.g. 'the reported debtors balance is within 3% of the actual figure at a 95% level of confidence'. However, there is a long practical, if not theoretical, tradition of sampling for quality control purposes (e.g. Stigler, 1977). 'Sampling, after all, is largely a matter of common sense, and the common sense approach has often resulted in more rapid progress in technique than has the more purely mathematical approach' (Yates, 1946:12). The concept of the 'representative sample' makes its first formally significant and controversial appearance in 1895 with Kiaer's work on the Norwegian population census, although the implications of this work did not emerge fully until many years later (Westergaard, 1932:263).

Sampling, like auditing, was from the very beginning a practice or craft before it became an object of theoretical interest. Indeed, sampling has always been intended to solve practical problems: 'a sample survey is an economic production process intended to make the most efficient use of limited resources in order to achieve specified goals' (Hansen and Madow, 1976:77). Over time, these practical origins conflicted with the values and background of an emerging body of elite professional statisticians (Porter,

1986:236). This group tended to argue that, in the absence of reliable information regarding the population as a whole, it was difficult, if not impossible, to know what 'adequate representation' really was. Sampling seemed to be paradoxical because one had to know the population in some sense before the sample could be credible. But if one knew the population then sampling was redundant.

Others, more sensitive to practice, recognized that sampling, albeit formally paradoxical, was nevertheless fundamental to experience itself (Kruskal and Mosteller, 1979, 1980; Stephan, 1948) and drew attention to the necessity of inference in a wide variety of areas where quality assessments were important, such as estimating crop yields. The Second World War provided a further stimulus to the development of sampling methods because of the need for munitions quality control (Vance, 1950).

As far as financial auditing was concerned, selective levels of detailed transactional testing were commonplace in the late nineteenth century; for example, a 'block test' was used in which the auditor might look at all the relevant transactions in a particular month. While such block tests were indeed a form of proto-sampling, they lacked statistically precise notions of 'representativeness', at least until the 1930s if not later. Hence, it is necessary to distinguish between a form of practice based on partial testing and the later emergence of a statistical discourse as a basis for rethinking the audit process. Long before auditors had become acquainted with statistical sampling, practical concerns forced them to be selective in their work.

Modes of evidence gathering and standards of proof represent styles of reasoning which become institutionally established, and this applies as much to financial auditing as it does to any other practice: 'Most professionals now believe that representative sampling gives more accurate information about a population than an exhaustive census. This was unthinkable during most of the nineteenth century. The very thought of being representative has had to come into being. This has required techniques of thinking together with technologies of data collection. An entire style of scientific reasoning has had to evolve' (Hacking, 1990:6–7).

Block testing made good sense in the context of tacit professional knowledge in the nineteenth century: conceptions of 'adequate proof' were implicit as an unarticulated consensus about what was reasonable. According to Justice Lindley's judgment in the *London and General Bank* case, 'businessmen select a few cases haphazard and assume that others like them are correct also.' Sampling also arises naturally from the discovery that internal controls can be relied upon. Taylor and Perry (1931), like Dicksee, consider it to be a 'waste of time' (and presumably money) to replicate every test that has already been done. However, there is 'no reference to sampling, namely, examining a few items and inferring that all of the items are equally well (or badly) handled' (Myers, 1985:55). Before the 1930s questions of operational scope were formulated negatively in terms of the amount of testing which could be curtailed, with 100 per cent as the benchmark.

Early American audits followed the British model of detailed checks of bookkeeping but over time they became more explicitly pragmatic and economic in focus (Moyer, 1951:5). There were also demands for a theory underlying the use of tests and samples (Kirkham and Gaa, 1939) and Stempf (1936) recommends the selection of a 'representative period' of transactions. Prytherch (1942) explicitly relates the problem of selective testing to statistical reasoning. In Britain the fifteenth (1933) edition of Dicksee's *Auditing*, edited by S. W. Rowland, introduces the concept of a representative sample: 'The items to be tested ought to be so chosen that they cover the whole field to be examined, or, in other words, they ought to be, in the statistical sense, *fair* samples of the whole group (Dicksee, 1933:49, emphasis added). Rowland died in 1946 but the seventeenth edition by Magee retains his formulation on sampling. By the time of the appearance of the eighteenth edition in 1969 by T. S. Waldron the formulation is supplemented by explicit references to statistically based sampling. Overall, it is through the problem of sampling that the economic dimensions of auditing become explicit; the auditor must stop checking where the marginal cost exceeds the marginal benefit (incremental confidence) of testing a further item: 'Between the detailed examination on the one hand and the balance sheet audit on the other, a new point of equilibrium was sought, an investigation comprehensive enough to inform the public and protect the accountant yet economical enough to justify the cost to the client' (Chatfield 1977:137).

The appeal of statistical rationalizations of the auditing process is cultural as well as economic. Clearly the independent development of statistical sampling as a body of knowledge in its own right is an important necessary condition for audit sampling. But this cannot explain the timing and reception of these ideas within audit practice. Early accountancy and auditing policy discourses in the USA were permeated by a scientific optimism (Miranti, 1986;1988) which was open to statistical ideas. This receptivity also coincided with a more general process of rationalization and formalization of accounting and auditing knowledge in the 1930s. The establishment of the Securities Exchange Commission in 1934 stimulated regulatory interest in audit priorities and methods and, following the famous *McKesson and Robbins* case in 1938, an SEC committee was established to review the quality of existing auditing standards which had been prescribed by the American Institute in 1936. This is a clear but rare example of regulatory attention to the system of audit knowledge which from this point on becomes explicitly codified.

If the rise of statistical sampling ideas within accounting and auditing policy was part of a broader construction and formalization of the knowledge base of practice, the story is nevertheless not free from conflict. Once external pressures for greater codification of practice gathered momentum, they were matched by internal pressures to preserve the boundaries of practitioner judgement. In short, programmatic demands for reform and for the introduction of new methods, like statistical sampling, always had and still have a problematic relation to the level of practical operations and to the interests of practitioners in preserving discretion.

Judgement and Formalism

From time to time financial auditing practitioners discuss the merits of 'structured' versus 'unstructured' audit approaches (e.g. Cushing and Loebbecke, 1984b; Mullarkey, 1984; Sullivan 1984; Francis, 1994). These debates are much more than theoretical; large auditing firms have periodically changed their entire approaches and audit methodologies as a consequence. But the issue goes deep to the heart of any professional practice and concerns the relative balance been trust in individual practitioner judgement and the need for conformity to formal and publicly defendable rules of conduct. Practitioners often react against increased formalization of the auditing craft while institutional pressures in the environment of the auditing system of knowledge (Chapter 2) demand more of it. Standard operating procedures also enable large auditing firms to control individual practitioners who often prefer inventive and *ad hoc* methods based on broad principles.

The rise of statistical sampling provides a good example of these tensions. Despite vague alignments with scientific ideals, the 'overall impression' approach to audit testing in which the auditor is 'in the capacity of a judge' (Staub, 1942:34), was an important counterpoint to the development of formal sampling. Practitioners needed to assert the mysteries of their art at the same time as they helped themselves to the impersonal scientistic rhetoric of the day (Boland, 1982). There were, and continue to be, concerns that audit could become a merely mechanical practice, thereby threatening the status of practitioners' expertise: 'nothing takes the place of judgement: the laws of probability are only a guide' (Prytherch, 1942:527).

In the post-war period, the appearance of texts and articles describing statistical sampling were an elaborate sales pitch to an army of practitioners unused to, and suspicious of, any mathematical basis for their craft. Sensitivity to these suspicions required an emphasis on the low level of mathematical knowledge required and assurances that the audit would not be merely mechanical. Furthermore, professional level 'technical guidance' tended to say very little about the substance of statistical sampling, preferring to leave this to the market for textbooks, such as those by Vance and Neter (1956) and Trueblood and Cyert (1957). The AIA itself had only developed meagre and statistically non-committal guidance to auditors.

The emergence of statistical sampling techniques therefore created tensions within the auditing system of knowledge. On the one hand here was an obvious practice to import into financial auditing, with a growing acceptance and legitimacy in other fields. On the other hand, professional judgement, despite the assertions of Trueblood and Cyert and others before them, was threatened. It is therefore not surprising that the actual use of statistical auditing practice, rather than its celebration in textbooks, is problematic. Gwilliam's (1987) review of research suggests that the texts of Trueblood and Cyert were well in advance of auditing practice. It is well known that many unskilled auditors did not understand how to deal with errors discovered in samples. This led to attempts to neutralize an error and explain it away, rather than follow the logic required by the statistics. Worse still, Elliott (1983) draws attention to the possibility that auditors work backwards from some desired outcome (e.g. sample size) to the determination of the required variables to generate that outcome (e.g. risk).

From this point of view, decisions in the audit process are rationalized and dressed up in the language of statistical sampling. There was progressive investment in a vague scientific rationality and in ways of talking about the audit process which did not threaten the discourse of seasoned judgement. A certain balance between the personal and the anonymous, the subjective and objective, the judgemental and technical, the concrete and the abstract is at the heart of professional expertise. Professional audit knowledge attached itself to the legitimate technical values of the day without becoming widely disseminated in a manner which would undermine the status of practitioner judgement (Abbott, 1988).

What is fundamentally at stake in this schematic history which is relevant today? The answer is that even the operational dimensions of auditing have certain vague programmatic elements which project an ideal operational form of the audit, a model around which actual audits can organize and represent themselves. Even though the concept of representation created analytical difficulties for professional statisticians, early forms of block testing could be representative simply because they were accepted as being so for many years, despite not conforming to strict canons of statistical method. The lesson is that what counts as reasonable procedure and evidence is grounded in an evolving practitioner consensus in which tasks and routines are given meaning within wider operational frameworks. And these frameworks evolve from the need to create an appearance of satisfying programmatic demands while controlling the audit as an economic product.

Risk Based Approaches to Audit

By the mid-1980s, statistical sampling in auditing had fallen out of favour. It seemed to be finally accepted in the USA and the UK that auditing could never be a science. In particular, there was a growing awareness that the conditions under which statistical samples are valid are often not met and, in any case, require prior decisions about precision and confidence levels. Furthermore, statistical sampling is usually only effective under conditions of low risk and typical error pattern[2] whereas auditors are increasingly interested in the high risk atypical errors. For example, they are more concerned with the rare but catastrophic potential of, say, corporate failure, than with the coolly calculated low risk associated with a large population of reasonably controlled transactions. Accordingly, in place of time consuming samples and tests in low risk areas, the view emerged that financial auditing must explicitly focus its work where it is most likely to generate assurance. This is the intuition which has driven the development of risk based approaches to auditing.

Holstrum and Kirtland (1983) and others developed and refined a model which has become a form of conceptual framework for thinking about the audit process and where risks may lie.[3] Most firms now adopt the language of risk, if not this model in its precise form, in their own methodologies (Turley, 1989:111). The attraction and durability of the risk based approach is not simply a function of its operational appeal as an aid to decision making for the individual auditor; it is also, and perhaps primarily, a basis for 'making sense' of audit work. Indeed, its vagueness is part of its operational attraction and as far as the existing body of practitioners is concerned, any innovation like this must also be continuous with existing operational habits.[4] Humphrey and Moizer (1990:229) observe that risk has become the new buzzword for audit and has been co-opted into a more general search for 'cost-efficiency' in auditing. In this way, the audit risk model replaces and subsumes the role formerly played by statistical sampling in promoting a scientifically rational image of the audit process. It also rationalizes a reorganization of audit work in terms of the assignment of 'risk factors'. Practitioners have been concerned about 'overauditing' which can be represented, as in Fig. 4.1, as a low marginal benefit to audit work. In this respect the model provides a framework for justifying a reduction in detailed transactions testing because there are compensating sources of comfort.

It must be emphasized, both in the case of sampling and the risk model that this is not an elaborate deceit by practitioners on an unsuspecting public. If the risk model is a marketing device it is not just for external purposes; concepts of sample and risk serve to reorganize practitioner self-understanding of operations. Practitioners are individually cynical about the 'newness' of the risk approach, as Humphrey and Moizer (1990) have

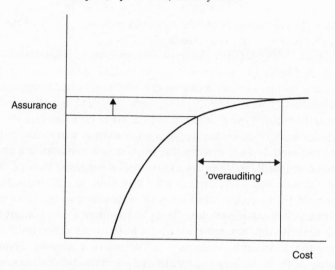

FIG. 4.1 Overauditing and the cost–assurance function

observed. But the significance of the audit risk model is not so much as a completely new operational basis for work but as a new framework for organizing these operations and as a basis for assuming an upward shift in the cost–assurance function (Fig. 2.1). Indeed, the very ambiguity of the audit risk model is its great strength in reworking the economic and epistemic bases of audit practice. Grobstein and Craig (1984) show how Ernst & Whinney applied the risk model non-quantitatively whereas Deloitte Haskins & Sells developed quantitative measures for all the individual risk factors. Yet in both firms the model provided an important unifying rationale for audit practice as a form of credible knowledge. The fact that the model is applied and interpreted very differently by different firms is of secondary importance as compared with its systemic meaning for the knowledge base of auditing. The model delineates a certain kind of practical logic which is simultaneously vague and formal. Furthermore, the risk model allows liability risk to be thought of in connection with operational matters. Audit risk is ultimately both the risk of a false audit opinion and also the possible economic loss that may result from legal action.

In conclusion, the view of both sampling and the audit risk model which has been sketched here attempts to go beyond a purely technical view of their function. Naturally, detailed routines and tasks can be developed which apply these forms of knowledge but this is often a case of matching particular judgements, hunches and intuitions formed under economic constraints to more abstract and formal metaphors of best practice. To say all this is to emphasize that the prevailing humble and craftlike nature of auditing is constantly being attached to models and frameworks which promise a new operational potential.

It is widely recognized that the financial audit process requires many different skills. Indeed, to read some textbooks one would have the impression of the auditor as a superman or woman with, in addition to core skills in accounting, skills in statistics, valuation, information technology, production processes, and a variety of other industry specific matters. In reality this cannot be so. Audits are normally conducted in teams with a mix of skills and levels of experience brought together for a common purpose. In the case of the emerging market for environmental audits described in Chapter 3, multidisciplinarity is the norm. Lawyers, engineers, and accountants may combine their skills in the environmental auditing process, often competing for hierarchical precedence (Power, forthcoming). Which skills are inside and outside the audit process is not clear in the case of environmental auditing. In Chapter 2 it was also suggested that audit opinions are a negotiation between auditor and auditee; this makes the distinction between the inside and outside of the audit process even more indeterminate.

In financial auditing, the core knowledge base is relatively stable and where a skill which is fundamental to the formation of a view on financial statements is very specialized, the opinion of a party external to the audit team is required. Indeed, professional guidance has been developed to deal with this possibility (APC, 1986 replaced by APB, 1995b).[6] The idea is that an auditor cannot be expected to have the detailed knowledge and experience of specialists in other disciplines but he/she is nevertheless obliged to form an opinion on the need for specialist knowledge and, in the case of a particular specialist, on their competence and objectivity. This formal guidance assumes that competence is normally indicated by technical qualifications, membership of a recognized professional body or even experience and general reputation in the market. Accordingly, existing institutional legitimacy in the form of professional qualifications provides evidence of the reliability of this specialist. In principle the auditor audits the specialist and not their work.

In the UK, perhaps one of the most common areas of reliance on other experts has been that of land and property. These valuations are normally performed by chartered surveyors who have an established professional status in the British system. Financial statements which incorporate such valuations must disclose the basis of the work as well as details about the valuers themselves. In addition to chartered surveyors, financial auditors also rely upon the work of actuaries who value pension funds and determine contribution rates (APC, 1990*d*). However, perhaps the most instructive case to consider is that of brand valuation.

Valuing and Auditing

The background to, and problem of, brand accounting in the UK has been well documented.[7] In the late 1980s, a period of intense merger and acquisitions activity, the accounting rules for business combinations and the enforcement of these rules by financial auditors evoked much criticism (e.g. Smith, 1992), especially where companies flagrantly exploited rules to enhance post-acquisition reported performance. The problem of brand accounting arose because companies with large amounts of goodwill in their consolidated balance sheets were faced with two undesirable possibilities within the existing rules in the UK: immediate write-off to reserves or capitalization and amortization. A number of UK companies, notably Grand Metropolitan PLC and Ranks Hovis MacDougall PLC, valued and capitalized their brands in the balance sheet. RHM also valued its internally generated as well as purchased brands.

The controversy centred on the question as to whether brands could be measured with sufficient reliability to be recognized on the balance sheet (Napier and Power, 1992). A report by the London Business School (LBS) (Barwise *et al.*, 1989) argued that, despite the assertions of valuers such as the specialist company Interbrand PLC, there was no general agreement about the validity of their valuation methodology. The methodology was neither 'totally theoretically valid nor empirically verifiable'. Furthermore, 'Verifiability . . . has implications for "auditability" since it is a necessary condition for recognition that asset valuations should be auditable'. In other words, there is a close link between the credibility of economic measurement for accounting recognition purposes and the auditability of such measures.

The LBS report argued that brand valuations are not auditable because all the 'auditors can really check is the process, not the book values'. Auditors can check any calculation to agreed procedures but cannot check the procedures themselves since they are 'not experts and cannot make such judgements'. But others were less sceptical (e.g. Sherwood, 1990:82–4). The auditor can 'verify the underlying facts' on which valuation is based; brand valuation is not an 'exact science' and it is 'better to be broadly right than precisely wrong'. In part the question is whether the auditor can reasonably just re-perform certain conventional calculations or whether she must try to inspect and form a direct judgement about the substantive inputs into the calculative process. However, on closer inspection, much of the controversy about the verifiability and auditability of brand valuations hangs on the *trust* in the expertise of those whose calculations are being revisited by the auditor. Furthermore, verifiability and auditability are not absolute properties of transactions themselves but are a function of the often changing limits of the auditor's expertise, the system of audit knowledge, and the credibility of other external specialists who might fill an expertise deficit.

The problem can be illustrated in terms of three possibilities. First, the verification of the valuation of marketable securities would be regarded as well within the normal competence of the financial auditor and he/she would rely on official price listings as an independent source of evidence.[8] Second, the verification of the valuation of land and buildings seems to fall beyond the knowledge base of the financial auditor but falls within that of chartered surveyors.[9] Third, in the extreme case a matter is beyond expert measurement and is therefore unauditable either by the auditor directly or by relying on other specialists. As far as brand valuation is concerned, there has been much heated debate as to which of these three possibilities applied. The problem is that an answer is not simply a technical question of the valuation method but also a question of the *social* position of the valuer.

The now defunct Accounting Standards Committee stated that 'A valuation may be regarded as verifiable if different independent valuers using the same information would be likely to arrive at a similar valuation' (ASC, 1990*a*, para. 3.2, echoed in ASC 1990*b*, para. 27). This consensus between different valuers is in principle an empirical question of the *actual* standard deviation among measurers (Ijiri and Jaedicke, 1966). In other words, there are no *a priori* grounds for saying whether a valuation technique is unreliable and hence unauditable; this is a function of the social consensus which supports its general acceptance. And how does the technique become generally accepted? Only if its practitioners are credible. And if the valuers are credible, their expertise can be relied upon and the numbers they produce become auditable. In this way the whole question of the auditability of measures of brand value rests on the credibility or otherwise of what the valuers were doing. Auditability is a function not of things themselves but of agreement within a specialist community which learns to observe and verify in a certain way (Hacking, 1983). Of course, the world may show that these community habits were defective and need revision, but a consensus will need to be reconstructed for any better practice.

The problem of brand accounting can expressed as follows. Instead of a story of struggles to identify relevant cash flows and apply an appropriate discount rate, there is a story of the social and institutional acceptability of organizations like Interbrand who have threatened accountants' monopoly of asset recognition. It was less that the valuation methodology for brands was too subjective, since this can be argued against any valuation basis which depends on projecting future earnings streams, but rather that these technical arguments were a smokescreen for doubts about the credibility of Interbrand (Power, 1992*b*). In short, brands were regarded as unauditable largely because Interbrand was not trusted.

The case of brand valuation is also generally instructive for a number of other reasons. First, it suggests that not only the programmatic ideals which demand auditing but also its technical operations have a social basis. Auditability cannot be defined; it is negotiated. And it is negotiated not just at the individual level between client and auditor but also systemically in terms of boundaries of audit knowledge. Second, brand valuation illustrates hierarchies of expertise (Dezalay, 1995*b*) in the professional field. The problem for Interbrand was not so much that their valuation method was intrinsically doubtful, since many accounting firms now pursue a commercial interest in selling very similar valuation services. It was rather that this company was encroaching on the territory of the accounting firms and had the audacity to make judgements about the quality of financial reporting.

From this point of view, a dry guidance document on how to rely on other specialists simultaneously reinforces an implicit hierarchy of expertise. Historically, this has shaped conceptions of the internal auditor as the poor relation of the external auditor, a relationship of dependence which is only now beginning to shift as regulatory attention to internal control increases (Chapter 3). Within the environmental auditing field, similar hierarchical struggles are also visible. In staking their claims to competence accountants must force applied scientists and engineers into the category of sub-contractable expertise: 'the environment is no different from other specialist areas such as property valuation or interpretation of legal agreements ... it is clear that risks of mis-statement arising from environmental problems are in many respects no different from many other financial statement risks' (ICAEW, 1992:106–7).

However, reliance upon other specialists, whether actuaries, chartered surveyors, engineers, lawyers and so on, is not simply a natural process arising from a division of multidisciplinary labour. It is the product of specific and often competing hierarchical relations between different bodies of expertise. In certain fields, such as environmental and medical auditing (Chapter 5), this makes auditability a competitive professional project. And in the field of VFM auditing, where there are constant debates about competence for effectiveness auditing (Glynn, 1985*a*:79), the issue is further complicated by the fact that the specialists with the capability to pass judgements on effectiveness are also the auditees.

The third important lesson to be drawn repeats the observation made in Chapter 2 that a certain proceduralization of the audit process acts as compensation for its essential obscurity. In the case of auditing brands or emissions to air, a certain kind of admission of ignorance by the auditor simultaneously normalizes the subordination of the valuer or chemical

engineer who may take on the status of reliable specialist. Forms of practice which may be complex and heavily qualified in their home specialist
contexts, tend to shed these doubts and nuances and acquire reliability the
more that they become distant from their context of origin. In this way the
auditability of problematic things is ultimately accomplished by chains of
reliance on insiders and outsiders in which trust in specialists and acts of
verification are increasingly difficult to distinguish. Brand valuations are
verified by trusting brand valuers. Reliance on other specialists makes a
certain style of verification possible, a style which trusts that somewhere in
the chain of opinion direct, unmediated checking has actually taken place.
In the audit process, alien bodies of knowledge can be imported and 'black
boxed' in Latour's (1987) sense.

This is not to say that specialist bodies of knowledge can always be black
boxed or that hierarchies of expertise are always stable. On the contrary
the field of knowledge is dynamic. The expertise of chartered surveyors
has been doubted,[10] actuaries and accountants continue to argue, the
climate is more receptive to brand valuations and internal auditors are
gaining institutional legitimacy. The auditability of environmental liabilities
will be another area where legal, scientific, and accounting based expertise
overlap and make the boundaries of the financial auditors' tool kit even
fuzzier. As the process of verification takes place in the context of an
increasingly large network of trusted specialists, things are made auditable
by constructing chains of reliance. Expertise acquires authority as a link in
the chain and this allows audits to be possible where they might ordinarily
be impossible. And, above all, auditing must never be allowed to be
impossible.

MANAGEMENT SYSTEMS AS AUDITABLE OBJECTS

In Chapter 2 it was suggested that as auditee organizations developed
their own internal systems of control, the external audit process became
more efficient by concentrating attention on these controls in the auditee
organization. Even though economic pressures may have driven auditors
to reduce the volume of their transactions work, the idea of reliance
on auditee controls is fundamentally plausible: if one can have confidence
that a system exists to control the completeness, accuracy and validity
of transactions between an organization and its environment, then it
is unnecessary to duplicate this work and look at the transactions in
detail. First order control exists in the organization and the external audit
function acts as a second order control of the first order control system;
audit is control of control. The risk based approach to auditing discussed
above is not really a fundamental departure from this conception;
instead of painstaking documentation of the whole system of transaction

controls, the auditor now tends to focus on *key* controls and particular risks.

What is an internal control system? The professional literature tends to distinguish between broad environmental or general controls (segregation of duties, organization structure, cultures of supervision) and more specific application controls for particular transaction cycles (authorization, accuracy, credibility tests). However, within financial auditing there has always been debate about the relevant boundaries of control systems. The emerging public reporting role regarding internal control (see Chapter 3 for the discussion of the Cadbury Code) has made this issue even more heated. If the auditor is not simply concerned with specific financial application controls, how far do her responsibilities extend? Are environmental management systems to be included under the scope of financial auditing? Are there significant financial risks arising from non-compliance with regulations?

In addition to these debates within financial auditing, the concept of a control system has been expressed in more general terms, abstracted from any specific organizational or institutional context. For any control system there must be a loop which formally corresponds to a certain learning potential. Organizations set policies and design procedures for implementing and measuring performance in relation to these policies. Results are fed back into the system in the form of reports, comparisons, etc. and remedial, corrective action is taken where necessary. On this view the internal control system is a form of structured self-observation. Internal audit is relevant as a practice which observes this self-observation process and is also a form of second order control. Internal audit can also perform tests on the system, as financial auditors do.[11]

All this would be of little general interest, a subject for practice manuals and textbooks, if it were not for the manner in which the systems audit concept has been at the heart of the audit explosion. In Chapter 3 it was argued that the managerial turn in regulation across a number of different areas has generated a quasi-public status for the internal control system. Indeed, the condition of an internal control system which, within financial auditing, was a means to a broader end, has now become more of an auditable object in its own right. Developments in quality assurance schemes are indicative of this general trend and reveal much about the operational logic of the audit society.

In the UK, the British Standards Institute (BSI) developed BS 5750 as a general model for a quality assurance system. The elements of such a system correspond to the model sketched above: it requires a statement of objectives, benchmark standards to operationalize these objectives, monitoring of actual performance against these standards, feedback of the results into the system itself via reports, corrective action as required. At such a level of abstraction there is something obvious and uncontentious about these ideas. They have existed for many years as part of the tool kit of systems consultants. However, BS 5750 (now subsumed under the ISO 9000 series[12]) has codified, formalized, and repackaged these elements to make a product in its own right. Auditing enters into this process in two ways. First as an internal monitoring mechanism which is part of the system and which feeds back results into systemic and operational matters. Second, as an external process of reporting on and validating the quality of the management system. It is this second process of certification which makes internal control systems public objects in their own right.

BS 5750 and similar schemes are voluntary. As indicated in Chapter 3, the ideal is to create internal commitments to improvement by building compliance structures from below. First, the process of preparation for registration should enable the organization to look critically at its objectives and the extent to which operational systems serve these objectives. Second, this process institutionalizes an ongoing process of constant improvement in performance, once this is defined by benchmarks. Third, the organization gains the reputational benefits of signalling its internal quality via the certification add-on. The power and no doubt attraction of BS 5750 is its lack of organizational specificity. Quality assurance systems can be applied to industrial and service companies alike, to universities and firms of solicitors, to the provision of health as well as arms procurement. Indeed, one can be very good, in a quality assurance sense, at doing morally questionable things.

In the field of environmental management the general principles of quality assurance have been adapted within BS 7750, *Environmental Management Systems* (BSI, 1992, 1993). In addition, the European Commission issued a Regulation on *Eco-Management and Auditing* (EMA) with a similar orientation (CEC, 1993). The structure of these two schemes have much in common although the latter is intended for EU industrial sites and the former may apply to any organization and, given its international counterpart in the ISO 14 000 series, has no jurisdictional restrictions. Both are voluntary schemes for which organizations may register in order to obtain the perceived benefits of official accreditation and publicity for internal arrangements.[13] Only EMAS provides for a (limited) form of public reporting, for which the opinion of an accredited verifier is required.[14]

The schemes focus on the quality of internal environmental management *systems* rather than the quality of the product or service itself as specified in standards. The operations of this system structure can be verified and approved by independent outsiders, certifiers for BS 7750 and verifiers for EMAS. In short, organizations decide on their environmental policy (e.g. reduction in energy usage), translate this into operational performance measures and implement a system to monitor and report the performance so defined and feed this back into the system itself. The idea is that not only does the environment in general benefit, but the company also gains a competitive advantage.

Both schemes require some kind of independent validation which connects the organization to other regulatory layers. In theory, regulatory and corporate programmes coincide in the structure of a system which serves internal economic and external regulatory goals simultaneously; the environmental management system embodies enlightened corporate self-interest, a new 'logic of plausibility' (Ladeur, 1994). But schemes such as this also redirect external regulatory attention away from 'deep' organizational process towards chains of abstract procedure (Simmons and Wynne, 1992:215). Like BS 5750, BS 7750 and EMAS abstract from performance in a substantive sense and emphasize system values and their auditability as ends in themselves. The schemes have been explicitly designed for performance standards to be a contingent input from organizations themselves. Similar tendencies are observable within quality assurance for higher education where the distinction between good teaching and good systems for monitoring teaching are blurred (see Chapter 5).

The abstract system tends to become the primary external auditable object, rather than the output of the organization itself, and this adds to the obscurity of the audit as a process which provides assurance about systems elements and little else. Many products and services have public, visible, and 'non-expert' criteria of whether they are good or bad, although usually after they have been purchased. Customers usually know when light bulbs work or when plumbing is defective. Of course, they also want to know this before they buy the product or service. In these circumstances, quality assurance certification acts much like a brand or label which signals that the product is 'fit for purpose'. The certification of quality is saying something directly about the products and services and in such ideal cases the auditability and certifiability of the quality system is a secondary process, a means to an end. The quality of the system is judged directly by judging the quality of the output.

However, in cases where output standards are ill-defined (true and fair financial statements) or controversial (such as environmental or medical performance) or even where they do not exist at all, the certification of quality assurance systems, by default, takes on a life of its own. At the extreme, system structures exist for the purpose of being externally verified (Halliday, 1993). For example, it has been suggested that environmental performance has come to be closely identified with having an (auditable) system (see Shaylor *et al.*, 1994) rather than first order standards. At the other extreme, this approach is said to enhance organizational learning: 'The environmental audits are designed to assure that quality programs are in place and working. The primary concern, for example, is not that a drum has been mislabelled, but determining *why* the drum was mislabelled' (Friedman, 1991:1321).

This shift in focus reflects a preference for compliance over deterrence based philosophies of control. But there is a risk that the environmental management system, intended to mediate and facilitate the auditing of output, becomes a mere 'surface' which makes a certain style of auditing possible, a style which tends to drive rather than follow the process. And here lies the potential expectations gap for environmental auditing. The public expects audit to contribute directly to substantive change, whereas systems change only contributes indirectly, depending on how an organization defines performance measures for itself. And while companies may wish to combine quality and environmental audits, these activities may point in different directions (Sammalisto, 1995). Quality assurance values may dominate or the environmental management system may be cut off from other management systems.

The information requirements of environmental management systems can be weakly or strongly interpreted. Forms of eco-accounting used by some German companies like Kunert reflect German technical traditions and a desire to integrate the data requirements of EMAS with *Ökobilanzen*. In this way, the management system is integrated into life cycle accounting for inventory analysis (Gelber, 1995). In other words, EMAS is an abstract shell which can be operationalized with quite different policies and information requirements. German commentary on EMAS has always reflected a concern that: 'sites with very different actual levels of performance [will] be given equal recognition under the scheme' (Hemming, 1993:5). Integrated environmental management as its worst ends up emphasizing formal relations between system elements rather than the standards to which the system and the organization might be held to account. Indeed, EMAS and BS 7750 have a thinly developed sense of accountability, which is the price to be paid for all voluntary schemes.

To conclude, the extension of quality assurance models to the environmental field exemplifies the manner in which the logic of auditing operates. The idea of a management system and its control structures is both an essential component of a form of audit knowledge which can justify the abandonment of direct inspection and also an institutionally legitimate practice for an auditee. A close analysis of the official documents in this area reveals much about how a 'logic of auditability' gives priority to the accreditation of systems of control, rather than standards, an emphasis with obvious cost implications for the auditor and clients. In this way the management system solves important epistemic and economic problems for auditing. The system provides an organizational reality on which audits can act and are therefore possible. The verifiable assertion, and hence the audit process, can be shifted away from the complexities of natural environment impacts to the workings of the management system. This is not to say that operational problems of auditing systems no longer exist. For example, in the context of the Cadbury Code proposals there are doubts about whether the 'effectiveness' of an internal control system can be 'objectively verified' (Piper and Jones, 1995) and the views of the APB and the Stock Exchange differ. But this problem gets solved by defining effectiveness in terms of the system components themselves, not what they do. The audit of management systems is cost-effective and gives off an image of control through acts of certification which are demanded elsewhere in the regulatory network.

CONCLUSION: MAKING THINGS AUDITABLE

For auditing practitioners 'making things auditable' is a deeply practical issue. It is what they do when they apply various techniques, routines, and experiences to an organization. This process is not a science; it is largely a matter of practitioner common sense and intuition. Of course, analytical techniques can always be better and mistakes in judgements can always be made; hence the demand that audit partners, like doctors, have experience. But formal knowledge is one thing, diagnostic skill is another. A whole research tradition has been developed to analyse and evaluate these judgement processes and to develop new methods which might improve them.[15]

When practitioners complain that an organization or area is unauditable they are usually referring to the quality of record keeping. An incomplete audit trail connecting individual transactions to financial statement aggregates will render these numbers unauditable; it will be impossible to prove that the number in the financial statements is complete, accurate and valid and the auditor is left with little choice but to qualify her audit report in some way. Other types of unauditability also exist. For example, contingent events which may or may not crystallize in the future are a special kind of uncertainty.[16] But the future can be made auditable in various ways. In some cases financial auditors need only insist that the uncertainty is fully disclosed in the financial statements and that the assumptions underlying the disclosure are reasonable. Instead of auditing the future, the auditor comes to a view about the quality of disclosure and, crucially, about the auditee system for generating the disclosure.[17]

However, making things auditable is not simply a question of implementing particular techniques in particular settings, where practitioners may display considerable ingenuity. It also concerns the general acceptance of these techniques as reasonable. One can naturally be concerned with how well or badly practitioners perform an audit relative to well defined standards. But there is also a question about where these standards come from and how they characterize a system of knowledge. The contrast I wish to make can be put as follows: the common sense view is that audit techniques are accepted by practitioners because they more or less 'work' whereas the systemic view is that techniques and procedures are perceived to 'work' because they have become institutionally acceptable ways of gathering and processing evidence. In short, the *production* rather than the *presumption* of practitioner common sense is the issue. Before individuals can judge they must at least be able to draw upon and frame those judgements in a taken for granted system of knowledge.

In this chapter, I have explored three very basic ways in which things are made auditable in this systemic sense: selective testing by sampling, reliance on other specialists, focusing on systems processes rather than outcomes. These three areas must be understood not merely as methods but as ways of making auditing economically and epistemically possible. All three cases show how crucial economic and cognitive problems for auditing are resolved while leaving the essential obscurity of the audit process untouched. All three also provide a basis for elaborating further detailed procedures, for making audits work in a systemic sense. The story of sampling shows how auditing drew on the language and legitimating force of statistical science to rationalize selective testing that was already in place. More recently, auditing has attached itself to the idea of risk analysis, again with cost motives as a primary driver. In both cases the image of equal, if not greater, assurance must be maintained.

In the second case of reliance on other specialists, audits are seen to work by the construction of networks of trust in which the knowledge of others can be more or less 'black boxed' and rendered reliable. More generally, trust plays a constitutive role in verification processes and will be discussed at greater length in Chapter 6. The third case of auditing systems is central to the concerns of this book. Audits become possible in complex environments by abstracting from that complexity and by operating upon a systems surface which in some cases has been designed with auditability in mind. Not only can audits work, but they can be exported to a wide variety of organizational contexts which can be sold the institutional benefits of system certification. In this way the management system is not only a technological construct; its elements have an essential public face which is offered for the purpose of accreditation and which makes a certain style of audit process possible.

This is not to say that 'making things auditable' is a seamless and smooth process and perhaps nowhere is this more evident than in the work of the European Court of Auditors discussed in Chapter 3. The Court was provided with an extensive auditing mission by the Maastricht Treaty requiring it to report on the accounts of the EU as a whole. It has always faced operational difficulties, not least the fact that basic transactional data for EU expenditure may be held not with the European Commission in Brussels but with the member state bodies who administer directly nearly 80 per cent of the EU budget (Harden *et al.*, 1995). In 1995 the incumbent president of the Court stated that 'we have decided to do direct substantive testing on the basis of a sample size which we could (just) handle with a confidence level of at least 95% and a materiality limit of 1%' (Middelhoek, 1995:266). It was predicted that this would yield 600 or so transactions for testing out of 360 000 (Pratley, 1995:252).

In this case, one cannot but be left with the impression that the statistics rationalize a decision to test a number of items predetermined by reference to resource constraints and what can 'just' be handled by the Court. The EU is made auditable in this way because institutionalized mechanisms for 'relying' on national audit institutions are imperfect and diverse (Hardin *et al.*, 1995:14) and because of a presumption that systems of control of the required quality do not yet exist. It is argued that if the Commission could demonstrate that it monitors and evaluates the activities of member states, then the Court could rely on this 'internal audit' function and audit the reasonableness of this work. At the time of writing, chains of procedure and reliance are beginning to emerge on the European stage and the Commission is developing its internal auditing resources (Pratley, 1995:252–3). This will make the external audit of the EU budget possible in a different way, a shift from sampling to systems.

Accordingly, it is not quite right to say that the EU is unauditable, although this is often suggested by critics. Rather, the EU is and must be 'made auditable' by defining the techniques that make this possible and by integrating them into the mechanics of parliamentary discharge of the EU accounts. The image management of Euro-auditing is constantly disturbed by scandals about fraud; intra-institutional blame is triggered; new commitments are established and gradually preventative systems and reliance on the systems of member states will emerge which restore the auditability of the EU. The essence of the Court's 'statement of assurance' is precisely the production of global comfort about the EU as a whole and it is this that attempts to link the results of tests on only 600 items to the mission of financial control. Auditing must always look as if it works but in this case there is perhaps no better illustration of the *imperfect coupling* between programmatic demands for control and the realities of operationalizing it.

In conclusion, making audits work is the constant and precarious project of a system of knowledge which must reproduce itself and sustain its institutional role from a diverse and humble assemblage of routines, practices, and economic constraints. The technological base of auditing examined here is only loosely coupled to different programmes and objectives and operates in its own space of rational procedure. But to say this is to leave open the question of the effects of audits on auditee organizations. Whether audits are or are not loosely coupled to their organizational environments as mere 'rituals of inspection', or whether there are nevertheless real impacts on core activities, is an empirical issue. In the desire to create certain appearances of their own functioning, audits have effects. In this chapter, the audit process has been considered from the inside, in terms of a logic of auditability which constitutes reasonable practice. But there is another very direct way in which audits work; by transforming the environments to which they are applied. It is this theme that must now be considered.

5

Making Audits Work: Auditees and the Auditable Performance

INTRODUCTION

In Chapter 4 it was argued that economic pressures exist for new 'techniques' to be acceptable and that audit cloaks its fundamental epistemological obscurity in a wide range of procedures and routines. From time to time audit practitioners have worried about the erosion of judgement and the imposition of too much structure on the audit process, but the history of financial auditing and the recent history of other forms of audit suggest that codification and formalization is continuing, particularly where new programmatic demands are made of existing skills. Of special significance is the emergence and exportation of the self-auditing management system as an auditable object. The hopes and aspirations articulated by governments and delegated to auditing institutions are progressively specified and operationalized by the creation and maintenance of such a management system.

So far the manner in which audit technique is made to appear reasonable and is harnessed to programmatic intentions has been considered. However, this is only one sense in which audits are made to 'work'. Of equal interest is the manner in which the audit process interacts with the audited domain. In this respect it is instructive to look beyond financial auditing and to consider the impact and consequences of some of the auditing practices stimulated and reorganized by the New Public Management agenda. The advantage of this focus is that these audit practices have often been introduced into organizational contexts where they have not previously existed or have existed only in an informal and undeveloped manner. Audit functions here less as a practice of verification and more as an explicit vehicle for change in the name of ideals such as 'cost effectiveness', 'efficiency', 'quality' and so on. This suggests a close relationship between the audit explosion and the need to install auditable performance measures. In short, audits work because organizations have literally been made auditable; audit demands the environment, in the form of systems, and performance measures, which makes a certain style of verification possible.

The discussion begins by considering some general criticisms of the NPM and their implications for auditing. Two extreme analytical possibilities are considered—decoupling and colonization—as a basis for assessing the effects of auditing in three different contexts. Auditing within higher education, medicine and, ironically, the regulation of financial audit share operational features and raise similar difficulties. In particular, the three cases illustrate the tension between a concept of auditable performance derived from quality assurance systems and one which is rooted in the specialist judgement and knowledge base of different service professionals. This is essentially a tension between audit and evaluation and this theme is considered explicitly in the context of performance auditing. Overall it is argued that audits work if they are themselves not too closely subject to their own values of effectiveness. Furthermore, there is increasing, if unsystematic, evidence of the dysfunctional side-effects of auditing and this suggests that audit must itself be evaluated rather than audited.

NEW PUBLIC MANAGEMENT: CRITICISMS AND REACTIONS

Chapter 3 suggested that the New Public Management was an assortment of ideas and orientations driving the reform of public administration. In different sectors and across different countries, elements of the NPM have been used selectively to suit particular needs. It is difficult to deny that enhanced financial control, the elimination of genuine waste and possibilities for fraud, and the creation of incentives to provide higher quality services are desirable as ends. No doubt there have been many benefits of this kind and there is a need for a balanced assessment of the impacts of the NPM in particular settings. However, the problem is that the NPM and the promotion of a private sector management style has been driven less by a sober empirical evaluation of consequences and more by faith in the presumed benefits of abstract management (Bogdanor, 1994) and a universalistic approach to administrative design (Hood, 1991:9–10). It is this insensitivity to side-effects and empirical consequences which has been the object of considerable criticism.

The attempt to separate service provision and governance arrangements, as described in Chapter 3, represents an intention to replace state bureaucracy with the managerial tools of accounting and audit (Self, 1993:159). In mimicking market structures, 'management' has emerged as a portable technical skill 'divorced from specialised experience and knowledge about particular subjects, equally applicable to the private and public sectors, and primarily concerned with the efficient use of resources' (Self, 1993:169). In the context of the criminal justice system it has been said that:

the attraction of managerialism as a political strategy is that it keeps the rhetoric of criminal justice intact while demolishing the structures which, however imperfectly, previously enabled their realization . . . there is now in the ascendant an ideology

which wholly legitimates the pursuit of administratively rational ends over substantive justice goals ... the auditing process has had a profound impact upon the
practice of criminal justice in Britain. ... At first sight ... the traditional structures
of accountability appear to be reinforced by the new system. The contrary view
argues that auditing undermines these traditional structures. Instead of officials
being responsible to ministers for their decisions, ministers are forced to rely upon
the professional values of accountants and auditors. ... Accountants are no longer
simply providers of financial information; they are at the forefront of decision
making. Policy making thus moves outside recognized political channels (Jones,
1993:192–9).

These and similar criticisms suggest that reforms in Britain, such as the
Financial Management Initiative, pose a radical challenge to the culture of
the organizations to which they are applied: 'Systems of administration,
control and evaluation, however technical they may appear, are also expressions of a series of underlying beliefs and values' (Neave, 1988:18). Some
of this challenge is undoubtedly intentional, such as the need to install
greater awareness of the resource implications of organizational decision
making. But equally there are unintended and undesired consequences.
One of the ironies of the NPM is that while it insists that 'public services
must invest much more heavily in the currency of measurable
outputs ... some fundamental aspects of NPM reforms themselves appear
to have remained almost immune from such requirements' (Pollitt,
1995:135). Indeed, the NPM can be characterized by a lack of self-
evaluation, except in relatively simple financial terms, and is committed
more, in the style of Gosplan perhaps, to making sure reforms work, or at
least look as if they do, than to self-evaluation. Hence there is a use of
consultants to *implement* all-purpose reform rather than to *evaluate* its
particular organizational effects (Laughlin and Broadbent, 1995).
    This is not to say that such a process of evaluation of reforms, such as
FMI or the separation of purchasers and providers in the NHS, would be
an easy matter. Quite the opposite is true. Rather, the point is that the institutional foundations of such an evaluation are slim and are dominated by
the need to show that things are working well, that objectives are being
achieved. Not only can this lead to the continuation of certain practices irre-
spective of mounting evidence that they do not work, but transactions costs,
a core element of the conceptual armoury of the NPM, actually rise: 'Each
side of this quasi-market relationship has to maintain staff with expertise
in the technical aspects of contracting in a way that was not necessary under
the previous administrative hierarchy, where trust and hierarchical authority substituted for detailed accountancy' (Pollitt, 1995:147).
    To conclude, the NPM is problematic because it puts itself as doctrine
beyond question. A broader based evaluation of the financial and non-
financial consequences based on sensitivities to the social and organizational context of reforms would be an intolerable policy burden, especially

where longitudinal pilot studies and cost–benefit analyses introduce delay and discussion. As part of this policy commitment, NPM based programmes also presume that the forms of audit on which they depend are efficacious and without unintended dysfunctional side-effects. The general argument of the sections which follow is that auditing works because it creates an environment of auditable performance and this leads to questioning the effects of imposing such auditable measures. Before considering three illus-trative cases in detail it is worth considering what may be at stake in these effects.

AUDITABLE PERFORMANCE: DECOUPLING OR COLONIZATION?

Accounting information systems do not simply describe a pre-existing eco-nomic domain but, to varying degrees, serve to constitute a realm of facts, to make a world of action visible and hence controllable in economic terms. Creative accounting practitioners have always known that profits can be 'what you like' and that for every financial accounting rule there is a way to frustrate the purpose of the rule while appearing to comply with it. Tax and accounting regulators engage in a constant struggle to catch up with these schemes. But the point about accounting and information systems goes even deeper than these preoccupations with 'fiddling' or discretion in rule interpretation. It concerns the mutual constitution of information systems and forms of behaviour, the multiplicity of ways in which account-ing information can be used, appealed to and even ignored.

There is a growing literature on the consequences of attempts to measure and report performance in accounting terms and to develop practices of comparison and evaluation around such measures. For example, it is argued that internal accounting creates a factual domain in terms of cost which allows state activity to be conceived explicitly in economic terms. Performance can be disciplined through such measures which are 'advanced in the name of their presumed potential rather than their practical pos-sibility or actual consequences' (Hopwood, 1984:176). A study of the intro-duction of diagnostic cost categories in medicine suggests the inherent 'decision ladenness of accounting numbers' (Chua, 1995:113) and their ability to influence what is regarded as significant. On this view economic reality is emergent and negotiated through figurative accounting practices which necessarily promise a control that they cannot deliver. Accounting becomes an expanding and self-preserving structure and builds the network of facts which make monitoring and audit possible. According to Chua, technically flawed accounting numbers command consent because they can hold together diverse purposes and because they have a kind of legitimacy which has little to do with their technical properties and much to do with the creation of a certain kind of window on operations, a window which allows one to trace the operational translations of political programmes into detailed costing systems.

At the most concrete level accounting practices depend on systems of classification embodied in books and records, manuals of instruction, computer printouts and so on. Transactions must be captured and recorded, invoices must be processed and, through selective assembly, aggregation and analysis, economic activity must be represented in a form which corresponds to programmatic demands for disclosure and performance measurement. In turn, these financial accounts can themselves provide a base for further calculation of performance and solvency ratios, ratios which often serve specific regulatory functions and which reinforce norms of performance. A certain kind of administrative objectivity is created whose logic is to standardize, which prefers rules over unfettered judgement and which hides its processes of selection. In this way, the factual environment of financial auditing is created:

To provide an account in . . . the auditing world . . . means adhering to descriptive devices (numerical and narrative) that are by and large conventional and arbitrary. They are neither right nor wrong but stand as coding or reporting standards that are 'generally accepted' as adequate for the task. They can be regarded as strategic representations, collectively validated by members, designed to put the organization's best foot forward (Van Maanen and Pentland, 1994:81).

If one accepts these broadly constructivist themes one must confront a simple question: how does this world of accounts and related forms of audit connect to other worlds, not just those for enhancing manufacturing performance but also those for teaching children, curing the sick, trading on derivative markets, policing the streets, prosecuting offences, enabling sustainable growth, and so on? Discussion can be organized around two extreme possibilities, both of which represent different kinds of audit 'failure' but which are never likely to be found in a pure form. The first type of failure is that the audit process becomes a world to itself, self-referentially creating auditable images of performance. The audit process is *decoupled* or compartmentalized in such a way that it is remote from the very organizational processes which give it its point. The second type of failure is that, regardless of intended changes to the audited organization, the audit world spills over and provides a dominant reference point for organizational activity. Organizations are in effect *colonized* by an audit process which disseminates and implants the values which underly and support its information demands.[1] The audit process can be said to fail because its side-effects may actually undermine performance.

Decoupling

In their classic article, Meyer and Rowan (1991) have suggested that formalized control systems have more to do with myths of control in the environment of organizations than with real improvements in operational efficiency. From this point of view the management system structure described in Chapter 4 is an 'institutionalized product' adopted primarily for external legitimation purposes; it rarely functions like its blueprint. The technical structure of such a system, its rules and procedures for ensuring the loop of self-observation, embodies norms which originate in the environment. The point is that while such building blocks of rational organization have an 'explosive organizing potential' (Meyer and Rowan, 1991:46) and can lead to new organizational structures, they can also be decoupled from core organizational activities in such a way that 'evaluation and inspection systems are subverted or rendered so vague as to provide little coordination'. Through the creation of compartmentalized organizational units for dealing with external assessment, audit and evaluation can be rendered ceremonial in such a way as to deflect a rational questioning of organizational conduct.

Meyer and Rowan regard external evaluation primarily as a destabilizing and delegitimizing activity that organizations will wish to buffer from their core activities. In this way buffering sub-units manage an interface with external assessors which leads, in the case of quality assurance, to the certification of formal systems elements. From this point of view, audits are 'rationalized rituals of inspection' which produce comfort, and hence organizational legitimacy, by attending to formal control structures and auditable performance measures. Even though audit files are created, checklists get completed and performance is measured and monitored in ever more elaborate detail, audit concerns itself with auditable form rather than substance. From time to time these ritualized audits are perceived to fail, inquiries take place and new technical guidance is issued which, depending on the audience, represents a radical overhaul (for the ears of regulators) or simply a codification of what most auditors do anyway (for the ears of practitioners).

Notwithstanding the analytical attraction of the motif of decoupling, the issue is ultimately an empirical one. One *prima facie* sign of decoupling is the creation or enhancement of organizational sub-units explicitly to manage the external audit process (audit committees, internal auditors, audit officers, etc.). Another would be the extent to which managers 'devote more time to articulating internal structures and relationships at an abstract or ritual level, in contrast to managing particular relationships among activities and interdependencies' (Meyer and Rowan, 1991:61). But there are also reasons to doubt whether pure decoupling in the sense described above ever takes place. Explicit attempts to compartmentalize the external audit process are expensive and 'efforts by clinicians to neutralize the impacts of reforms can be crude and counterproductive' (Ezzamel and Willmott, 1993:125). This means that the external audit process is rarely sealed off from the rest of the auditee organization, despite strategies with that intention. Internal audit officers may 'change sides' and may use their new found power to advance internal changes. The external audit may even be desired by parts of the organization to exercise leverage over other parts. And ways of talking around audit processes inevitably percolate into other areas of organizational life. In this way the external audit process cannot remain permanently buffered.

Colonization

The other extreme to consider is that the values and practices which make auditing possible penetrate deep into the core of organizational operations, not just in terms of requiring energy and resources to conform to new reporting demands but in the creation over time of new mentalities, new incentives and perceptions of significance. In short, against the image of decoupling, audit processes may contribute to the construction of a new organizational actor (Laughlin, 1991). On this view the supposed, and perhaps questionable, distinction within organization theory between the front stage of formal performance and the back stage of informal process is eroded as formal elements, such as accounting operations, become ingrained in habits and classifications for control purposes.[2] At the extreme, the organization aspires to be omniscient and 'employees enjoy the loyalty of others. They welcome audits, reasonable monitoring, and documentary proof of their activities' (Marx, 1990:5).

The diverse programmes which fall under the umbrella of NPM have a certain kind of colonization as an explicit goal. The intention is not only to remedy weaknesses in financial control practices but also to challenge the organizational power and discretion of relatively autonomous groups, such as doctors and teachers, by making these groups more publicly accountable for their performance. In this way VFM auditing is explicitly a vehicle for organizational change. However, colonization is rarely successful and monolithic for a number of reasons. The institutional environment of organizations is not usually homogeneous and consistent. Different institutional logics of evaluation exist. Financial and non-financial conceptions of performance live uneasily side by side, as do the governance demands of rules and of economic efficiency. In addition, different professionals articulate competing claims to expert problem solving (DiMaggio and Powell, 1991); accountants are naturally more comfortable with matters of economy and efficiency rather than effectiveness. Accordingly, the processes of organizational change demanded by the NPM and its auditing agencies produce varying forms of conflict and resistance, of which explicit decoupling strategies are one.

What is ultimately at stake in the question of colonization is the possibility that auditing is a 'fatal remedy' (Sieber, 1981). The point is not just that audit may be decoupled ritualistically or that it permeates the auditee organization totally. It is rather that the imposition of audit and related measures of auditable performance leads to the opposite of what was intended, i.e. creates forms of dysfunction for the audited service itself. This issue is ultimately an empirical matter. As the following three case studies show, much depends on the relation between relatively consensual internal structures of self-evaluation, which have always existed in varying degrees of formalization, and forms of external audit with a probative orientation towards external audiences (taxpayers, citizens, shareholders, and so on). In short, do auditable standards of performance come, or are they perceived as coming, from inside or outside the organization? The example of UK academics will be considered first.

MAKING AUDITEES: RESEARCHERS AND TEACHERS

Since the mid-1980s a new theology of 'quality, efficiency and enterprise' has emerged in higher education. Explicit strategies of 'financial compression' (Neave, 1988:12) have been accompanied by a considerable number of institutional changes, most notably the replacement of the University Grants Committee (UGC) with the University Funding Council (UFC), subsequently renamed the Higher Education Funding Council (HEFC) (there is a separate agency for Scotland). The UGC had effectively acted as a buffer between the state and universities whereas the HEFC is more explicitly an agency of central government. Like the UGC before it, the HEFC provides funding to universities by way of a block grant and in the past this was calculated and notionally split between teaching and research. Since the mid-1980s, the HEFC has begun to introduce evaluative mechanisms to control the allocation and use of these (diminishing) funds.

These institutional changes signalled a fundamental shift in evaluative philosophy which may be found in many other areas, a shift from process based local forms of self-evaluation to standardized measures of output. New evaluatory mechanisms and indicators have been created to operationalize quality initiatives in teaching and research and with new information demands new patterns of authority have emerged. For example, Vice Chancellors (VCs) in universities now assume the role of chief executive overseeing policy and resources committees and academics can no longer dabble in managerial roles which fit uneasily with an older value base. Universities are being forced to be more entrepreneurial and specialized educational consultants have emerged as part of a new market for advice. These changes reflect what Neave has called the 'evaluative state', an attempt to enhance the self-government of universities leaving state agencies with a monitoring role. The question is whether these measures are intended to build 'consensus around those options that evaluation may reveal or whether the purpose of evaluation is to bend a recalcitrant academia to what the government deems to be "the new reality" ' (Neave, 1988:16). The evaluative mechanisms which exist at the time of writing can be broadly divided between research and teaching.

Auditing Academic Research

As part of its control over the element of the block grant for research, the HEFC conducts Research Assessment Exercises (RAEs). These 'audits' are intended to rate academic subject areas in universities on the basis of the quality of their research and to allocate central government funds accordingly. The first such exercise was conducted in 1986 and was subsequently repeated in 1989, 1992, and 1996. Over time as the assessment process and its classifications have developed, increasing amounts of research money have been allocated in accordance with the results. However, the precise link between RAE results and funding depends on complex formulae with caps and safety nets to ensure that the results are not too drastic. This means that the apparent economic logic of RAEs is heavily compromised by other more pragmatic values. Many commentators regard the RAEs as creating explicit pressures for separating research and teaching universities and for providing incentives for raising private research funds. In particular, there seems to be a long term trend to shift the mix of funding from the block grant system towards organizations, such as the Economic and Social Research Council (ESRC), who are purchasers of research.

The programmatic intention of these arrangements is to focus on the accountability of research funds both in the sense of quality and of financial control. Regarding the need to control the use of research funds, the HEFC (1993) explored the possibility of timesheets for academics. The intention was to focus on the accountability of research monies but, as the report from a firm of management consultants suggested, accountability could be operationalized in a number of different ways. There was an explicit desire to make research funds auditable and the consultants, Coopers and Lybrand, proposed a scheme which was detailed enough to provide the HEFC with assurance but not so demanding as to be unacceptable to the academic community (Coopers and Lybrand, 1993).

The specific timesheet proposal reflects a more general trend: the need to measure at an appropriate level of detail to make auditability possible. This is a level of detail which has little to do with accuracy or even representational faithfulness, but which reflects a certain legitimized style of technical elaboration. Audit requires not just an auditable reality but one which reflects institutional myths about the appropriate level of formality (see, Power, 1996b). Nothing came of the proposals for academic timesheets. Many VCs were dismissive of the prospects of minute monitoring and the

HEFC itself was unenthusiastic. But the programmatic aspirations which drove the HEFC to explore this mechanism exist elsewhere in the system and show how rhetorics of auditability, measurement and accountability are intertwined.

One of the unintended but predictable consequences of the RAEs has been to create incentives to teach less and write more. According to Trow, the RAEs have created subtle 'accountings' for research staff with little knowledge or desire to understand their costs and impacts. Staff in the former polytechnic sector are now under pressure to engage in research for the first time and there are visible transfer markets for research academics in the run-up to such exercises (which only increase the costs of research as a whole). More problematic still, it has been argued that the RAE is in fact a 'fatal remedy' in terms of its impact on existing research culture. Cycles of research have changed in favour of publication in prestigious journals rather than books. Scientists are changing research habits,[3] and a whole menu of activities for which performance measures have not been devised have ceased to have official value. Editing books, organizing conferences and, paradoxically, reviewing and facilitating the publications efforts of others fall out of account.

In the context of natural scientific research, the perennial issue of harnessing science to wealth creation has taken a new turn. Science policy in the UK (White Paper, 1993) has imported many of the hard managerialist elements of the NPM (Trow, 1993). Sherman (1994) has shown how the patent has come to occupy a central position in the performance measurement of science, stimulating Intellectual Property and Technology Audits to maximize exploitative opportunities which have not been recognized by scientists themselves. In addition, the programmatic values of VFM have been applied to science with the imperative of maximizing returns on public funds. Such a manner of governing science and rendering it auditable represents a fundamental shift in the fulcrum of evaluation with consequent impacts on the conduct of science. In short, research must now be organized to be assessable.

A study of the implementation of Total Quality Management (TQM) in a North American scientific laboratory demonstrates the consequences of using inappropriately deterministic performance measures in contexts like fundamental research, where there is high uncertainty of outcomes. Defensive anxiety and escalating distrust of unscientific TQM experts are the product of 'inappropriately detailed management systems' (Sitkin and Stickel, 1996:210) leading to deskilling and heightened in-group/out-group perceptions. There is also a tendency towards 'more boring but patentable paths in . . . research.' However, Law and Akrich (1994) suggest that these images of colonization are too crude to capture the complexity of adjustments to outside forces. In their study of a laboratory subject to an increasingly commercial framework, in which users are replaced by customers and the good seller must control costs, ideals of VFM are not sufficient to displace traditional senses of getting the job done. The growth of courses in financial management for scientists suggests at least the longer term emergence of hybrid experts.

Overall, tensions remain about the role of science, the mix of applied and basic activity and the timescales for evaluation and accountability to peers, patrons, and publics. The UK white paper has stimulated discussion on the necessary conditions for innovation, on the relation of science to wealth creation and on the relation to the citizens whose taxes support scientific endeavour. In this sense the formerly self-evident values of a self-regulating 'big science' have been challenged by a new alliance of managerial ideals and radical populism (Fuller, 1994). Add to this related concerns with scientific fraud and one has all the conditions for making science into an auditable object.[4]

Teaching Quality Audits

At the time of writing the institutional arrangements for teaching quality assurance in higher education are, to say the least, confusing. The Committee of Vice Chancellors and Principals (CVCP) established an Academic Audit Unit (AAU) in 1990 which was subsequently transformed, in name at least, into quality audit under the control of the Higher Education Quality Council (HEQC), owned jointly by higher education colleges and universities. The HEQC has a broad management brief concerning itself not merely with teaching quality but with quality *assurance* more generally for the whole organization. These arrangements also overlap with another set of evaluative mechanisms, this time quality *assessment* conducted by HEFC bodies in England, Scotland, and Wales at the level of academic departments. Needless to say there has been much discussion about these arrangements given such an obvious overlap. And behind theological debates about the difference between assurance and assessment VCs seem to be reluctant to give up control of the evaluation process.[5]

Willmott (1995:1019) has noted that the AAU was originally concerned with internal systems of quality assurance[6] and its preoccupation with formal structure resembles the environmental auditing field. Even when academic standards were perceived as high by an AAU visit, there were criticisms of the internal system for controlling these standards, particularly where it depended too much on trust. Pressures were created to adopt a certain management style which, in Willmott's view, were corrosive of old ideals without themselves being effective.

Overall, universities have created 'buffer' elements which mirror and track external regulatory institutions and which present a legitimate face. For example, in 1992 the London School of Economics created an internal academic audit unit to mirror the AAU. In 1994 this was subsumed within the teaching quality assurance committee to liaise with and respond to the HEQC on quality matters and on matters of teaching quality assessment under the HEFC. In short, auditing initiatives stimulate the creation of internal sub-organizations or compartments. From this point of view, audit is always a 'layered' activity organized around systems of control. For example, teaching quality assessments were initially self-assessment based and the HEFC emphasized the quality of systems in place to allow credible self-assessment. Such moves to stimulate consensual self-auditing are visible in other areas and the model is borrowed explicitly from BS 5750: standards are set by universities and colleges and quality is intended to be a measure of achieving those self-determined standards.

Unsurprisingly, this process of institutional adjustment and the realization that teaching quality relates to systems rather than to actual teaching has led to conflict. It has been suggested that 'the British Government is motivated more by its desire to control the academic community than by its quest for top quality higher education' (Trow, 1993). From this point of view, these self-auditing arrangements have been installed with a view to discipline rather than learning. A 'hard' managerialism has displaced trust and 'elevates institutional and system management to a dominant position in higher education'. Performance criteria and mechanisms of continuous improvement have been created which are intended to operationalize abstract ideals of accountability as well as to provide a competitive element.[7]

VCs themselves have often been resistant to quality initiatives, expressing concern about league tables, and the HEQC, an agent of the new regulatory mood, is nevertheless hesitant about directly linking quality initiatives to funding, preferring instead to emphasize local diversity. There have also been complaints about the quality of auditors, appeals about assessments and growing resistance to the increased and uncosted bureaucratic demands (paper mountains and red tape) of quality auditing. Heated debate on these matters has taken place in the pages of the *Times Higher Education Supplement*.[8]

A fundamental problem concerns the ineffectiveness of quality assessment initiatives in a climate of fiscal restraint. Despite indicators of rising standards, the public success story, there is also evidence that staff are covering up falling standards[9] consequent upon rising class sizes and associated administrative burdens. In short, the quality assurance process is decoupled as an expensive ritual. Equally, there is distrust about how performance indicators embodied in quality systems for teaching will be used, particularly those which emphasize student feedback and which simplify the significance of student reactions with a 'dipstick approach'.[10] Trow (1993) points to different orientations to teaching (delivery, challenge, scholarly exploration, and creation) which co-exist, whose diversity necessarily

defeats single model assessment and whose effects cannot always be measured when students are still students. The drift towards delivery philosophies of teaching, supported by hard managerial assumptions, is
transforming teaching from a relationship into a transaction which can be
made auditable in isolation. Trow argues that while the creation of adequate
procedures for complaints are important, teaching ultimately depends on
appointing competent teachers whose motivation is independent of
attempts to audit them. The performance culture of rewards and penalties
is a refusal to trust this motivational guarantee with the result that teaching will be orientated to the expectations of the customer rather than to
shifting and transforming those expectations.

Academics as Auditees

Supporters of the new managerialism and auditing argue that complaints
about bureaucracy tend to hide the fact that existing systems of control
were always inadequate and that the new world refuses to defer to self-
appointed professional authority. Audit is a legitimate demand and the
requirement that universities impose mechanisms for self-review is not
unreasonable. Against this positive view Parker and Jary (1995) have
argued that this is leading to the progressive *McDonaldization* of the university. Even ritualized compliance has a percolative second-order impact
(Laughlin, 1991) in which orientations to teaching and research have been
affected and colonized by a hard managerialism. However, academics in
their new role as auditees are hardly 'totalized' and 'docile' subjects and
Pritchard and Willmott (forthcoming) argue that there is also resistance to
easy imbibing of commercial discourse.

   Between these extremes of managerial colonization and resistance there
is a continuing struggle ('debate') about teaching and research quality as
the auditable object. The concept of quality has hovered uneasily between
definitions which emphasize outcomes and those which emphasize the
processes for determining outcomes. Such arguments are not just semantic
but have implications for the way in which quality can be monitored.
Instead of superficial audits and hard managerialism there are demands
for 'real' evaluation with a social scientific base in order to make the side-
effects of audit visible. In contrast to myths of productivity gains, 'it has been
a case of academics reluctantly cutting per student class contact times,
teaching much larger classes, reducing the number or length of written
assignments, sacrificing time for research and scholarship, and so on'
(Pollitt, 1995:142).[11]

   In conclusion, questions of audit colonization and decoupling in the field
of higher education are complex and ongoing. There is much evidence for
both. Assessment systems damage intra-departmental relations as crude
languages of evaluation trickle into local administrative deliberations. At

the same time a game is played and individual departments are coached to make themselves auditable.[12] The mechanics of research and teaching assessments are instruments of central oversight and control which are simultaneously dependent on the creation of layered self-assessment structures. Assurance and comfort are passed upwards between internal and external auditors. Whether such arrangements really do build on existing consensual cultures of self-auditing, thereby growing from the bottom up, or whether auditing is perceived as externally and crudely imposed is a fundamental issue which recurs in the medical context.

MAKING AUDITEES: DOCTORS AND NURSES

Medical auditing is hardly a new practice. Like many other elements of the audit explosion it is partly the product of reassembling existing routines and harnessing them to new programmatic intentions. Thus within medicine there is a long tradition of case reviews, data gathering and attempts to improve diagnostic practice and patient care (Pollitt, 1993*a*; 1993*b*). Formalized medical auditing seems to have originated in the USA although British doctors have tended to prefer *ad hoc* approaches to evaluation based on the interlinking of medical records (Dent, 1993:257). Although transatlantic influences have percolated into British medical practice, most audit work has been locally specific and institutionally indistinguishable from first order clinical practices. However, in the past ten years as particular elements of the National Health Service have been subjected to NPM style reforms, the meaning and practice of medical auditing has begun to change.

The most significant structural innovation in the field of health care provision has been the creation of quasi-markets for medical services. The intention is to stimulate more effective use of increasingly limited resources by creating an element of competition between those who supply medical services (hospitals and general practitioners) and those who must now explicitly purchase those services (health authorities and general practitioners). This separation of purchasing and providing institutions reflects NPM ideals of autonomization and disaggregation. It is through elaborate contracting arrangements that purchasers can exert control over the nature and quality of the medical services which they wish to purchase from newly constituted entities for provision (hospital trusts and fund holding general practices). It is also within this created space for contracting that medical auditing in the UK is evolving beyond its humble and obscure origins. For GPs some form of audit has become a condition for the payment of certain categories of income and regional Medical Audit Advisory Groups (MAAGs) have been created (out of audit enthusiasts) with a quasi-consulting role to visit practices and encourage the audit cycle.

It is hardly surprising that these reforms have been the subject of massive debate, criticism, and comment. The politics of health care provision has always been intense and fears persist that the creation of these new managerial markets will undermine the whole ethos of health care on which the NHS is based (e.g. Self, 1993:140–1). Furthermore, there is evidence of complaint by medical practitioners themselves and of resistance to market based changes which intrude on their professional autonomy (e.g. Broadbent *et al.*, 1992) even though, as the manager–clinician interface evolves, distinctions are increasingly blurred (Ezzamel and Willmott, 1993). Since the late 1980s these broadly based reactions and reservations have begun to focus on medical auditing as it has started to assume a more prominent programmatic role.

Between 1989 and 1994, approximately £220 million was allocated specifically for the development of medical auditing practice broadly defined as 'the systematic, critical analysis of the quality of medical care, including the procedures used for diagnosis and treatment, the use of resources, and the resulting outcome and quality of life for the patient' (White Paper, 1989).[13] The proposed operational structure for auditing resembles that of the management system described in Chapter 4: objectives and standards must be defined, practice must be observed, results of observations must be compared with standards and there must be feedback with the aim of improvement. However, in the medical context, in contrast with environmental audit, the idea of audit is indistinguishable from this management process as a whole. And behind vague definitional issues, and the conceptions of quality assurance in medicine which they embody, lie complex tensions. Notably, these tensions are revealed in the form of hierarchical struggles between medical practitioners and emergent managers over the control of the evaluation process (Pollitt, 1993a:162). Who decides on objectives and who is the audit intended to serve (Nolan and Scott, 1993)?

Medical Autonomy and Decoupling Strategies

Professionalism may be characterized in part by the self-control of quality (Pollitt, 1990:435). Nowhere is this ideal of self-control so firmly entrenched as it is in medicine. As Pollitt has argued, the NHS context shows clearly the politics of quality assurance in which practitioners have sought to resist not only managerial definitions of quality but also managerial participation in the definition process. According to Pollitt, quality as an issue is diversely and 'tribally' interpreted by virtue of its vagueness and this has implications for the style of quality auditing considered to be appropriate.

Initial challenges posed by the possibility of external evaluation of medical practice were transformed and defused by the Royal Colleges who, in a series of publications, articulated a conception of medical audit which

was voluntary, local and the preserve of medical specialists with no disciplinary implications. Even a formalized system of peer review like that
existing in the USA was preempted (Pollitt, 1993a:163). This strategy
can be interpreted as a form of 'inverse decoupling'. Instead of defusing
external evaluatory initiatives by ritualistic compliance, the mechanics
of evaluation are co-opted into core practices and made invisible to
external monitoring agencies, other than by assertions that audit has taken
place. In short, medical audit was initially more the preservation of the
internality of existing evaluation practice and less the internalization of
external initiatives. The initial use of earmarked money for research
purposes indicated a refusal to distinguish between auditing and learning
processes more generally: 'most of us are happy with . . . "low grade audit":
simply collecting interesting information and using it to help us to improve
the care we give.'[14]

Decoupling strategies have also been driven by a willingness to delegate
audit activity to medical practitioners. Without a tradition of knowing what
to 'do' with audit results, purchasers have tended to be content with the fact
that an audit was done rather than with knowing *what* exactly was done: 'so
long as some form of audit was being performed, nobody outside the clinical staff were interested in the results or the methods.'[15] Decoupling also
has its origins in practitioner suspicion about the new wave of audits, particularly given the perception that medical audit was already operating as
a successful part of practice and did not require extension or formalization
(Laughlin *et al.*, 1994:104). There is also evidence of resistance by general
practitioners (Broadbent *et al.*, 1992) resulting in minimalist and formal
responses to audit rather than in utilizing it for cultural change. However,
these formal responses necessitate administrative changes and the creation
of resource intensive absorbative functions (Laughlin *et al.*, 1994).[16]

Is this a story of successful professional decoupling of audit initiatives?
Or, even in this form, is the practice of medical audit a Trojan horse for
more disciplinary machinery? There has been much discussion on the shape
and development of medical auditing by practitioners. Much of this has
been concerned to maintain the conception of audit as a learning process
to facilitate professional development, a bottom-up, holistic process led by
professional activity (Nolan and Scott, 1993). These views have been reinforced by general suspicion that a more abstract and standardized form of
medical auditing would be nothing more than cost-cutting in disguise.

Managerial Colonization

Audit could never continue to exist as a private clinical activity and 'even
soon after [medical] audit was established, the potential for audit to operate
in a wider environment was recognised' (Exworthy, 1995:31). Packwood *et
al.* (1994) echo this view and draw attention to the growing encroachment

of public accountability demands within medical auditing, building on a fragmented and messy, though largely consensual, base of existing routines and practices. Medical audit has begun to emerge as a management priority, particularly as purchasers and providers learn new roles, as hybrid doctor–managers are created and as pressure for multi-discipline representation increases. Of course, management involvement is explicitly and officially premissed on sensitivity to practitioner autonomy and workloads: 'successful audit takes place in a culture that does not attribute blame' (quoted in Exworthy, 1995:78). But the emergence of audit committee structures is a clear signal of a trend: greater management involvement in the purposes, processes, and results of medical audit. And many practitioners remain suspicious of this involvement and of the possibility of a routinization of medical practice (Black and Thompson, 1993:850).

The case of psychotherapy practitioners, as newly conceived providers of services to purchasers (health authorities and general practitioners), illustrates the disturbing potential of audit.[17] The development of audit for psychotherapeutic services is consistent with developments in other specialties. However, where psychotherapy differs is that there is a long and extreme practitioner history of controversy about effectiveness. Different schools of thought and practice exist together with competing professional sensitivities about the nature of care and the meaning of outcomes. The introduction of audit has heightened tensions in the field for a number of reasons.

First, a suspicion of external management encroachment exists, as it does in medicine more generally, and there are the usual preoccupations with preserving autonomous self-audit structures. However, these reactions are amplified by concerns that, in the absence of demonstrable criteria of auditable performance based on successful clinical outcome, psychotherapeutic services may face a crisis of demand. Second, audit has intensified longstanding practitioner tensions about 'measurable change'. There are general worries about an incompatibility between short term audit cycles and the longer term cycles of therapy. There is also another key issue: whoever gains control of the audit process can legitimate their concept of therapy over rivals by building it into accreditation processes. In short, the prospect of audit has heightened inter-professional rivalries, supporting Dezalay's (1995*a*) argument that regulation is a stake in professional competition.

Ultimately the question of colonization hangs on the management of tensions between managers and clinicians (Gain and Rosenhead, 1993:11), a process which is constantly developing. Although audit can be hijacked for internal purposes, anxieties persist about its uses in the future (Black and Thompson, 1993:854–5). Pollitt (1993*a*; 1993*b*) argues for an explicitly institutionalized decoupling or 'insulation' to provide a buffer between internal and external audit arrangements. In this way there can be a clear distinction between medical self-reflection and accountability. But it remains to be seen whether such a clear distinction can be maintained, especially as the evidence from other audit contexts suggests the existence of institutional pressures to combine these roles and to ensure the external visibility of internal control. However, at the time of writing it is too early to say whether decoupling or colonizing tendencies or, most likely, a mix of the two, will harden into institutionally stable arrangements. What can be said with some confidence is that, as with financial and other forms of audit, medical auditing remains a contested field.

Medical Audit: A Contested Terrain

There can be little doubt that the application of NPM based reforms, and the role of medical audit as an instrument of these reforms, has constituted an enormous environmental disturbance to health organizations. This much was probably intended. The problem for medical auditing is that, despite many attempts at definitional closure (Dent, 1993:263), it is likely that it will need to satisfy multiple expectations, particularly where it is coupled to external review processes (Exworthy, 1995:101). Operational definitions and textbooks have been created to develop the principles articulated by the Royal Colleges.[18] Contracting functions continue to evolve and the normative and operational boundaries of medical auditing are far from being fixed. Indeed, as in the case of financial auditing discussed in Chapter 2, a certain lack of clarity about the role of medical audit allows it to express clinical and managerial aspirations simultaneously, aspirations which are themselves blurred. For example, Nolan and Scott (1993:760) point to the continuing ambiguity of the Department of Health definition of medical audit.

Some argue that medical audit serves accountability programmes imperfectly because so much information remains private. Again the parallels with other forms of auditing are striking: audit often does not coincide with information release, especially where practitioners control the process. Furthermore, even its internal use value has been criticized: audit cycles remain incomplete, it is impossible to attribute change to audit and patients' (the customers?) perspectives play little role. All in all medical audit is a fragile practice which can be 'readily ignored or omitted, its results argued away as idiosyncratic, its insights seen to be duplicated by other sources, its purposes conflicting, with no perceptions of any serious detriment to medical practice resulting from its absence' (Packwood et al., 1994:310). But supporters of medical audit contend that such doubts about the operational role of audit are likely to be self-fulfilling, leading to further non-completion of cycles and increased medical complacency (Black and Thompson, 1993).[19] Faced with evidence of operational weaknesses, enthusiasts are pressing for more resources and status (Thomson and Barton, 1994).

The field of medical audit is evolving and the meaning of the practice is being negotiated between increasingly overlapping medical and managerial concerns. Purchasers are learning to be 'principals' who must monitor their contracts and hybrid professionals in multi-discipline teams are constantly demanded. The language of quality assurance and the need for performance indicators which focus on outcomes is also taking shape. It is here that the concerns of medical practitioners echo those of academics and critics of quality assurance. The medical profession, like all professions, tends to prefer evaluation orientated towards quality of process (Dent, 1993:262). As medical auditing becomes part of a quality assurance system, it concerns itself with the auditable object of managerial capability rather than directly with care itself and this cannot but impact on medical autonomy. In addition there are operational worries about crude forms of performance measurement: 'the need to introduce audit in short order will make easily collected, quantifiable data very appealing' (Nolan and Scott, 1993:762).

Medical auditing was never initially intended as a public accountability device and practitioners have worked hard to maintain its status as a heuristic tool to improve practice. As it is slowly moving into the orbit of public accountability new managerial demands are made of it with the expectation that older roles can be maintained. Inevitably, the medical quality assurance system is emerging as the primary auditable object: 'the changing environment of CA [clinical audit] has meant that purchasers and provider managers are not necessarily concerned with quality of clinical care *per se* but increasingly with the systems established to ensure that quality is developed and maintained' (Exworthy, 1995:95).

In conclusion, medical audit seems to moving inexorably away from its local, *ad hoc*, bottom-up origins towards a more standardized, national framework, a process which necessarily weakens local professionals *vis-à-vis* newly created auditors: 'Top down models generally apply a generic instrument administered by outside assessors, whereas bottom-up systems are generated and largely applied by practitioners themselves' (Nolan and Scott, 1993:762). As bottom-up schemes make contact with, and are transformed by, top-down accountability requirements, the audit process may heighten conflict, especially where direct impacts on clinical decision making can be demonstrated. Yet, like other audits, the value of medical auditing becomes harder to demonstrate the more it is disengaged from local learning processes. It is rather a practice that must be made to work.

MAKING AUDITEES: FINANCIAL AUDITORS

In the two cases considered above, higher education and medicine, one can see something of the belief in the reforming and revelatory power of auditing (McSweeney, 1988). From this one might conclude that one cannot audit audit itself, that it puts itself beyond the possibility of evaluation of its costs and benefits. However, this is only partly the case. Even though the audit explosion has been accompanied by the a prioristic faith of the NPM, it is nevertheless the case that the audit of audit takes place. Indeed, it is perhaps an inevitable extension of the logic of making things auditable discussed in Chapter 4 that it should arrive back at the doors of accountants themselves, who are often accused of being the agents of the NPM. The audit of audit discussed below demonstrates that the logic of auditing cannot be easily identified with a conspiracy of the large accounting firms and has more to do with the broader shifts in regulatory philosophy discussed in Chapter 3. Accountants are clearly agents of this shift; but they are subjects of it too.

The history of financial auditing presented in Chapter 2 tells a story of crisis driven developments in the regulation of auditors, a dialectic of failure in which standards of technical practice have been codified and codes of ethics have been formalized. As accountants, and the firms in which they operate, have become more explicitly commercial in orientation there have been greater demands for regulation and almost constant preoccupations with the problem of independence. Many institutional structures have been created as a consequence of these pressures for reform. Despite the myth that independence is a 'state of mind' there is now in the UK a Chartered Accountants Joint Ethics Committee (CAJEC) and a Joint Disciplinary Scheme (JDS) for determining and enacting policy in the sphere of ethics and professional behaviour. The JDS has always been controversial, criticized both for doing too much and too little.[20] At the time of writing the Chartered Association of Certified Accountants (ACCA) signalled their intention to withdraw from it on grounds of cost and the fact that it was contributing to the discipline of members of other institutes. The feeling that these self-regulatory arrangements have been falling apart[21] has led to the search for new structures with greater independence from the professional bodies and greater legitimacy and effectiveness (Mitchell *et al.*, 1991).

It was argued in Chapter 2 that where a product or service is ambiguous, it is to be expected that practitioners will invest heavily in ethical codes and procedures. In other words, the guarantee of quality in 'inscrutable markets' is somehow to have trust in the people. But equally these people must be competent and there is a need for the knowledge base discussed in Chapters 2 and 4 to be credible and enforceable. While the UK Auditing Practices Board and its predecessor body have been concerned with articulating and codifying best audit practice, they have not been concerned with enforcing practitioner compliance with technical standards. In the UK this task has been entrusted to the Joint Monitoring Unit (JMU), essentially an inspectorate for audit quality.[22] The JMU was created for the purpose of financial services regulation (Cooper *et al.*, 1994) and was restructured and given further resources to fulfil its new role in 'guarding the guards'. The ACCA created its own regulatory body.

Following the European Eighth Directive on the regulation of auditors, the UK adopted various monitoring requirements into the Companies Act 1989. Section 25 of this Act requires the auditor to be 'registered'.[23] The numerous requirements relating to the regulation of registered auditors' competence and integrity were delegated to the professional bodies. An important effect of the Eighth Directive measures was to strengthen arrangements for the regulation of firms rather than individuals. It is the firms who must ensure that partners and staff are 'fit and proper' persons. This means that a layered regulatory system has been created and that the primary object of regulatory interest is the organizational control system at the level of the firm. This mix of enabling legislation and delegation to professional structures reflects more general commitments to private government coupled to state oversight (Chapter 3), exercised through the requirement that professional bodies report to the DTI on the operation of the scheme.

The Problem of Small Practitioners

The operational problem confronting the JMU resembles that of any audit: how can it be done economically and credibly? Initially a stratified sampling approach was adopted reflecting the skewed nature of the population of firms engaged in auditing. Of nearly 9000 firms it was decided to make 250 visits to those having at least one listed client and 150 visits to the rest. However, it is in relation to this second category of smaller firms that the JMU has encountered most difficulty. From its earliest days under the Financial Services Act the JMU had encountered problems with the auditors of investment businesses regulated under the Financial Intermediaries and Money Brokers Regulatory Authority (FIMBRA). Following the fraud related collapses of Barlow Clowes and Dunsdale Securities (Chapter 2), concerns were raised about the competence of auditors to practise in a complex area when they only had one or two FIMBRA clients.

If there were operational problems for the JMU itself in dealing with small firms, given its own resource constraints, small firms nevertheless complained bitterly about the costs of regulation, costs which they argue were disproportionately high for them and for which the benefits were at best doubtful. Registration fees had been raised in the early 1990s to pay for the new regulatory system and to provide the £4 million budget for the

JMU. Constant worries about rising membership costs and concerns about the nature of control exercised by the professional institutes demonstrate the heterogeneity of the UK accountancy profession as well as the distinctive and powerful position of the large firms. Not only did these regulatory initiatives heighten big firm–small firm tensions, they also created difficulties for professional institutes as organizations in their own right as they struggled to reconcile the dual role of regulator and trade association.[24]

The early years of JMU appear on the surface to have been a regulatory success and paint a picture of a strong inspectorate unafraid to be critical. In its first annual report, the JMU reported that very few firms were up to the mark and overall there seemed to be a high level of unsatisfactory inspections.[25] One might expect this from a body wishing to establish its legitimacy early on. But in the joint ICAEW/ICAS/ICAI report to the DTI of 30 September 1990, it was emphasized that the JMU is not just an inspector in the deterrence mode. It also plays an advisory and educational role in assisting firms to improve audit quality. The regulatory style is that of a cooperative process attempting both to win over practitioners to the benefits of being 'inspected' and also to convince the DTI of its regulatory credibility. Nevertheless, the JMU was never free of the criticism that the quality audit it promoted was based on the large firm model and was inappropriate and expensive for smaller firms.

There are numerous ironies surrounding the work of the JMU. First, while auditors themselves have always pushed the added value of the audit process, many small practitioners would not buy such stories from the JMU when they came to be audited themselves. Second, given that the JMU faced similar operational problems to auditors, it seemed reasonable to ask whether JMU inspections were themselves of sufficient quality. Third, the regulatory initiatives, of which the JMU was a part, showed up deficiencies in the professional institutes' knowledge of their members. And fourth, the problem of auditing small practitioners may have been decisive in steering the UK to accept in principle the abolition of the small company audit against the longstanding resistance of the Inland Revenue. At a stroke the number of entities requiring JMU visits was cut. Overnight audit quality became *more* auditable.

Making Audit Quality Auditable

Some of the criticisms of the JMU by small audit practitioners are similar to those relating to quality assurance more generally. For the quality of auditing to be itself auditable, it was necessary for the JMU to inspect firms' own quality assurance systems, i.e. their systems for inspecting their application of, and compliance with, auditing standards. This systems approach is endorsed by Holden (1995:21), the ex-head of the JMU: 'the whole focus of future monitoring should be around the effectiveness of the firm's quality assurance review.' Audit quality assurance is therefore an internal audit process which is occasionally validated by JMU inspectors. Auditing, like higher educational teaching, is only auditable if the quality systems approach is taken. Once this approach is adopted then documentary appearances are vital. One of the most common audit failings identified by the JMU was a failure to perform a 'close down review'. Literally this means a failure to finish the audit but in fact it is impossible for the JMU to distinguish between a failure to finish the audit and a failure to write up the audit as finished.

The bureaucratic excesses about which small practitioners complained were reflected in new markets in which they could buy standard working papers and advisory publications on how to manage a visit from the JMU. Some accountants, like academics and doctors, recognize the ritualistic and expensive nature of the process. The JMU makes practitioners get the file looking neat and one senior practitioner complained that 'Countless hours are spent "upgrading" files, not to produce evidence of their audit opinion but to satisfy voracious JMU inspectors'. He/she goes on to suggest how it is possible that model files may be created for bad audits and calls for a review of 'actual work carried out', rather than just the file.[26] Ironically the quality assurance approach conflicts with auditors' own self-image that good auditing is a function of experienced professional judgement, which by definition is self-policing. The JMU can only observe and audit this judgement process at one or two removes by observing the control systems. Audit judgements are made auditable by creating these compliance systems. The big question is do audits really improve? It is difficult to know since the quality assurance of financial auditing does nothing to overcome the essential epistemic obscurity of audit. Criteria of effective auditing which are independent of procedures would be needed for this (Chapter 2).

To conclude, there is some evidence of costly ritualistic compliance for JMU quality assurance purposes. However, it is striking that whereas researchers and doctors and many others are being pushed towards *outcome* based auditable performance measurement, auditors themselves are being inspected in terms of their *process* because the outcome of the audit process, the production of assurance, is obscure and defies measurement.[27] When Day and Klein (1987:232) argue that the notion of performance as outcome is 'genuinely difficult and elusive' resulting in a drift towards a process which is the preserve of the professional, they could have been describing a situation in which the audit of financial auditing currently finds itself. One could say that the audit of quality finds its natural home in the context of financial auditing.

IN SEARCH OF THE AUDITABLE PERFORMANCE: AUDIT,
EVALUATION, AND EFFECTIVENESS

In all the specific cases discussed above a common pattern is visible.
Existing structures of self-reflection on practice, which have traditionally
been *ad hoc*, local and under the control of practitioners themselves, have
been harnessed to regulatory initiatives in the environment. Despite explicit
pleas to differentiate learning and accountability, internal and external
auditing, one can discern the steady transformation of internal control cultures into externally auditable objects. Auditees have adopted strategies to
deal with these developments but, formally at least, systems with very
similar general features are being developed in diverse contexts to provide
an auditable surface for the organization. It is not that self-auditing is giving
way to external auditing but that both are being reshaped to 'fit' each other;
audits must always work.

A crucial part of this reshaping is the construction of auditable performance which can be embodied in a management system and which may be
reported to external parties. I have already suggested that financial auditing values have influenced the development of financial accounting. Is this
direction of influence true more generally for the NPM related changes in
the public sector? Does auditability drive performance measurement? Day
and Klein (1990) have suggested that 'hard data is a basic tool of inspection' but the point can be turned on its head. Data which are inspected will
seem hard, since 'hardness' is a function of institutionalized acceptance. To
put the point another way, performance must be constructed in such a way
that it can be measured, audited, and communicated to external agencies
in a legitimate, rational and, yes, 'hard' form.[28]

As the case of timesheets for academics demonstrates, the actual mechanics of constructing measures which conform to ideals of replicability, calcu-
lability, visibility, portability, and legitimacy can be done in many different
and contestable ways. Day and Klein (1987:92–5) draw attention to the well
recognized problem of defining objectives and performance for public services whose outputs are difficult to identify (e.g. education, research, policing, auditing). Where the specialist knowledge base of the practice itself is
complex (medicine) and/or internally controversial (social work, psychoanalysis) these problems are compounded. Attempts to grade casualty
departments in terms of the length of time patients wait to be seen, day care
centres in terms of throughputs of the elderly, schools in terms of examination results and so on all have a certain plausibility. It is widely accepted
that such factors should play some role in an evaluation of the organization. But as 'measures of the measurable' in abstraction from local complexity, there are problems. As Klein and Carter (1988:14) put it,
'performance is a contestable notion' and much depends on the particular
characteristics of the service organization. The significance of a measure

may also lie less 'in the practical use that has been made of it so far than in the messages sent out by its production' (Day and Klein, 1990:29). For example, are installed performance figures ends in themselves, a basis for nuanced internal debate, or a first step towards deep cultural change in an organization?

Klein and Carter (1988) distinguish between outputs and outcomes and define effectiveness as the relation between the two. Outputs are often service activities and can be problematic to measure. Outcomes are the impacts or consequences (intended and unintended) of these outputs and it is often equally problematic to identify them and connect them to outputs. In the examples considered so far one can discern a tendency to obliterate this distinction and to abandon the causal demands of outcome based measures. Accordingly, performance measurement gravitates towards outputs and the systems for producing them; it is around these measures that a certain style of management control can be exercised unencumbered by the contingencies of how such outputs might relate to desired outcomes. In other words, the difficult connection between service activities and outcomes can be ignored in favour of the (more auditable) intermediate outputs of the activities, such as examination results or average waiting times for patients. And where these outputs are also problematic, there is a further tendency to drift towards inputs, such as costs, which are readily auditable.

The distinction between outputs and outcomes and the tendency for 'performance' audit to drift towards outputs is a crucial issue. What is at stake is the compatibility of two logics, broadly that of auditing on the one hand and that of evaluation on the other. Coupled to these two logics are questions of turf and of power to define what counts as adequate performance. One logic has developed from a home base in input auditing, focusing on the regularity of transactions, towards the audit of measurable outputs. The other, though not without problems and much less coherent than audit as a practice, is traditionally more sensitive to the complexities of connecting service processes causally to outcomes. The audit explosion represents a systematic shift from the logic of evaluation to that of auditing, a shift which puts auditing itself beyond evaluation.

Audit and Evaluation

Preoccupations within public sector services with needs, inputs, and professionally supervised processes came under increasing criticism in the early 1980s. Managerial imperatives began to displace both professional evaluative structures, such as peer review, and methods rooted in the social sciences. In comparison with evaluative practice, which often generates conflict and ambiguity, audit is attractive for its apparent objectivity. However, audit in new contexts is not merely neutral verification but an agent of change which creates the organizational basis for internal and external verification of economy, efficiency, and effectiveness. The rise of the Audit Commission and its emphasis on performance measurement and audit is paradigmatic of this managerial agenda.

The Audit Commission has already been described in Chapter 3. Its role as an agency of change became explicit in the late 1980s as it began to encourage the development of internal performance measures and systems for financial management (Henkel, 1991:205). Over this period a more integrated audit concept emerged. Through programmes of special studies to develop subsequent VFM auditing guidance, the Commission attempted to install the possibility of auditability in target organizations. However, it was initially a weak body and 'in its early years, the Commission was undertaking local "value for money" audits with substantially the same type of expertise (that of accountancy) as had been deployed on the much narrower functions carried out by its predecessor body' (Henkel, 1991:183). Slowly the Audit Commission developed new advisory roles and acquired confidence in the area of effectiveness and performance measurement, applying variants of the conceptual toolbox of management consultants, such as McKinseys. Without doubt, the Audit Commission has thrived in an institutional environment in which questions of politics were converted into questions of resource management.

The economic order of local government had to be changed before it could be regulated and the development of performance indicators was essential to this. However, operational relations between the Audit Commission, local authority elected council members and non-elected executive officers were and remain variable and complex. Day and Klein (1990:56) emphasize the 'dependence of the audit on the professional expertise of those being audited', suggesting that audits are essentially collusive in nature and that 'pure policing' is never possible. Accordingly, relations with auditors are not always antagonistic and much depends on the internal political and administrative style within the local authority itself. High conflict tends to give a high profile to the audit report but equally such reports can be used selectively and are not stereotypical cost cutting documents.

Despite these qualifications and complexities, the work of the Audit Commission provides a powerful model for inspectorates such as the SSI and HAS which grew out of organizations oriented towards 'professional enlightenment rather than ... political accountability' (Day and Klein, 1990:58). The accountancy base of the Audit Commission undoubtedly gives it a legitimacy which other evaluators lack: 'the techniques of presentation, the deployment of argument and the choice of language and symbol played a significant part in the acquisition of authority on the part of the Audit Commission' (Henkel, 1991:224). The Commission's unique 'combination of technical modelling and political argument' (Henkel, 1991:216) characterizes a dominant audit style which emphasizes the importance of clear and measurable objectives within a strong managerial system of control. In contrast, organizations like the SSI have to manage the tensions created by standards of performance for an area, social work, which is traditionally rather insecure about the professional basis of what it does and in which professional process based values often conflict with external assessments oriented towards outomes.[29]

Although the SSI exists somewhat in the shadows of the Audit Commission and could never be transformed into a financial auditing body, its development suggests an emergent hierarchy between audit and evaluation, an issue which goes to the heart of value for money auditing and which casts the construction of auditable performance in terms of inter-professional struggle. Where outcomes, and hence effectiveness, are ambiguous or controversial for professionals themselves (such as in psychoanalysis or social work), cost imperatives and output measures tend to dominate the language of evaluation. In the climate of NPM the logic of performance audit encodes a hierarchical relation between cost considerations and non-financially based evaluation. In this way, the development of auditable performance measures is much more than a technical issue: it concerns the power to define the dominant language of evaluation within this hierarchy (Day and Klein, 1987:238). When Day and Klein (1990) argue that the essential tension between cost and quality could be solved by joint inspections, they underestimate the territorial issues at stake and this tendency for the three Es to be related hierarchically such that economy and efficiency values 'oversee' those of effectiveness.

As noted in Chapter 3, the operational relation between the three Es within the structure of value for money auditing attempts to steer a path between the financial logic of economy and efficiency and the more elusive set of skills required to formulate judgements about effectiveness, the performance auditing component of VFM audit. Initially it seemed that accountants were reluctant to stray beyond their expertise; in a VFM study of the care of children, there was no attempt made to draw conclusions on the relative merits of different methods of child care (e.g. fostering, residential care) even though these methods had clear cost implications (Kimmance, 1984:243). The relative merits of such methods, in terms of the objective of providing children with a chance to develop in a stable environment, were perceived as a matter for professional social workers to determine. Accordingly, accountants are not crudely unaware of problems of measurement in complex service organizations (e.g. Kimmance, 1984:236) and as Henkel (1991) has observed, many VFM auditors were caught between the restraints of their competence and a desire for impact.[30]

The question of the knowledge base of performance auditing has a long history, particularly in the USA where both audit and evaluation have been and are important resources for the GAO. Rather than trying to draw absolute analytical distinctions between audit and evaluation one should pay attention to *how* the distinction is used and to what end. For example, Chelimsky (1985) distinguishes between the two practices as follows. Audit focuses on verification, i.e. the correspondence between some operation and certain standards to which it should conform. In contrast, evaluation has two streams focusing on cost-effectiveness on the one hand and the assessment of programmes in influencing outcomes on the other. From this point of view audit is a normative check whereas evaluation provides empirical knowledge and addresses cause and effect issues; audit is orientated towards compliance as a normative outcome whereas evaluation seeks to explain the relationship between the changes that have been observed and the programme. Without normative standards of conduct, audit is undermined. Hence the importance of standards of performance which create a normative template to make an operation auditable. In contrast it is argued that evaluation is much less affected by ambiguity about standards of performance and objectives.

On this view performance can be *audited* when clear performance measures and standards of performance exist (Flint, 1988). Otherwise performance can be evaluated in the two ways described above. Furthermore, Chelimsky (1985:501) describes the 'cost-effectiveness' aspect of evaluation as an 'auxiliary, not an alternative approach' to the evaluation of performance. Accounting skills are important here but essentially subordinate. The Financial Controller and acting director general of DGXX in the European Commission offers a hierarchical view of the relation between audit and evaluation in direct contrast to that of Chelimsky. He uses the distinction slightly differently and reserves the term evaluation for the assessment of outcomes in contrast to the audit of cost-effectiveness. Although forms of self-evaluation are viewed as a necessary threshold for any spending to be taken seriously, cost effectiveness auditing sits *above* them and takes into account whether such self-evaluation programmes exist:'I'm not going to do the evaluation. I'm going to make sure that evaluation is being done' (Pratley, 1995:261).

Even though Roberts and Pollitt (1994) draw attention to the crude nature of cost-effectiveness analysis, especially where it substitutes for a broader based evaluation of the relation between outcomes and intentions, it nevertheless satisfies the regulatory mood of the times.[31] Conceiving of performance evaluation primarily in terms of cost-effectiveness overcomes the problems of an evaluation community whose epistemology is constructivist, and therefore less useful for policy purposes (Henkel, 1991:179), and brings evaluative practice closer to the domain of accountants. Equally, as Hepworth (1995) suggests, as performance auditing moves closer to evaluation, accountants will lose their hold on the work. Hence the contestability of performance evaluation has implications for different professional groups. In exploring the differences and commonalities between performance audit and evaluation, Pollitt and Summa (1997) draw attention to the greater rights of access and legitimacy of audit bodies like the NAO in the 'web of power' and the greater occupational distinctiveness of auditors as compared with evaluators. Although evaluators may have formal freedom to define objects of investigation, performance auditors increasingly work well beyond their original remits with an evidential style which is non-research based and procedural in form. Typically the audit feedback process embodied in a formal management control system reflects a naively mechanistic and self-corrective view of organizational change, with levels of often highly ritualized calculative specificity.[32]

To conclude, I have used the motif of the 'auditable performance' to suggest that the development of audit practices and the design of performance measures are not independent. This has always been true for financial auditing and accounting and in Chapter 4 the extreme case was suggested where it was the performance of the control system itself which was the relevant auditable performance. In the case of VFM auditing, and the audit of effectiveness in particular, the whole notion of performance, and hence of auditability, is contested and problematic. There are tendencies to favour the administrative objectivity of auditable measures of performance which are replicable and consistent even if they are essentially arbitrary. This is preferred to the nuances, ambiguities and qualifications which surround evaluation in all its guises. In the end, the problem has much to do with the nature, extent, and impact of management intervention in the operational judgements of service providers such as teachers and doctors (Pollitt, 1990:438). In the audit society the power to define and institutionalize auditable performance reduces evaluation to auditing.

CONCLUSIONS: AUDIT AS FATAL REMEDY?

In this chapter it has been argued that auditing and the development of concepts of performance are mutually constitutive. This is because performance is itself an ambivalent concept which can be anchored in terms of the functioning of a management control system or in terms of measures of output, which could figure in such a system, or in terms of outcomes which would remove assessment of performance from managerial and hence auditing control. The power of auditing is therefore to construct concepts of performance in its own image. The effects of this power were considered in three cases which suggest varying degrees of decoupling and colonization for the audit process. In the case of the audit of effectiveness, a part of value for money auditing, it was argued that concepts of performance were contestable in terms of competing primary orientations towards audit and cost control on the one hand and the evaluation of out-comes compared to intentions on the other. The mood of the NPM is such that audit tends to dominate evaluation and that performance tends to be measured in terms of auditable outputs.

The lesson of regulatory history is that, in the end, all experiments in control fail and lead to further reforms: 'Good monitoring systems are hard to design. Getting the right information about the agent's performance, without drowning the principal in paper, is difficult. So too is developing a feedback system that gives the principal the needed information without interfering with the agent's work' (Kettl, 1993:29). But auditing cannot just be understood in such formal and technical terms. Accountability and per-formance are constantly elusive, discipline-specific (Sinclair, 1995:221) and problematic as more elaborate, expensive and intrusive surfaces for control are constructed with little knowledge of their potential consequences. Accounting and audit practices exist in a process of near constant change, tossed to and fro between the demands of different and often contradic-tory programmes.

Decoupling and compartmentalization are the rule because individuals are infinitely more complex and adaptable than normalizing attempts to measure and control them; a substantive, messy rationality always reasserts itself over formal, technical rationality (Ezzamel and Willmott, 1993:127). And yet formal colonization is also always the rule because new forms of organizational language become institutionalized, percolate into domains even where active decoupling is pursued and become interpretive schemes which shift motivations (Laughlin, 1991). Somewhere between these extremes the gains and losses of the audit society must be evaluated. The key question is not just whether there are intended gains to be weighed against unintended side-effects but whether elements of decoupling and colonization lead to 'reverse effects' (Sieber, 1981) in which original goals of financial control and effectiveness are actually frustrated and undermined.[33] In the context of 'gesture politics' with little interest in the longer term effects of intervention, systematic mechanisms do not exist to understand reverse effects, especially those which affect disenfranchised groups. Furthermore, where objectives are vague and unclear, and they usually are at the level of political programmes, the question of whether reverse effects have even occurred will itself be contestable.

In the case of auditing some reverse effects can be suggested. An increase in pointless information systems leads to 'inspection overload' (Day and Klein, 1990) and misdiagnosis (in contrast to official deregulatory and mini-malist myths). Decoupling strategies are exacerbated but there is also a decline in organizational trust which creates an inhibiting and 'anxious pre-occupation with how one is seen by others' (Roberts, 1991:366). It has also been said that the rise of the performance related contracts has led to irrevocable damage to cultures of trust (Day and Klein, 1987:235). New games are created to demonstrate quality and substantive performance declines: 'formal controls instituted to enhance trust by increasing performance reliability can undermine trust and thus deter achievement of the very goals they were put in place to serve' (Sitkin and Stickel 1996:197). Superficial commitments to empowerment reinforce forms of exclusion and auditors are captured or co-opted into turf battles, thereby forgetting the original intention of the programmes they serve. As the means becomes the end, there is a continuing overcommitment to create politically acceptable images of control. 'Off the shelf' (Nolan and Scott, 1993) audits are used to represent the auditee organization so as to make its activities less heterogeneous, less complex, and less uncertain.

These adverse effects are constantly eclipsed by the programmatic imperative that audits must work. In this respect one might compare this imperative with that which informed the detailed output targets of the former Soviet Union. This was a situation characterized by pathologies of 'creative compliance' (McBarnet and Whelan, 1991), poor quality goods and the development of survival skills to show that, often impossible, targets were achieved. Games are played around an 'indicator' culture where auditable performance is an end in itself and real long term planning is impossible.[34]

To conclude, there is a need to recognize these 'regulatory paradoxes' which surround audit and a need for ways to evaluate the audit explosion which are sensitive to the incentive effects through which micro-rationalities can subvert macro-rationality (Sunstein, 1990:432). The creation of an academic transfer market by research assessment exercises is a good example: the RAEs may be a fatal remedy for the university sector by stimulating behaviour which increases the costs for the sector as a whole. Grabosky's (1995a) solution to such 'counterproductive regulation' is better monitoring but this does not help when it is the monitoring itself which is counterproductive. The solution, if any, lies in making the effects of auditing visible. This means that audit will need to be evaluated rather than audited, a move which requires a prioristic policy making to rediscover the complexities of cause and effect. Even though audit has been *audited*, the power of auditing is itself one of the institutional barriers to the *evaluation* of audit.

Overall, the discussion of auditable performance measurement suggests how 'the anxious ruler tries to make his phantasies come true by way of a mixture of minute controls and rigorous isolation' (Van Gunsterten, 1976:142). Undoubtedly the programmatic faith in auditing reflects wider social anxieties and a need to create images of control in the face of risk. This will be considered in greater depth in the concluding chapter.

6

Audit, Trust, and Risk

INTRODUCTION

In this concluding chapter, I explore some of the more general implications of a society which is increasingly committed to observing itself through various kinds of auditing practice. Common sense suggests that it is often useful for operations to be checked by different people and audit practitioners are not trying to be deceptive when they speak of the benefits of the assurance that auditing provides, even if they cannot be precise about these benefits. Supporters of auditing argue that it is foolishly romantic to imagine that individuals can be entirely trusted with economic resources; they must be made to give an account of their actions and this account must be checked for its veracity. In short, auditing exists because of the way societies are and the way individuals are constituted; economic analyses suggest that it emerges naturally from the demand for third party enforcement of business contracts.

The previous chapters in this book have attempted to probe deeper into this view. One might agree with Lee (1993) that auditing arises from the common human need to alleviate anxiety but it remains to be asked where these anxieties come from and in what other ways they might be addressed. Societies and their institutions change. When directors were generally regarded as trustworthy and shareholders were perceived as largely ignorant of business matters, financial audit existed in a very limited form. Despite being ruffled by the occasional scandal, cultural consensus about the expertise and honesty of directors remained intact until the 1930s when, as Chapter 2 suggests, the financial audit began to assume a major regulatory function which was constantly extended and adapted in new directions. Audit may therefore seem obvious or natural under certain circumstances but the history of the institutions through which it is realized provides a reminder of its specific form.

It has been emphasized that auditing is not merely a collection of technical tasks but also a programmatic idea circulating in organizational environments, an idea which promises a certain style of control and organizational transparency. From this point of view audit may be less a rational response to the need to reduce transactions costs and more a temporarily congealed taste or fashion which escapes conscious design

(DiMaggio and Powell, 1991:8). This taken-for-granted aspect of auditing, its persistence as a self-sustaining system of practical knowledge, has been the concern of the previous chapters. The underlying social theory is more that of routine or institutionalized practice rather than rational choice, cognitive congealment rather than efficient adaptation. Standardized elements, such as the auditable management system discussed in Chapter 4, represent the rationalizing tendencies of audit to reproduce ever more formal auditable structure, regardless of demonstrable effectiveness. Auditing has the character of a certain kind of organizational script whose dramaturgical essence is the production of comfort.

So what does it mean when a society commits ever more financial and intellectual resources to the production of comfort through auditing? This concluding chapter addresses this question in terms of four interrelated themes, themes which are familiar to social scientists: democracy, surveillance, trust, and risk. The discussion begins with a consideration of the democratizing potential of audit. Is the discourse of empowerment and choice which motivates programmatic demands for auditing really more than rhetoric? Do audit reports contribute to democratic ideals and provide a basis for public critique? If not, what does accountability mean when it is operationalized by auditing? Even though auditing has a problematic relation to democracy, the audit society is far from being the 'surveillance society' (Lyon, 1994). The relation between ideas of surveillance, inspection, and audit is considered and it is argued that the rise of audit represents a distinctive shift in the self-inspecting and evaluating capacity of society. This shift has important implications for the third theme: trust. The audit society is only superficially a 'distrusting society'. Indeed, auditing is a practice which must be trusted and which is also itself, of necessity, trusting.

In conclusion I argue that the audit explosion reflects a distinctive response to the need to process risk. Auditing threatens to become a cosmetic practice which hides real risk and replaces it with the financial risk faced by auditors themselves. Where the audit process is defensively legalized there is a risk of relying too heavily on an industry of empty comfort certificates. The audit society is a society that endangers itself because it invests too heavily in shallow rituals of verification at the expense of other forms of organizational intelligence. In providing a lens for regulatory thought and action audit threatens to become a form of learned ignorance. Does the rustle of paper systems, the 'symbolic atmosphere in which men calculate', provide only slogans of accountability and quality which perpetuate rather than alleviate organizational rigidity (Wilensky, 1967:191)? I conclude by speculating on ways of progressing beyond these difficulties and of re-evaluating audit practices in such a way that the worst of these tendencies may be avoided.

AUDITING, ACCOUNTABILITY, AND DEMOCRACY

In Chapter 3 it was argued that programmatic initiatives for auditing were formulated in terms of accountability to taxpayers, to shareholders, to customers, to future generations, and so on. The general idea is that the audit process, and related forms of accounting for performance, open up organizations to independent external scrutiny and thereby provide a basis for enhanced control by those parties with the legitimate right to exercise it. Such parties are described as stakeholders in the language of corporate governance. However, much depends on the manner in which these programmatic demands for accountability on behalf of stakeholders are operationalized. Of particular importance is the style and use of the various forms of report which auditors provide. Do they enlighten, inform, influence, and enable criticism and substantive change? Or is the giving of an audit report intended to bring inquiry to an end?

Certification or Information? Comfort or Critique?

Some forms of inspection produce certificates in the form of licences whose message is fairly clear: the organization, individual, or other object is 'fit' for a defined purpose and has met certain minimum standards (of safety, product quality, cleanliness, schooling, prison care, and so on). The licence is either issued or withheld and the public is entitled to trust that minimum standards are in operation. Escalatory possibilities exist for the revocation of licences and there are usually requirements for remedial action and other sanctions. The point about such certificates is not to engage in communication but to provide a one-way signal—fit or not fit for purpose.

At first glance audits seem to work this way. Many of the audit practices discussed in this book report very little about the auditee, at least publicly. The financial audit report is an attempt to communicate the fact that some minimum standards for the corporate financial statements (not the company itself) have or have not been achieved. These standards are defined by what is commonly known as Generally Accepted Accounting Practice (GAAP) which should function for accounting in the same way that minimum standards of roadworthiness operate for cars. However, the difficulty is that the financial audit report is not quite a licence in the sense described above. Certainly all large companies must have such a report but they are not prevented from trading or being listed on the stock exchange if the auditor issues a negative report, i.e. if the accounts are 'qualified'. Furthermore, these qualified audit reports are not explicitly connected to a regulatory machinery of escalation in Ayres and Braithwaite's (1992) sense. Financial auditors simply issue a report to the shareholders of a company which contains a professional opinion.

Is this financial audit report simply a quality label or does it actually contribute to greater information and understanding of the particular audit process which has been undertaken? There has always been pressure on financial auditing to say more in its reporting (Olson and Wooton, 1991) and there has been a more or less constant discussion about the relative merits of short standardized reports versus longer unstandardized narratives. New forms of words have emerged from these criticisms (e.g. Stevens, 1981:99–105; APB, 1993) but they tend to say only a little more about audit in general and do not provide specific details about the particular audit. Furthermore, a certain style of describing what audit is not (*not* insurance, *not* certification, etc.) has contributed to a loss of confidence in what is really being said by financial auditors. In reality, the financial audit report, although narrative in form, functions more as a quality label. Such labels only work as unambiguous signals of fitness for purpose if there are clear public standards of what quality is or, in cases where quality requires highly specialized judgements, there is social trust in the experts producing the label. Such trust is usually institutionalized by certification arrangements for those providing the quality label. In other words, labels are created for those doing the labelling.

Quality labels like the financial audit report may also create 'expectations gaps' between those who read and those who produce them. What is actually implied by the quality label and is a notion of 'fitness for purpose' clear? If auditors believe that the financial statements provide a 'true and fair' view what does it mean? And are companies registered under the BS 7750 scheme saying by means of a kitemark something about their management systems or something about the substantive environmental performance of the organization?

The quality label style of much audit reporting contrasts with a longer form of narrative reporting and commentary which may well be concerned with compliance with minimum standards but which also reports details of the case in hand. Value for money audit reports tend to be long and non-standardized. This is also the case for the inspectors' reports of the DTI (Russell, 1991) and other bodies. However, the issue is not simply one of the length of narrative forms of reporting; much also depends on the tone of reporting and the use to which reports are put. The quality label style of audit reporting exists to communicate comfort. In these circumstances, when the auditor is dissatisfied, the only option is to refuse to provide the label, i.e. to exercise 'exit' rather than 'voice'. Even for financial auditing which allows for a negative label, such a public critique in the form of a qualified audit report tends to be a last resort.

At its worst, public audit reporting amounts to little more than a 'negative assurance' label which is sanitized, cautious, and unhelpful and which often provides only a 'bland regurgitation of financial data'.[1] Audit compliance statements under the Cadbury Code arrangements discussed in

Chapter 3 provide an example of empty reporting which does not even rise to the level of negative assurance (Piper and Jones, 1995). The problem is compounded by vagueness in the requirements of the code and caution by both the APB and directors about making statements on the effectiveness of internal control. Directors prefer to state that they have reviewed the system but with little or no indication of the results of this review (Chambers, 1996). In the end, it is confusing to know what is being reported both by directors and by auditors in this context, if anything is reported at all.

These difficulties point to the fundamental issue. Do audit reports exist to produce certificates of comfort or are they essentially adversarial? Many of the audits described in this book produce internal criticisms of systems since this is the 'added value' which practitioners promote, however their public role tends to be to stabilize the institutional image of the practice in question. Certification rather than non-certification must be the rule; comfort rather than discomfort must be produced. Exceptionally, VFM audit reports have greater potential for adversarial reporting, a feature they share with state inspectorates. However, it has also been suggested that the NAO has a distinctive tension to manage in this respect since the issues selected for audit must be sufficiently controversial to attract parliamentary interest but not so much so as to split the Parliamentary Accounts Committee (PAC) on party lines (Roberts and Pollitt, 1994).

The pressures to produce comfort are great; too much critique may lead to the sacking or censure of an auditor. For example, the US GAO found itself subject to political inquiry after it had been critical of military contracting arrangements (Mosher, 1979). The history of the European Court of Auditors also reflects tension and conflict with the European Commission. In drawing attention to systems weaknesses 'fundamental aspects of the Court's criticism have not always been well understood' (Middelhoek, 1995:266). By 1995 adversarial attitudes seem to have softened and criticism has become institutionalized in the 'réunions contradictoires' (Harden *et al.*, 1995:17–18).[2] This suggests an emergent common purpose between the Court and the Commission and a shared commitment to a culture of improved financial management. However, it remains the case that auditor 'success' in detecting fraud in, say, agriculture creates wider political tensions within the EU.

To conclude, the adversarial potential of different forms of auditing described above can be a destabilizing force, creating conflict with auditees and producing political problems for regulatory authorities. In contrast where audit arrangements emphasize the production of comfort, this reflects an institutional need for auditing not to be too 'successful' in finding problems and in producing discomfort by reporting these problems. This tension between comforting and criticizing has deeper implications for the role of auditing as a basis for public dialogue.

Accountability and Dialogue

Auditing quality labels or certificates, unlike inspectors' reports, do not invite or provoke public dialogue; they are not designed to support public debate or to connect the audit process to wider representative organs or to further machinery of regulatory escalation. This is not surprising given the emerging regulatory style discussed in Chapter 3 which seeks to build regulatory compliance from below. For example, environmental audits may well be beneficial in terms of stimulating improved management systems, cost savings, greater legal compliance and so on but it is less clear how they really contribute to the empowerment of external parties. Even the EU environmental auditing scheme (EMAS), which requires auditors (external verifiers) to validate and report on a limited environmental statement, is primarily a 'management tool' with regulatory spin-offs.

Most audit reports are labels in the sense discussed above. They do not so much communicate as 'give off' information by virtue of a rhetoric of 'neutrality, objectivity, dispassion, expertise' (Van Maanen and Pentland, 1994:54). This means that the audit process requires trust in experts and is not a basis for rational public deliberation. It is a dead end in the chain of accountability (Day and Klein, 1987:244). Although the audit explosion has occurred in the name of improved accountability, this is largely a form of 'downward' accountability which 'is invoked in order to resist upward accountability; giving an account is seen to be a way of avoiding an account' (Day and Klein, 1987:171). In short, more accounting and auditing does not necessarily mean more and better accountability.

Corporate financial audits are formally intended to serve the goal of shareholder control by linking the operations of corporate boardrooms to the decision making calculus of distant financiers. Academic audits have as one of their goals the empowerment of a hitherto powerless student body. Medical audits are conducted in the name of patients. In this way, audit expresses the promise of accountability and visibility to these stakeholders. But this promise is at best ambiguous: the fact of being audited deters public curiosity and inquiry and the users of audits are often just a mythical reference point within expert discourses. Audit is in this respect a substitute for democracy rather than its aid:

the emphasis of public policy has been to respond to complexity by setting up new institutions of accountability . . . this may, in turn, bring about excessive complexity in the machinery of accountability and at the same time create dead ends. So, why not concentrate less on formal links or institutions and engage more in a civic dialogue to recreate at least something of the high visibility and directness of the face to face accountability (Day and Klein, 1987:249).

To conclude, the operational reality of auditing has a problematic relation to the democratic ideals which drive it. Most audit reports and their related accounting statements function as labels which must be trusted. They do not form a basis for communication and dialogue. Paradoxically, the audit society threatens to become an increasingly closed society, albeit one whose declared programmatic foundation is openness and accountability. So does this mean that these ideals are simply a cynical cover for something more sinister? Is auditing closer to a form of policing and surveillance than is commonly imagined?

AUDIT, SURVEILLANCE, AND INSPECTION

Practices of inspection and surveillance have a long history. The panopticon, borrowed by Jeremy Bentham from his brother Samuel, and made famous by Foucault as a metaphor for the disciplinary society of self-inspection, has provided a powerful image of social control.[3] The ideal form of surveillance is the totally observed and known individual who ends up as a self-observing and self-disciplining agent (Miller and O'Leary, 1987). Surveillance in this sense is orientated explicitly towards control rather than evaluation, towards prevention rather than learning, towards pure visibility rather than, say, a form of confessional accounting.

Surveillance is rarely pure observation, even if this remains a 'policing' ideal. Mediating technololologies play a significant role both in realizing particular forms of surveillance and in designing away the possibilities for deviant behaviour which create the need for control in the first place. Files may be created which attempt to capture every conceivable fact about a person[4] and at the extreme a 'maximum security society' increases the 'ratio of machines as monitors and controllers relative to humans' (Marx, 1990). However, such techno-fixes to control issues are rarely delivered. For example, data banks are only necessary conditions for a 'supervisory eye' which requires considerable institutional support to be effective.

Even though surveillance is often more disorganized than the panopticonic metaphor suggests and despite the fact that claims for disciplinary control are often exaggerated (Lyon, 1994:128), it raises complex normative issues about individual privacy. Technologies of surveillance may always be functionally imperfect but their desirability can always be contested. One reason why the idea of surveillance evokes reactions which audit does not is that surveillance tends to take the human individual as its primary object rather than the organization and its sub-systems of control. This is the case even though financial auditors are trying to 'audit the people'.

Surveillance also suggests a form of first order control whereas it has been argued that audit has become a form of second and third order control of first order systems. In this sense audit could be applied as a form of quality assurance for security and surveillance systems. Auditors also make use of surveillance systems. For example, financial auditors frequently need to form a view on the adequacy of physical and programmed controls over assets and over data integrity to prevent theft and fraud. As forms of organizational surveillance for security purposes are developed to prevent and detect financial loss, auditors need to assess their effectiveness as part of their normal work.

To conclude, audit and surveillance emerge from different programmatic ideals. Programmes for order maintenance may range from coercive policing at one extreme to regulatory practices with precise compliance norms to those that have a softer edge in which the regulatory result is negotiated and consensual (Shearing and Stenning, 1987*a*). From this point of view surveillance can be located at the more coercive end of the programmatic spectrum. Chapter 3 described the overlapping demands arising from changes in public administration, regulatory style, and from quality management which have little to do directly with security and policing agendas. Rather, military and policing systems and the programmatic commitments which support them are themselves subjected to value for money audit. The audit society is therefore hardly identical with the surveillance society and, to the extent that institutionalized mechanisms of surveillance are becoming subjects of auditing, may even subsume it. But a crucial issue is whether auditing itself institutionalizes wide ranging forms of practice in the form of an observation of other observation practices. In short, does the audit explosion herald an 'age of inspection' (Day and Klein, 1990)? To answer this question it is necessary to consider how practices of inspection have been institutionalized.

Auditors and Inspectors

The emergence of audit bodies in the UK described in Chapter 3 parallels the creation, consolidation, and reassembly of inspectorial institutions. For example, the Social Services Inspectorate and Her Majesty's Inspectorate of Pollution were created in 1985 and 1987 respectively. These and other organizations are diverse and constantly evolving (Rhodes, 1981) and the difference between audits and inspections cannot simply be defined by pointing to the activities of inspectors and auditors. Day and Klein (1990:5) argue that it is not really a question of which agencies and entities actually call themselves inspectorates but of the operational models which drive them: 'The notion of inspection is ambiguous and slippery precisely because it may (and usually does) involve a mix of methods and styles: the pure or ideal inspectorate, which automatically enforces a set of norms or benchmarks, exists only in the textbooks.'

Inspection is rarely a case of unmediated contact with things, although factory and prison inspections are close to this. What matters is what is inspected and the inferential technologies through which this is accomplished. Day and Klein talk of the 'age of inspection' as the 'act of examining what is happening' and even include under the concept of inspection audit institutions like the Audit Commission. Audits inspect accounts and systems elements. Equally the audit is also a negotiated result around notions of the true and fair view, value for money, best practice, and so on. In this sense 'an audit inspection represents a dialogue' (Day and Klein, 1990:22). Audits and inspections therefore share an interactive potential that is not suggested by the concept of surveillance. For example, in many contexts inspection is a less adversarial and more negotiated process than is commonly imagined, especially where statutorily based standards are unclear. Whereas for policing the nature of transgressions are relatively unambiguous, regulatory offences are often less clear cut and create incentive problems for inspectors who adopt 'an attitude of legal defensiveness, a concern for adequate documentation rather than substantive achievement, and a degree of rule bound rigidity' (Kagan, 1984:58).

Enforcement in inspections, like that of auditing, tends to take the form of 'interpersonal bargaining within the context of a license (sic), a consent, or permit, and often takes place in morally uncertain territory in which values, technology and business intersect' (Manning, 1987:298). It has also been suggested that factory inspectors gravitate towards easily prosecutable and well defined, usually *ex post*, offences at the expense of risks with more contestable causal structures (Hawkins, 1992). This is because the inspector faces certain reputational risks where prosecution is unsuccessful. Within auditing practice there are similar attempts to retreat into procedural and defensible certainties but much depends on the manner in which performance is defined and the manner in which audit procedures can be 'mapped' on to these rules of performance. Much also depends on strategies of retaining discretionary interpretations of the scope of audit. Unlike inspectors who fail to discover a health hazard which causes loss of life, auditors may have greater leeway to negotiate the facts of failure (Chapter 2).

This interactive and behavioural dimension of auditing and inspection makes it difficult to distinguish definitively between them. However, in terms of orientation towards management systems of compliance and control one can distinguish broadly between an auditing style and an inspecting style. The former increasingly takes the management system as its primary object whereas the latter focuses more on the substantive conduct of the inspectee. This distinction also suggests a systematic drift from classical inspection to an audit style of monitoring (Power, 1995*a*). Even though inspectorates and audit bodies differ greatly in their knowledge bases, there is a convergence towards a common managerial model which emphasizes the encouragement of internal compliance systems. For example, Day and Klein's study of three inspectorates in the UK suggests tendencies to converge towards a single audit model, exemplified by the Audit Commission. However, the process of convergence is uneven.

The Health Advisory Service was characterized by a more experiential form of inspection, emphasizing the 'texture of daily life in homes, with managerial issues brought in as an obligatory afterthought' and with often implicit standards against which compliance might be judged (Day and Klein, 1990:57). In contrast, the Social Services Inspectorate readily adopted a more managerial and collaborative style despite its extensive inspectorial powers.

A drift from an inspection style to an audit style of oversight does not mean literally that auditing will explicitly replace inspection. Indeed, in the USA the Environmental Protection Agency (EPA), which has generally encouraged voluntary audit practices, maintains that 'environmental audits evaluate, and are not a substitute for, direct compliance activities . . . audits do not in any way replace regulatory agency inspectors' (EPA, 1986:111–12). This reflects the EPA's strengths in, and commitments to, its own in-house arrangements for inspection rather than delegated audit, at least in the environmental regulation area. In contrast the UK seems more willing to delegate state regulatory functions to voluntary audit schemes and consultants, stimulated in part by criticisms of Her Majesty's Inspectorate of Pollution (HMIP) for carrying out too few inspections[5] and for possessing too much discretion under the EPA 1990.[6]

The telling difference between an auditing and inspecting style of control concerns the substitution of internal for external agencies of inspection where the external inspector or auditor checks the system for self-inspection. There have even been explicit calls for change in this direction. For example, Braithwaite (1984:139) argues that government inspectors 'ensure the quality of your records, not the quality of your deeds' and compliance records are sometimes written up in advance of doing the work. He argues that while the superior internal epistemological power of the internal quality controller will not always be used by a company, such self-inspecting arrangements are still the best chance of effective regulation. This shows that inspectorial or audit independence is just one value among others and it is being argued that the advantages of internalizing the enforcement of compliance outweigh the disadvantages. From this point of view, inspection and external audit should eventually collapse into a quality assurance function, an audit of arrangements for self-inspection. What is at stake in such a transformation of regulatory style?

Internalizing Inspection and the Problem of Independence

Despite the similarities between the practices which are called inspections and those which are called audits described above, there are also important differences. Inspection practices have been designed with institutionalized options for escalation. For example, prison inspectors are entitled to pay surprise visits to prisons and possess a detailed agenda for determining compliance with the requirements for prisoner care. Prison conditions are literally observed by inspectors and remedial action may be demanded.[7] Dawn raids by tax authorities are another extreme example; one would hardly call them audits. And perhaps the fact that the idea of a 'nuclear audit' is not a comfortable one reveals much about an intuitive distinction between audit and inspection. Are some things just too important and risky to be audited only?

Socio-legal research provides reminders about why such escalatory options may not be taken when they should, but nevertheless such options exist. In contrast, audits often operate in environments where escalatory machinery deliberately does not exist (voluntary schemes) or is uncertain in its functioning (adverse public reporting). For this reason pressures for voluntary system improvement rather than external sanction have emerged as the primary corrective tool. Even though inspection practices may adopt more of this audit style in their mode of operation and may start to trust more in the self-inspecting capability of regulated organizations, it is the existence of formal possibilities for *independent escalation* which marks an operational boundary between audit and inspection.

There is a deeply held view that without independence, audit has no value. External audit is often regarded as superior to internal audit for this reason alone. However, it is important to distinguish between two senses of independence, *organizational* and *operational*, since much of the debate has focused on the former (Wolnizer, 1987). Arrangements for the organizational independence of external auditors concern the manner in which the auditor is appointed, the development of ethical rules to ensure impartiality and the never-ending question as to whether the provision of advisory services compromises the audit role.[8] In general the problem of organizational independence is to design an incentive structure together with a range of escalatory possibilities such that auditors or inspectors will not be deterred from using the available enforcement options when necessary.

Compared to organizational independence, operational independence has more to do with the audit process itself and has been relatively under-discussed. Here the concern is less with the *willingness* of auditors to take up escalatory options as the more fundamental question of their *capability* to do so. It is possible to make a further sub-distinction between *informational* and *epistemic* independence. The former has been much discussed in regulatory literatures and refers to the problem of information asymmetry between regulator and regulated. To the extent that auditing must always trust at least some of the representations of senior management and other internal sources of information, the auditor is always informationally dependent. This is despite the fact that attempts will be made to obtain independent external corroboration of this information. Inspectors of factories, prisons, schools, and chemical plants will often be in a very similar position and it is argued that inspectorates and supervisors at the top of the regulatory pyramid lack detailed knowledge of the regulated domain and engage in 'regulatory bluff' as a result (Hawkins, 1984). To a large extent an interactive regulatory style has emerged as a practical solution to this problem of informational asymmetry. Informational independence is therefore a problem for both auditors and inspectors and it may be desirable to trade-off organizational independence to overcome this difficulty, as Braithwaite recommends.

The question of what I call *epistemic* independence is different from the above and echoes a number of issues raised in Chapter 2. Where clear rules of auditee conduct and robust techniques for determining compliance with these rules exist, the audit process is epistemically independent of the auditee. The auditor may be dependent on some information from the auditee but the basis on which conclusions are drawn is independent. This may be because the evidence of compliance or otherwise is amenable to direct observation or inspection without the cooperation or assistance of the auditee, as in the case of prison inspection.

Forms of inspection with clear standards of performance and criteria for determining compliance or breach will be epistemically independent. They may adopt an interactive style for information gathering purposes and they may negotiate on a wide variety of matters such as remedies and whether to prosecute. But they are less dependent on 'mutually negotiating' what actually counts as a breach or a problem. Epistemic independence means having a knowledge base which is independent of the inspected party. Such a knowledge base will only be a necessary condition for taking up escalatory options for enforcement but it can be hypothesized that the greater the epistemic dependence of auditors or inspectors, the more likely that these escalatory options will be compromised.

With a drift from audit to inspection and an increasing regulatory emphasis on self-inspecting capability, there is a loss of epistemic independence at the level of the external monitor, whether this is called an auditor or an inspector. Where the external emphasis shifts from compliance to the 'effectiveness' of systems for determining compliance, there is a corresponding shift in the knowledge base and focus of the external monitor. Some, like Braithwaite, may regard this as desirable; the gains to compliance outweigh the losses in terms of the epistemic dependence of the external auditor.

To summarize: the audit explosion does not herald a new age of inspection or surveillance. It reflects a more general transformation of monitoring style, a style which is evident in state sponsored inspectorates themselves. As regulation and the monitoring of compliance is passed down the control hierarchy into organizations, the character of external monitoring changes. State inspectorates in the UK are slowly redesigning themselves towards a capability for installing and monitoring effective control systems in target organizations. The internalization of inspection through systems reflects a loosening of central state inspection and audit activity and an increased trust in the improvements to compliance from auditable management control systems is emerging as part of the 'normative climate of organizations' (Shapiro, 1987*a*:207). One might say that audit is a paradoxical and complex combination of surveillance and trust (Reiss, 1984:29).

AUDITING AND TRUST

Whatever trust is, it is widely agreed that it easier to destroy than to create and 'climates of trust' are only noticed after their demise (Baier, 1994). There is also a growing feeling not only that organizations are theoretically undersocialized as strings of transactions and contracts but that the rise of contracting expresses a loss of faith in the 'binding power of obligations' (Tyler and Kramer, 1996:3). The concept of trust has a long philosophical history and continues to be analytically and empirically elusive in the context of organizations. Can we talk of 'swift trust' (Meyerson *et al.*, 1996) for one-off transactions? How does formal organization substitute for trust (Sitkin and Stickel, 1996:197)? And is a society justified in trusting trust (Gambetta, 1988*a*)? These questions have implications for the way in which auditees and auditors are or are not trusted.

Distrusting the Auditee

In Chapter 2, it was suggested that audits are demanded in the context of relations of accountability between two parties and the existence of operational difficulties for one party to monitor the activities of the other. This characterization of the source of demand for audit is widely accepted and it expresses the core programmatic value of auditing—its capacity to operationalize and realize accountability. Without that element of legitimate reciprocity owed by the agent to the principal, auditing would really be a form of one-way surveillance. What makes auditing auditing is the legitimate requirement for one party to give an account of those actions relevant to its relation to another party.

The entrusting of resources by principals is therefore a founding concept for auditing. But these principals and agents define a social relationship where there is no longer a form of embedded face to face trust; trust is rather more impersonal and depends itself on a chain of 'cool strangers' (Baier, 1994:117) who require new guardians of trust (Shapiro, 1987*b*). This means that financial auditors are social control specialists who oversee the proceduralization of information flows to principals in the form of accounting and disclosure requirements. In short, auditing is demanded under circumstances where resources are entrusted but where trust is also lacking and must be restored by the audited activity. Audits exist to negotiate and represent the accountability of autonomous agents; if these agents were not autonomous audit would be unnecessary. So audit only exists because social and economic trust has already been distributed and where the relevant principal has already been identified.

From this point of view audit is a 'second order trust relationship' which polices trust (Shapiro, 1987a:212). And only trust can really guard this growing population of guardians of trust:

one of the ironies of trust is that we frequently protect it and respond to its failures by bestowing even more trust . . . [with the cycle of] . . . new strains of deviance and new procedural cures, one gets the feeling that the original agency agenda has become distorted along the way. . . . By creating guardians of trust, we foster all kinds of ancillary certifications or guarantees of trustworthiness . . . that are readily manipulated yet are now essential to principals who have abdicated their distrust to these new guardians (Shapiro, 1987b:649, 652).

From this point of view the audit society represents tendencies toward an inflationary spiral of escalating trust in nth order guardians.

As Chapter 5 suggests, critics argue that many of the audit related changes which have taken place in the public sector in recent years reflect institutionalized distrust in the capacity of teachers, social workers, and university lecturers to self-regulate the quality of their services. Although these groups may be partly to blame for being increasingly excluded from the dominant discourses of control, the assumptions sustaining audits often deny the trust that exists between practitioners and those they serve: 'Evaluation and inspection are public assertions of societal control which violate the assumption that everyone is acting with competence and good faith' (Meyer and Rowan, 1991:59).

Assumptions of distrust sustaining audit processes may be self-fulfilling as auditees adapt their behaviour strategically in response to the audit process, thereby becoming less trustworthy. However, relatively little is known about the side-effects of auditing on the diverse organizational groups to which it is applied. Complexity lies in the fact that 'trust comes in webs, not in single strands, and disrupting one strand often rips apart whole webs' (Baier, 1994:149). In Chapter 5 some evidence was provided that tacit organizational understandings and expectations have been disturbed by demands to provide auditable accounts of an activity and individual incentives have changed in response to formalized measures of auditable performance. There is also evidence that the very quality of service or output which the audit process is intended to enhance is itself damaged, even though goals of efficiency and cost-effectiveness are achieved.

Overall the audit explosion has ambivalent implications for trust. On the one hand, there is the suggestion that audits create the distrust they

presuppose and that this in turn leads to various organizational pathologies, if not 'fatal remedies'. Where the solution to these pathologies of distrust is yet more and better auditing, yet more guardians of impersonal
trust, then one has the audit society in a nutshell. On the other hand, there
is also a need to recognize a form of silly or naive trust which ignores the
evidence of corporate history (Hatherly, 1995a). Recent experiences in the
financial sector in the UK and elsewhere suggest that 'escalating distrust'
(Sitkin and Stickel, 1996) is probably justified.[9] However, if one takes this
view, the problem of trust in the context of auditing is shifted yet again; one
needs to trust the auditor and the audit process itself.

Trusting the Audit Process

The relation between auditing and trust becomes even more complex when
one considers the audit process. In response to the question 'how effective
is the technology employed by inspectors, regulators, and other surveillants'
(Shapiro, 1987b:647) a different order of trust is visible. Chapter 4 suggested
that at some stage in the audit process trust must always be invoked, for
example, in auditor colleagues, in other experts, in forms of documentary
evidence or in management assurances about system integrity. Philosophies
of audit have stated that the auditor is entitled to rely on, i.e. trust, management representations since the audit process must start somewhere.
Auditability has also been defined in terms of a good client control culture
(Stevens, 1981:80–1); this means that good clients are those that can be
trusted.

This last point is significant. Developments in financial auditing in the
wake of management frauds suggest that auditors are trying to audit 'the
people' up front in the process; auditing is trying to trust a little less but is
nevertheless dependent on the internal control culture of the auditee to
make the audit possible in the first place. All this means that within financial
auditing the balance between planning, evidence, and review processes is
changing. The evidence process is being squeezed from one side by reporting compliance requirements, which are often regarded as excessive, and on
the other side by economic pressures to front load assurance by assessing
the trustworthiness of management. The external audit of management
systems is essentially a form of trust in self-audit and self-assessment capability and the development of such systems, such as the BS 5750 scheme, is
an attempt to build trustworthiness into organizations. It is this tendency
and the role of an audit process preoccupied with systems values which has
been the critical focus of this book.

It is clear that trust can never be eradicated in social arrangements.[10] The
audit society is not simply a distrusting society; rather, it reflects a tendency
not to trust trust. This means a systematic tendency towards uncritical trust
in the efficacy of audit processes, a trust which results in the absence of

evaluation of the audit process itself noted in Chapter 5. In the audit society, institutionalized trust, which differs from the trust of ordinary individuals, is bestowed on the auditor and is displaced from other organizational locations. Trust is increasingly 'vested, not in individuals but in abstract capacities . . . the modes of trust involved in modern institutions . . . rest upon vague and partial understandings of their "knowledge base"' (Giddens, 1990:26–7). Another way of putting this is the suggestion that 'Fundamentally auditing involves the certification of the unknowable. . . . Rituals of copying numbers allowed the underlying indeterminacy of the US mortgage market to be auditable i.e. something auditors can be comfortable with' (Pentland, 1993:611–12).

Events like the crisis in the US Savings and Loans industry show that society can choose to withdraw its trust in auditors' certification of the unknowable. And, as the emerging debate on the regulation of derivatives or the continuing controversy about Lloyds names suggests, it may also push auditors into more 'unknowable' areas. The reliance on monitors such as auditors to restore trust involves a potential regress to nth order trust relations which is resolved institutionally by the creation of supervisory arrangements, such as the Joint Monitoring Unit discussed in Chapter 5.[11] However, these arrangements leave intact the 'vague and partial understandings' of the audit knowledge base.

The 'accepted vulnerability' of principals to the possible ill-will that their trust in both agents and auditors involves does not mean that it is always easy to tell when trust is violated (Baier, 1994:103). For example, in the case of auditors with high discretion it is difficult to determine whether they should have been trusted or not in any particular case, as Chapter 2 argued. But Baier also reminds us that being trusted involves noticing that we are trusted and ensuring we do not generate excessive expectations which may lead to loss (Baier, 1994:134). So should a society really trust a practice which does not take steps to ensure that it does not create excessive expectations? Audit may be trusted to produce and reaffirm trust only because its real nature is widely misunderstood.

To conclude: trust relates to the institutionalized rhythms of account giving: 'we usually combine trust on some matters with careful checks on others. . . . One pathological case is the shrinking of the trust dimension to near zero, along with a commensurate expansion of the area where constant checking and testing is going on.' (Baier, 1994:139). This is essentially the pathology of an audit society. To avoid this one needs to know how to trust trust itself (Gambetta, 1988a), in other words how to know when to demand or not demand an account. Trust in the sense of an absence of all accounting can never be an absolute value: trust may be naive and auditable accounts fully justified. Knowing when to trust trust in this sense requires at least a kind of 'intuitive auditing' and mental accounting, the primary task of which is to 'monitor the on-going stream of interactions and exchanges that constitute, quite literally, the give-and-take of a hierarchical relationship, and which provide, in turn, the raw data from which inferences about trust and distrust are forged' (Kramer, 1996:218). The problem is that the audit society eclipses this meta-auditing. In place of reflection on the need for auditable account giving, there are increasingly formalized rituals of accounting and verification. And this means that trust in auditing may be risky.

AUDITING AND RISK

So far it has been argued that the audit explosion reflects a transformation of inspectorial style with ambivalent democratic credentials which demands trust in auditing. With trust there is always risk; they are complimentary concepts (Giddens, 1990:34–5) and 'trust presupposes decision making in a situation of risk' (Lorenz, 1988:197). If there were no trust in managers, teachers, doctors, and so on, there would be no problem of risk associated with their behaviour, i.e. the possibility of unexpected adverse outcomes. To the extent that regulatory systems have an inherent tendency to trust the supervisee, they are always at risk (Moran, 1986:85) and these risks create burdens for the enforcement machinery because expectations are raised that control is possible. 'Symbolic legislation' (Dwyer, 1990) may be created which, in appearing to give a solution, actually generates its own pathologies in the form of equally symbolic enforcement practices oriented towards the production of comforting labels.

Audit has emerged as a certain style of processing risk 'not so much because new kinds of risk have come in to being but because society has come to understand itself and its problems in terms of the principles of the technologies of risk' (Ewald, 1990:147).[12] This means that the audit society by definition is one which has come to understand the solution to many of its problems in terms of audit. Audit is a normalized 'style of analysis, and a way of categorizing and breaking down objects, tasks, and needs' (Ewald, 1990:151). As this normative commitment hardens into the routines of practice a new regulatory common sense is formed and risk is absorbed into programmes for its management.

Auditing and the Remanagerialization of Risk[13]

The programmatic idea of auditing partakes in a broader politics of fear and anxiety.[14] The mission of sustaining systemic control must continually be reaffirmed and reconstituted in the face of events which threaten its credibility. This process of reaffirmation reflects anxiety about the mission of regulation and the renewal of faith in the audit function is crucial in suppressing it. As argued in Chapter 2, within the politics of failure there is a continual re-intensification of available instruments of regulatory control. Audit cannot be permitted to fail systemically and must be immunized from radical doubt; if audit is to function credibly in the processing of risk then trust in audit must be constantly affirmed and supported.

To say all this is not to say that risks are fictional or invented by regulators. On the contrary, the dangers of pollution, financial loss, wasteful expenditure, poor medical diagnosis, defective products, and so on are real and affect individuals in tangible ways. However, the institutional mechanisms for dealing with these dangers and classifying them as risks to be managed are varied and it is this social construction of risk *management* which suggests that: 'Nothing is a risk in itself: there is no risk in reality. But on the other hand, anything *can* be a risk; it all depends on how one analyses the danger, considers the event' (Ewald, 1991:199). The audit explosion suggests that audit is emerging as a powerful institution of risk processing.

The concept of risk is normally associated with probabilistic calculi of an abstract and quantitative nature: 'The natural scientific conception calculates risk in a quantitative fashion, transforming risks into bloodless, dispassionate probabilities which are sometimes so remote as to defy lay comprehension' (Hawkins, 1992:293). In Chapter 4 it was suggested that the theoretical development of risk models in auditing have something of this character. However, while such abstract models may rationalize and motivate risk control practices, two other related ideas of risk are also realized. The first shapes and organizes the intuitive decisions of auditors. For example, judgements are made that the segregation of duties is inadequate, that systems of control have design weaknesses, that cheques need two signatories, that there must be an inventory of hazardous substances, that teaching methods must be reviewed internally and so on. This is the technical repertoire of auditing which is relatively decoupled from formal probabilistic risk assessments. It is a knowledge base constituted from a limited set of routines (sampling, observation, inquiry) which are loosely coupled to higher bodies of abstract statistical knowledge.

The second idea of risk concerns the risk to the auditor. Auditing, particularly financial based auditing, is permeated if not dominated by legal risk.[15] Legal risk enters the audit process as liability exposure and this creates a certain mode of conducting and representing the audit process in working papers in a *defendable* manner. As discussed in Chapter 2, legal risk also leads to systemic representations of the scope and capability of audit in official documents in order to maximize discretion, and hence defence capability. Since legal processes rarely question the body of knowledge as such, only the enactment of it, defendability is not only a matter for individual auditors but involves the development of a body of proceduralized knowledge, conformity to which counts as executing best practice.[16]

In sum, the growth of auditing as a risk processing institution is that of a practice which is only loosely related to statistical conceptions of risk and which is increasingly permeated by defensive mentalities which corrode the production of assurance. Nevertheless a certain style of risk management is normalized which steers managerial energies in a particular way. Furthermore, as Chapters 4 and 5 emphasized, the recognition capabilities of audit are always relative to an overriding logic of auditability which is necessarily partial and which gravitates, for economic and epistemic reasons towards the 'control of control'. By this I mean that audits are generally indirect methods of control which act primarily upon control systems which, to varying degrees, have been created for the audit process. And, as argued in Chapter 5, audit is a style of risk processing which in many cases is not neutral with regard to concepts of individual and organizational performance but shapes them in crucial ways. In short, there are risks associated with trusting audit to process risk and these must now be considered.

The Risk of Auditing

Is the audit explosion the product of an institutionalized delusion, a refusal to confront the politically uncomfortable policy reality of loss of control, and the creation of ritualized cover up as a response? In Chapter 2 it was suggested that the particularization of audit failure and the rewriting of official guidance may be cosmetic strategies to preserve the existing order of risk management. Images of control over pollution and derivatives, of higher quality teaching, of improved financial management, and so on get manufactured by an audit process which necessarily insulates itself from organizational complexity in order to make things auditable and to produce certificates of comfort. For example, environmental audits have a problematic relation to ideals of sustainability; at worst they are a form of environmental tokenism. Improvement gets defined in relation to a system loop and not in relation to environmental protection itself (Brophy *et al.*, 1995:129). Something may well be better than nothing but it should not be imagined that environmental auditing represents the basis for any paradigm shift in corporate cultures, although this is often claimed. Self-regulated rates of improvement do not bear any necessary relation to notions of sustainability which require observable changes in the natural environment rather than the organization (Brophy *et al.*, 1995:130).[17]

In Chapter 5 it was suggested that audit might be a 'fatal remedy' because of its incentive effects on auditees. Another dysfunctional possibility is the effect on alternative styles of data gathering and reporting. For example, just as rumours of the great salad oil swindle had circulated before the full extent of the fraud became officially public (Wilensky, 1967:89), it seems that the Barings Bank exposures under derivative contracts were also known outside official channels of communication and reporting. Regulatory responses to such failures of intelligence tend towards greater investment in formal, generalizable systems of control rather than the development of non-standard capabilities for acting on informal sources of intelligence.[18]

The post failure picture is always similar: 'trust in conventional arrangements' and chains of institutionalized (false) confidence screen out the signs that were evident elsewhere. Just as the salad oil case illustrated 'the vulnerability of highly institutionalized organizations to information pathologies' (Wilensky, 1967:92–3), the secondary banking crisis in the UK reflected fragmented institutional structures and 'institutional jealousies' which prevented the assembly of signs for rational diagnosis (Moran 1986:91).[19] Excessive reliance on the financial audit function was a contributing factor: 'the influence of auditors as a professional group lay in their assumed capacity to simplify publicly the complexity of modern company accounts into clear, conventional signs of the financial soundness or otherwise of an enterprise' (Moran, 1986:95). In fact the audit signature had 'more limited and ambiguous meaning' than regulators imagined or wished to acknowledge.

Social interventions to avoid pathologies tend to result in more control of a similar type. This can lead to 'increased exploitation of bureaucratic resources, goal displacement, and provocation—that is, less *actual* control' (Sieber, 1981:198). As an institutionalized practice auditing 'tends to be self-perpetuating regardless of relevance to or achievement of goals. This disjuncture between means and goals is enlarged by scarcity of resources, ambiguity of goals, status anxiety of agents, cultural emphasis on efficiency and technique, and sub-cultural emphasis on an exclusive possession of skills' (Sieber, 1981:208). At worst auditing tends to become an organizational ritual, a dramaturgical performance. The problem is to determine what aspects of audit practice achieve 'an instrumental aspect, and can be shown to have such an impact, and what aspects serve to dramatise and define social values, to set apart certain social relationships for evaluation and control, and to reassure society of the merits of regulation' (Manning, 1987:311).

The problem of the epistemological obscurity of audit means that it is difficult to disentangle instrumental effects from a certain staging of control; audit practice is a form of social control talk. The idea of audit and the policy discourse through which this idea is articulated is a source of power 'for guiding and justifying policy changes and for insulating the system from criticism . . . to reassure the powerful about their intentions' (Cohen, 1985:115). The idea of audit also stimulates the never ending search for the 'Golden Goose of effectiveness' and for 'systems that work' (Cohen, 1985:177, 195). In this way the idea of audit provides a good story and 'good stories stand for or signify what the system likes to think it is doing' and support and increase self-confidence (Cohen, 1985:157).

The risk of audit is not simply that it does not work and leads to fatal remedies, although one can assemble evidence for this. Rather, it is that, in the process of continuous movement and reform which it generates, it is also impossible to know when it is justified and effective. In essence this is the message of this book: audit has put itself beyond empirical knowledge about its own effects in favour of a constant programmatic affirmation of its potential. Can anything be done to correct this?

CONCLUSIONS: BEYOND AUDIT?

Evaluation, assessment, checking, and account giving are part of everyday human interaction (Broadfoot, 1996:3). They are sometimes explicit, always varied and usually take place as part of the tacit understandings which constitute social life. Although an examination of these micro-exchanges has not been undertaken in this book, the possibility of such an analysis provides an important reminder: if account giving and auditing in a general sense are a deep part of the social fabric, it makes no sense to be against them on *a priori* grounds alone. However, when attention is focused on the manner in which forms of checking are specifically institutionalized and formalized, on their methods and consequences, then these practices become a legitimate object of critical inquiry.

This book offers a diagnosis where hitherto there has only been presumption. If the analysis errs too much on the side of criticism and polemic, this has been necessary to provide a counterweight to official stories. While there is much more empirical work to be done, it is clear that in the UK and elsewhere during the 1980s and early 1990s auditing acquired an institutional momentum which insulated it from systemic inquiry. The mood which has led to the reshaping of the public sector in recent years could not be described as very sensitive to empirical inquiry. But this is equally true of the financial sector where the machinery of supervision and audit are constantly being refashioned in response to each crisis.

The motif of the 'audit society' which provides the title of this book suggests where the audit explosion may be heading and points to a set of tendencies and potentials. These tendencies are far from being monolithic. Different traditions of evaluation and control, appeals to collegiality and trust and doubts about the efficacy and cost of auditing provide a discourse of resistance. There is also scepticism about programmatic ideals of 'performance' and 'quality' and the technologies through which they are made operational. But despite these critical developments a certain intellectual and political vigilance is still required because, as Chapter 3 argues, the audit explosion has emerged from deep structural changes in organizational governance. While accounting practitioners and others may be opportunistic there is no grand supply side conspiracy which drives the rise of audit. There is rather a series of interrelated programmatic shifts in styles of government which commonly presuppose the necessity and benefits of auditing in its various forms.

The question which must be brought back to the surface in every particular case is whether the tail may be wagging the dog and, in the process, whether audit provides deluded visions of control and transparency which satisfy the self-image of managers, regulators and politicians but which are neither as effective nor as neutral as commonly imagined. Against official images of a technical fix I have counterpoised the possibility that audit emerges more as a new form of image management. Rather than as a basis for substantive change, it is a practice which requires social trust in the judgements of its practitioners and which is only superficially empowering to the notional publics which give it its purpose. And when audit fails, or is presumed to fail, strategies exist to insulate it from radical enquiry about its role and operational capability. Worse still, audits may turn organizations on their heads and generate excessive preoccupations with, often costly, auditable process. At the extreme, performance and quality are in danger of being defined largely in terms of conformity to such process.

Against this sceptical view there are two main counterarguments. First, it can be said that the evidence in this book is insufficient and heavily selective. To some extent this charge is reasonable. The analysis attempts scope rather than depth; I have tried to look at audit in a number of different contexts, thereby sacrificing considerable specificity. Furthermore, although an attempt has been made to draw out general features of the audit explosion, much of the empirical material is UK based. Whether the arguments in this book can be exported into other national contexts is not yet clear. I think that they can, but such an analysis must wait. As for being selective, I am less bothered by such a charge. I leave it open for critics to provide equally selective counterbalancing evidence. This project inevitably reflects a personal point of view, a series of interpretative pre-judgements which no doubt affected the way evidence and arguments have been constructed. Such selectivity always exists and methodological purity is one, perhaps unattainable, value among many others. This book is not intended as the final word and I shall be content if others find it useful, interesting, and provocative.

The second counterargument is that, the problems described in this book notwithstanding, auditing practice in all its guises is still the best option available for achieving cost-effective incremental assurance about a wide range of activities. The knowledge base of audit may be obscure and professional institutes may invest extensively in defensive guidance documents but, in the final analysis, audit represents a form of pragmatic 'muddling through' with experienced professionals giving it their best shot. There can be no guarantees of assurance or control, nor can assurance be tightly quantified in a manner that would give it an appropriate aura of objectivity.

There is much to be said for this pragmatic modesty and, quietly, this is the view of most practitioners. But the selling of audit has not taken place so modestly: audit is a practice which in every sphere where it operates must necessarily talk up expectations at the very same time as it may suffer from so doing. I have argued that the 'expectations gap' is not so much a problem for auditing as its constitutive principle. More generally, the audit explosion has actually closed off avenues of official scepticism and modesty; auditing has become central to regulatory programmes. It is too greatly needed for many of the changes which have taken place for an open and fundamental diagnosis of benefits and dangers. Diagnosis is necessary and yet constantly deferred by a range of other localized and procedural issues which occupy regulatory energies.

Do the arguments in this book have any implications for policy makers? It would be wrong to conclude simply that less auditing is desirable. The issue is rather a question of organizational design capable of building in 'moral competence' and of providing regulated forms of openness around these competences (Selznick, 1994). This view is actually consistent with the growing enthusiasm for self-organization and responsive regulation but it also requires mechanisms for higher level reflection on instruments of control, on the mix between internal and external audits and on the consequences of audit arrangements. In this respect the problem of governance is not just a question of first order knowledge and control, but also of second order knowledge and sensitivity about the side-effects of the instruments of knowledge.

Borrowing from Sieber's (1981: Chapter 12) recommendations it may be possible to develop criteria, performance indicators perhaps, by which audit could evaluate itself. For example, audit could be judged in terms of: empathy with and understanding of the auditee; its capacity to reflect on cultural bias; the strength of its orientation to original goals to avoid displacement; its understanding of the possible exploitative strategies by auditees; the existence of provisions for rebuilding auditing agencies; the creation of forms of evaluation which are sensitive to regressive effects; possibilities for bringing auditees into the audit process. Would all this simply be an ironic extension of auditing and a further step towards the audit society? The experience of monitoring arrangements for financial audits suggests caution, if not pessimism, about the capability to build an ongoing process of self-evaluation into audit practice. However, 'it may be the better part of pessimism to create some organ of assessment to test, monitor, evaluate, and codify not only the unanticipated outcomes of large-scale social interventions, but the organ of assessment *itself* (Sieber, 1981:216).

Being fit for auditing, being auditable and ready for compliance visits, says little about fitness for any other purpose or about the dangers that societies face. If the big dangers always lie outside organizational capabilities for formal inspection, then forms of control and communication which are low on institutionalization and high on environmental responsiveness are needed. There can be no guarantees of success in relying on such *ad hoc* sources of intelligence and accounting but they can be distinguished from auditing in terms of a primary orientation to *discomfort*. Rather than being caught up in rituals of certification they are oriented towards 'dirtier' data processing (Marx, 1984:79), such as improved public interest access and institutionalized opportunities for whistleblowing (Vinten, 1995). In addition, improved liability mechanisms may be better ways to internalize externalities, especially if the real accountors for externalities of businesses are victims rather than costing systems (Jacobson, 1991:1335).

The demands of such ongoing reflexivity would be great, requiring sensitivity to obscure sources of auditee system maintenance, such as trust, and a constant preparedness to redesign the audit process. In some cases it may be necessary to accept that there is no pent up demand for auditing arrangements and that markets or other mechanisms may be forms of effective influence. Reflexivity will require an institutionalized confidence to dismantle as well as construct audit arrangements. Regulatory sensitivity about what makes organizations like schools and hospitals effective is necessary, a sensitivity which involves decisions about how to leave individuals alone to get on with their work as much as about how to monitor them. This in turn will require a recognition of the manner in which practices are perpetuated isomorphically because they have become legitimate and not necessarily because they have been even moderately effective in achieving goals.

The politics of regulatory failure described in Chapter 2 must become reflexive if it is not to reproduce itself in ever increasing structures of regulatory complexity with ever greater demands for monitoring. In effect regulatory politics would need to 'go empirical' and this would require some institutionalization of social scientific knowledge of the manner in which instruments of supposedly neutral verification can transform the contexts to which they are applied. And as this knowledge of consequences grows, so too would the possibilities for debate and discussion about whether they should be intended or not. In this way, audit would become part of a broader organizational learning process rather than an empty ritual of verification for merely disciplinary purposes.

It is important to recognize that such an institutionalized capability for evaluating audit which avoids reproducing the very problems it is intended to solve could only be created by a confident society. This would be a society capable of knowing when to trust, when to trust trust and when to demand an audited account. This would also be a society which wants to know the dangers it faces before creating risk management practices which simply fragment responsibility for these dangers (Beck, 1995). It would be a society which was capable of a certain honesty about the prospects for social order and about the instruments available for bringing it about. A preparedness for discomfort would be necessary and this would clearly require a distinctive political culture. Audit currently operates in a regulatory space where regulators and politicians do not wish to be encumbered by systemic doubts about audit; they need to be reassured that it works or can be made to work better. Empirical knowledge creates discomfort and is needed to institutionalize disturbance.

On the back of these speculative proposals, it must be borne in mind that the audits described in this book are part of an organizational order which is itself constantly changing. The emergence of corporate networks, in which clearly definable groups give way to a multitude of related parties, is already creating problems for traditional financial auditing. Companies and states are legal fictions in a 'grand web' of employees, suppliers, regulators, customers, and many others (Kelly, 1995:188). Such developments suggest a long term drift away from central control capabilities towards an encrypted network economy which is literally 'out of control'. Developments in information technology will create new possibilities for deviance as well as control. If there really is to be a real time culture, *ex post* practices of verification begin to look redundant (Elliott, 1995) as compared with a multi-partite network of interacting, real time self-auditing elements. In the field of derivatives regulation this seems to be the most likely future as control is cultivated internally from the bottom up. In the future it is not just that internal audit will eclipse external audit but that the internal/external distinction, constructed on the basis of the monolithic ideal about independence, will become redundant. Internal auditors will play regulatory roles at the same time as internal control functions are contracted out to external agencies.

Finally, the way societies call individuals and organizations to account says much about fundamental social and economic values. Power is this ability to demand accounts, to exercise control over performance, while at the same time remaining unaccountable (Day and Klein, 1987:9). Such accounting arrangements are necessarily contingent and varied, ranging across formal and informal, financial and non-financial, detailed and aggregated measures of performance. Auditing operationalizes a balance of liberty and discipline which is not shaped simply by objective economic necessity or common sense. Rather, even in its most mundane techniques, it reflects a complex and not always consistent constellation of social attitudes to risk, trust, and accountability. The motif of the audit society reflects a tendency for audit to become a leading bearer of legitimacy and this must be so because other sources of legitimacy, such as community and state, are declining in influence. So the audit society is a symptom of the times, coincidentally a *fin de siècle*, in which a gulf has opened up between poorly rewarded 'doing' and highly rewarded 'observing'. In this book I have tried to create some understanding and a little discomfort about this growing industry of comfort production.

NOTES

NOTES TO CHAPTER 1

1. It was estimated that 30 per cent of US national income consisted of the information sector, a fact which supports the concept of the 'information society' (Beninger, 1986). Although one could develop similar kinds of quantitative indicators for regulatory activity (e.g. Wilson, 1984:211), this is much more difficult for the audit society. Audit expenditures as a proportion of national income would be low and would not capture what is at stake in the rise of auditing; the audit society is a society of auditees rather than auditors.
2. Hence the motif of the 'audit society' overlaps with that of the 'age of inspection' (Day and Klein, 1990), the 'evaluative state' (Neave, 1988), and assessment (Broadfoot, 1996).
3. In fact Rose and Miller have a third concept, that of 'rationalities' of government, which I have tended to collapse into the idea of programmes. In this sense my use of the distinction does not correspond analytically to theirs, but is sufficient for the arguments of this book.
4. For example, the field of financial accounting has accounted for itself through the development of conceptual frameworks which emphasize users. This sits uneasily with ideals of public accountability.
5. Books are not the only way to be critical. Members of professional institutes may revolt, scandals may demand public enquiry, new forms of competitor practice may evolve and markets for practices may fail. In addition academics themselves play different roles. Some work for government enquiries, some lead private campaigns and many, particularly in accounting, provide services to support the official account of the practice. They operate in what some accounting theorists have called 'the market for excuses' (Watts and Zimmerman, 1979). Critics also establish 'straw men' as a kind of fabricated meta-account for rhetorical purposes. Sometimes these critics meet producers of official accounts in seminars. And sometimes the producers of the official accounts concede the point in private over a few drinks but nevertheless continue to push their own account. It is what they are paid to do.

NOTES TO CHAPTER 2

1. For an account of the power of the large firms, see Stevens (1981).
2. For a wider discussion of early forms of audit see Chatfield (1977) and Wolnizer (1987:35–9).
3. See Kindleberger (1978: Chapter 5) who reminds us that share support schemes and fraudulent or stolen collateral are not inventions of the 1980s.
4. This section is based largely on Power (1992a).

5. In the famous *Kingston Cotton Mill* case (1896) it was ruled that the auditor could rely upon a certificate of the value of stock (rather than taking stock himself) only if he could trust the company official giving it.
6. There has always been a problem about how judgements concerning the state of internal control determine the level of further substantive transactional work.
7. Future historians will be in a difficult position since most working papers for audits are retained for a short period (seven years or so) for legal reasons and then destroyed. Even if an archive of such working papers were retained, there would still remain methodological problems for historians about what they really say about practice.
8. This material is based on Power (1993*a*).
9. Russell (1991) argues that critical DTI reports are part of the learning process for the audit profession. In contrast Cousins *et al.* (1993) maintain that such investigations, under government pressure, have often suppressed important information.
10. Jensen and Meckling (1976) assume such a function for monitoring expenditure. Increasing assurance is coupled to decreasing effectiveness of further costs.
11. This section is based in part on Power (1993*a*).
12. See Alborn (1995*a*:281–2) who also draws attention to the image of plague and disease which informed nineteenth-century discourse on financial matters. Contemporary references to the 'contagion of derivatives' suggest that little has changed in the choice of metaphor.
13. Alborn (1995*b*) suggests that the erasure of an ethical discourse from banking had already occurred in the nineteenth century.
14. Meyer and Rowan (1992) refer to this style as 'fragmented centralization'. Moran (1991:15) describes very similar ideas in terms of 'meso-corporatism'.
15. The FSA has also impacted directly on accountants and accounting firms in their capacity as investment advisers. See Cooper *et al.* (1994).
16. The Companies Act 1985 requires the auditor to report explicitly if he or she believes that proper books and records have not been maintained. However, 'proper' is not defined in detail and while it might include internal controls in general, there is a tendency to distinguish bookkeeping from other forms of control.
17. These arrangements are more or less the same in the FSA and the Building Societies Act 1986.
18. It is not just auditors who have responded cautiously to new responsibilities. Regulators such as SIB and the Bank of England have said that they will not feel obliged to communicate with auditors. See 'Regulators attack role as informants' *Accountancy Age* 18 January, 1996.
19. Martens and McEnroe (1991) report on the development of audit guidance on auditors' responsibilities for the detection, evaluation, and reporting of illegal acts. In contrast to the story I have told in the UK context, they suggest that it was the legal profession which acted to resist an expanded audit role.
20. This section is based on Power (1996*b*).
21. The idea of a system of knowledge should not be taken too strictly. Bourdieu's (1990*a*) concept of a field is equally applicable. The idiom of system, as used by theorists such as Luhmann, is preferable since it invokes the image of *self-reproducing* elements of knowledge and this is suggestive in the auditing context.

22. Some audit procedures are proprietorial and remain at the in-house level. See Fischer (1996).

NOTES TO CHAPTER 3

1. For a comparative exploration of this diversity see Hood (1995), who argues that the rise of NPM is less typically a function of 'Anglo-American' conservatism than is commonly imagined. For the specific case of Australia, see Parker and Guthrie (1993).
2. For a comprehensive overview of the issues in the USA, see Pildes and Sunstein (1995).
3. It should be remembered that it 'is a long haul from academic theories to actual public policies. Academic ideas become simplified exaggerated or diluted along the way' (Self, 1993:69).
4. It should not be assumed that accounting requirements have suddenly been imposed on the public sector. Accounting practices have been intimately linked to certain conceptions of government and have supported the attribution of financial rationales to a wide range of practices (Miller, 1990:316). Governments have always resolved problems of their authority in conjunction with problems of knowledge and to the question 'how can the state know, and thereby manage, itself and its subjects?' political arithmetic emerged as an answer. The counting of subjects and their characteristics has come to symbolize the intimate relation between forms of calculation and the cognitive competence of the state (Rose, 1991). In recent years, this general link has become visible in the increasing dependency of government on accounting and audit practices. For example, the introduction of accrual and asset accounting in the UK state sector has clear implications for requiring a return on capital to be calculated and reported.
5. This broader concept of accountability has even been applied reflexively to regulation itself. See Boden and Froud (1996).
6. Although reference is made to North America for illustrative purposes, this section reflects the UK emphasis of the whole book and is not an attempt to provide a comparative analysis. Whether the arguments advanced here are valid for other countries, such as Germany or France, I cannot yet say.
7. For a history of the independence of state audit in Britain see Funnell (1994).
8. Unsurprisingly perhaps, the NAO has also begun to absorb private sector philosophies of audit. For example, it has published private sector style operational standards and the NAO has begun to appear in 'league tables' with the large accounting firms. See *Accountancy Age* 30 March, 1995.
9. Fielden (1984) raises the question whether there should be just one supreme audit body in the UK.
10. A separate body, the Accounts Commission, was created for Scotland.
11. See 'White Knight of Auditing' *Accountancy Age* 16 February, 1995, 16–17.
12. VFM auditing is not so well established in the EU. The European Court of Auditors has developed VFM work only on the back of its regularity orientated systems work (Harden *et al.*, 1995). The culture of financial reform implicit in the NPM has been relatively late to emerge at the EU level.

13. For example, see Glynn (1985*b*) who suggests that legislation in Australia extended the role of audit but not as far as effectiveness reviews which were conducted by another department. Similar developments occurred in New Zealand. In Canada, there was a shift from financial audit in the mid-1970s toward comprehensive audit (value for money audit). The office of the Auditor General in Canada held conferences on the subject and developed guidance for sub-issues of effectiveness and efficiency auditing. Radcliffe (1995) analyses the reception and adaptation of these ideas in the province of Alberta.

14. It is worth bearing in mind that notions of 'programme effectiveness' and VFM, although analytically related, have been shaped in very different political and institutional spaces. The former came to prominence in the 1960s when the GAO was given resources to monitor the implementation of *expanding* federal programmes. VFM has taken hold within a context of fiscal *constraint* and the normative environment provided by the NPM. It is not just that the NAO is smaller than the GAO in terms of resources but that it has come into existence, and its role has been shaped, under fundamentally different conditions, conditions in which waste and inefficiency are driving a reform process and reshaping the mission of auditing.

15. It is worth bearing in mind a tension between the role of VFM auditing in making judgements about effectiveness and the role of markets. The more that state bodies begin to assume corporate ideals, even to the extent of outright privatization (Harden, 1993:37), the more that it is a market rather than an audit which judges organizational performance. This is to say that VFM auditing and markets are different mechanisms for controlling effectiveness (Hepworth, 1995). And the rise of VFM auditing suggests the artificial nature of many of the new 'markets' which have been created by NPM programmes.

16. According to Dunsire, system stability is maintained by the exploitation of rival, antagonistic forces which are self-correcting and which spare the need for cumbersome forms of implementation and enforcement. Dunsire conceptualizes this regulatory style in terms of a balance between steering from above and self-organization from below which is not 'implementation heavy' and which embodies possibilities for organizational learning. In short, people cannot be governed unless they are also self-governing, a point which also lies at the heart of Rose and Miller's (1992) work.

17. Although, it has been suggested that the multiplication of 'stakeholders' threatens to become meaningless and that the socially responsible business is a 'loose cannon' (Brittan, 1996).

18. Of course, it can be argued that notions of 'defect' are not very well defined. Furthermore, as the sociology of technology informs us, there is nothing 'natural' about product design and concepts of 'fitness for use'. So ideas of quality itself are profoundly social in character. Notwithstanding such doubts, I wish to work with the contrast between a technical standards orientation towards quality and a systems approach.

19. One should not overstate this point. In parallel with this generalization of the quality concept, there has also been an explosion of product specific standards in areas such as safety. Such standards have emerged in the so-called 'self-regulatory' space between the state and industry and organizations like the

British Standards Institute have acquired the multiple roles of quasi-regulator, industry mouthpiece, lobbyist and technical advisor.

20. BS 5750 provides the model for the International Standards Organization. The ISO 9000 series on quality assurance was being developed at the time of writing.

21. For example, in September 1994 a conference was organized by the South Bank University, London and the British Standards Institute on the theme of 'Quality *in* Auditing' (emphasis added). So quality assurance preoccuptions are re-entering the financial auditing field. At the same time 'the quality audit represents a new market offering growth opportunities for the public accounting profession' (AAA, 1993; Brewer and Mills, 1994). If accountants can provide quality assurance services for their own financial audit product, then why not in other areas?

22. For similar arguments in the German context see, 'Wieso ISO?' *Suddeutsche Zeitung* 14 February, 1996.

23. 'Environmental audits evaluate, and are not a substitute for, direct compliance activities . . . audits do not in any way replace regulatory inspectors' (EPA, 1986:111–12).

24. Scientific expertise has been perceived as insufficient and in need of sup-plemetation by management expertise. Inspectorates, such as HMIP, have found themselves subject to criticism for lacking such skills.

25. See Rousseau (1988) on the French experience of delegated self-monitoring coupled to government inspection.

26. Even banks are co-producers of environmental regulation (Grabosky, 1994a:436). In the UK the National and Westminster bank has played a leading role and has conducted its own internal environmental audit. In Germany, Deutsche Bank has also been promoting Öko-audit for *Mittelstand* companies.

27. Orts (1995) describes EMAS as a pure example of the 'reflexive law' concept.

28. From 1 August, 1995 the NACCB has been absorbed into the United Kingdom Accreditation Service (UKAS).

29. This was a burden which generated pessimism about the penetrability of sub-systems and about the often perverse effects of direct interventions (Sieber, 1981).

30. It has been suggested that these new enthusiasms for autonomy and compliance based styles of regulatory enforcement forget the experiences of regulatory capture. But capture theory itself was relatively indifferent to compliance costs (Wilson, 1984:220).

31. Braithwaite and Fisse (1987:230) argue against the effectiveness of control at the associational level. The ideal of 'enforced self-regulation' requires the integration of operational and financial auditing into one internal compliance system, as Exxon has done. External controls by association bodies, such as the ICAEW, still have the status of 'outsiders attempting to pull the levers of intracorporate controls' even though they can regulate membership rights.

32. Similar issues apply in the case of inspectorates who must always manage 'conflicting values of stringency and accommodation' (Hawkins and Thomas, 1984:7) and work out a strategic mix of policeman, politician, and con-

sultant (Kagan and Sholz,1984). See Chapter 6 for a further discussion of this issue.
33. See McInnes (1993) for an explicit suggestion for greater substitution between internal and external auditing.

NOTES TO CHAPTER 4

1. This section is based on Power (1992*a*).
2. Some indication for this is the fact that, as a trainee, one of my first assignments involved the extraction of a sample from a population of purchases. Having just completed a course on how to take samples, senior staff members were happy to let me do this. But the fact that I was so junior meant that I was being assigned to a low risk area. Statistical sampling became irrelevant as I experienced more difficult audit areas where the primary risk was that of understatement.
3. The audit risk approach is a simple multiplicative probability risk model which can be specified as follows:

$$UR = IR \times CR \times AR \times TD,$$

where

UR is the (ultimate) risk that the financial statements are materially mis-stated after completion of the audit.

IR is the (inherent) risk of material mis-statement (errors or irregularities) occurring in the process of preparing financial statements, without consideration of control procedures.

CR is the (control) risk that the system of internal accounting control will fail to detect a material mis-statement given that it has occurred.

AR is the (analytical review) risk that review procedures will fail to detect a material mis-statement, given that it has occurred and has not yet been detected by the system of internal accounting control.

TD is the (test of detail) risk that substantive tests will fail to detect a material mis-statement, given that it has occurred and has not been detected by the system of internal accounting control.

(*Source*: Gwilliam, 1987:190–1). For criticisms of the model see Cushing and Loebbecke (1984*a*).)
4. When I was employed by Deloitte Haskins & Sells in the mid-1980s, the Business Review and Planning Approach was introduced (BRAP). The idea was to do away with heavily standardized working papers and lead schedules and to motivate attention to risks in the planning process. As I recall it, the internal marketing of BRAP claimed that it was new but also not new; it was an 'innovation' but it was also 'common sense'. This is an anecdotal illustration of the politics of technical change in a large accounting firm.
5. This section is based on Power (1996*b*).
6. Similar guidance exists in the USA.
7. The background to this debate has been extensively analysed elsewhere (see Barwise *et al.*, 1989; Napier and Power, 1992).

8. It is worth bearing in mind that the prices on the official list may not refer to actual or recent transactions. They are public 'market prices' by convention, a convention which the auditor can accept as objective.
9. Even here the valuation of properties is highly conventional, often based on comparator properties and relative pricing rather than any fundamental calculation.
10. See 'A Revamped Red Book', *Financial Times* 4 November, 1994.
11. When the external auditor relies on the work of the internal auditor, the former acts in the capacity of third order control, i.e. control of the control of control!
12. BS 5750 influenced the development by the International Standards Organization of ISO 9000.
13. Throughout discussion and debate about the nature and scope of environmental audit, attempts have been made to abandon the word 'audit' and to talk of reviews, surveys, assessments and so on (e.g. Welford, 1992, who distinguishes many types of environmental audit). Some companies 'have deliberately chosen not to use the word audit, sometimes at the expense of legal or financial staff. Others use "audit" specifically to lend credibility to their programmes' (ICC, 1991:4).
14. The environmental statement under EMAS must include *inter alia* an assessment of all significant and relevant environmental issues and a summary of figures for material and energy consumption and waste generation, together with any other significant effects. For a detailed analysis of these schemes, see Hillary (1993) and Woolston (1993).
15. For a critique of this tradition see Power (1995*b*).
16. A legal judgment in 1996 against the firm of Ernst & Young regarding the audit of a Lloyds insurance market syndicate has raised the possibility that these organizations may be 'unauditable'. This means a number of things. First, that audit firms may simply think the risk–return ratio for this kind of work is just not worth it anymore. Second, the court has taken issue with the accepted system of techniques for dealing with insurance syndicates. By doing so it is literally true that what was auditable becomes unauditable.
17. Auditing difficult areas usually rides on the back of accounting guidance. For example, Financial Reporting Standard 8 (ASB, 1996) dealing with the accounting for transactions with related parties leaves the audit process essentially dependent on representations from the Directors. Substantive techniques to detect the understatement of transactions with related parties are at best crude and much depends on luck.

NOTES TO CHAPTER 5

1. This binary classification of colonization and decoupling is too simple and obscures many other possible auditor/auditee relations, such as cooperation, anomie, and collusion (see Day and Klein, 1990:39). However, it provides a useful analytical overview.
2. See Bourdieu (1990a) who argues against the idea of the 'informal' somehow lying behind the formal. Within codification there is a constant two way process in which zones of informality are assembled and disassembled.

3. See 'Poor Research: Ranking Blamed' *Times Higher Education Supplement* 4 December, 1992.
4. See Power (1994c:375). See also Shapiro (1992) who analyses data audits conducted by the US Food and Drug Administration (FDA) on sub-contracted tests. Evidence of unperformed, falsified, and modified data and lack of audit trail is reported. More generally, these results increase the momentum for the introduction of quality systems into laboratories.
5. See 'V-Cs Reject Quality Red-Tape' *Times Higher Education Supplement* 22 January, 1993. It is likely that a new agency will emerge from the joint deliberations of the CVCP and the HEFC.
6. See Husbands (1992) who compares the institution based approach of the AAU with the subject based approach of the Dutch.
7. It is no surprise that environmental auditing can be grafted on to these arrangements. BS 7750 for universities is now a realistic option and it was reported that Warwick University were undertaking an environmental audit. See *Times Higher Education Supplement* 4 February, 1994.
8. See, for example 'Tripping on Red Tape', *Times Higher Education Supplement* 12 December, 1992; 'Concern at Pointless Quality Rules', *Times Higher Education Supplement* 9 April, 1993; 'Universities Balk at Review Team Costs', *Times Higher Education Supplement* 17 September, 1993. Howarth (1995) has argued that HEFC and CVCP 'seem determined to impose time-consuming methods of "assurance" (based on short-term observations of practice) and "audit" (based on organizational paperwork).'
9. See 'The Parts Assessors Can't Reach', *Times Higher Education Supplement* 4 February, 1995.
10. See 'Feedback that Is Hard to Swallow', *Times Higher Education Supplement* 25 December, 1992.
11. It has also been argued that evaluative systems devalue and compress time for public policy intervention (Puxty *et al.*, 1994; Willmott, 1995).
12. See 'Beaten with a Yardstick', *Times Higher Education Supplement* 11 February, 1994.
13. I shall use the term medical audit in a broad sense. However, there is a distinction to be drawn between clinical auditing, relating to the entire cycle of care, include nursing and out-patient arrangements, and medical auditing which has a narrower diagnostic focus (see Exworthy, 1995). The present discussion does not rely on these distinctions.
14. Private correspondence with a medical practitioner, October 1994.
15. Private correspondence with a medical practitioner, October 1994.
16. Similar absorbative, decoupling strategies are visible in schools' responses to the 'Local Management for Schools' (LMS) initiative, which was introduced in the wake of the 1988 Education Reform Act (See Broadbent *et al.*, 1993; Shearn *et al.*, 1995).
17. These observations are based on my experience and discussions as a participant at a workshop on 'Audit and Psychotherapy' at the Tavistock Clinic, London, January 1995.
18. An editorial in a medical journal is typical, calling for multidisciplinary practice and defining audit by distinguishing it from its financial namesake. See 'Constructive audit' *Palliative Medicine* 1990 4(1).

19. A study of 379 audits at the University of Newcastle Centre for Health Services Research showed that while 80 per cent of audits identified the need to alter practice, this was only attempted in 40 per cent of cases. 90 per cent of audits were incomplete.

20. Practitioners have complained about high subscription costs and the JDS has found itself unable to conduct its own investigations following the closure of BCCI. See 'Critical Smoke Obscures Disciplinary Reforms' *The Financial Times* 8 August, 1992.

21. See 'In the Twilight of Self-Regulation', *Accountant* October 1994, 7.

22. Prior to the formation of the Audit Commission, there was an inspector of audit charged with developing local government audit practice. The Commission assumed this role (Kimmance, 1994:228).

23. Initially, 10 000 registrants were expected covering 900 000 companies. See 'Auditors Pay for Registration' *Independent* 16 October, 1990. On the technical problems of compiling the audit register, see Fearnley and Willet (1995).

24. See 'Accountancy Body Faces Legal Threat' *The Financial Times* 31 May, 1991; 'The Institute Prepares to Flex its Muscles' *The Financial Times* 4 July, 1991; 'Touche attacks ICAEW audit role' *The Financial Times* 1 May, 1992.

25. A similar story was told by the regulators for the ACCA and the Association for Authorised Public Accountants. See 'Auditors Called to Account' *The Financial Times* 3 February, 1993.

26. See 'JMU Needs to Rethink Regulation Strategy' *Accountancy Age* 25 January, 1996. Whether this view is representative of small practitioner sentiment is unclear.

27. In this respect it is interesting to note that the NAO audits the Audit Commission and the NAO is itself audited by the firm of Clark Whitehill (whose methods would be audited by JMU). Bowerman (1994*b*) has argued there is no in-depth VFM audit of the Audit Commission and little attention to effectiveness issues for these auditors other than in terms of identified savings. This is because audits are audited, not evaluated!

28. It could be argued that within UK financial reporting for private sector organizations there have been attempts to make auditable performance 'softer' by de-emphasizing single figure measures of performance and by encouraging experimentation with a new narrative form of reporting, the Operating and Financial Review.

29. It should be noted that questions of colonization apply equally to bodies like the SSI which, like the Audit Commission, was also able to define policy through the process of inspection (Day and Klein, 1990:30).

30. There has been much debate about the appropriateness of an accountancy background for effectiveness audit work, often with half an eye on the pluralistic skills base of the GAO (Pendelbury and Sherim, 1990:179). Whereas financially based auditors themselves felt they could do effectiveness audits, this view was not shared by senior management in the auditee (Pendelbury and Sherim, 1991). From a different perspective, Harden (1993:36) has suggested that the concept of ministerial responsibility encourages a focus on efficiency and economy.

31. Despite, and perhaps in reaction to, the audit explosion there has been a resurgence of interest in evaluation (see Laughlin and Broadbent, 1995). In the UK

a new journal was established in 1995 to coincide with the inception of the UK Evaluation Society. The evaluation tradition is heterogeneous as compared with auditing and the establishment of such a society, which has a European counterpart, is an attempt to institutionalize, formalize, and legitimize the field. I am grateful to Christopher Pollitt for pointing out to me that at the first conference of the European Evaluation Society in the Hague in 1994, auditors were the largest single identifiable group. This suggests that auditors themselves will play a large role in the institutionalization of evaluation.

32. These criticisms of audit must be balanced against a naive enthusiasm for evaluation as an alternative. There is a longstanding tradition of criticizing evaluation. For example, in the context of schools and medicine, Ivan Illich has been a prominent critic. See also Sieber (1981, Chapter 2). So the contrast with auditing is not intended to imply unconditional support for evaluation against auditing. It has even been suggested that 'Evaluation talk is not nonsense but meta-nonsense, a more or less random arrangement in chapters, boxes, arrows and flowcharts of phrases such as: data collection points, needs assessment scales; goal progress charts; the hierarchical pyramid of goals, subgoals, basic objectives and action objective; programme completion criteria; programmatic activity evaluation forms; follow up assessment; outcome comparisons' (Cohen, 1985:179).

33. Marx (1981:236–7) provides one of the most dramatic examples of the 'reverse effect' of performance measurement: 'When the police organizations' system of performance evaluation, reward and promotion emphasizes quantitatively measured productivity (as tends to be the case in more professional and bureaucratized departments), there may be a strong incentive for police facilitation of crime to meet monthly quotas.'

34. I am grateful to Professor R. Amman for alerting me to this sovietological comparison with the UK.

NOTES TO CHAPTER 6

1. See, 'Time Value was Added to Due Diligence Reports' *Accountancy Age* 30 November, 1995, 10.

2. See 'Commission takes it on the Chin' *The Financial Times* 15 November, 1995 which reports on the European Commission reaction to criticism in the Court's annual report and its first 'Statement of Assurance'.

3. Samuel Bentham was the first and only 'Inspector General of Naval Works' in 1796 and was extensively preoccupied with management control, fraud prevention, and value for money issues at Portsmouth Dockyard. The panopticonic ideal provided for a physical reorganization of working space to 'make things inspectable' (See Ashworth, 1996).

4. During the tenure of my fellowship at the *Wissenschaftskolleg zu Berlin*, I visited the old *Stasi* headquarters on Frankfurterallee. Although many files of agents and victims have been destroyed, the sense of this project of data gathering right down to the most banal facts of personal life is still very strong. Unlike auditors, the Stasi had no principle of data relevance or even sampling. This made the police state staggeringly expensive and it buckled under the weight of its

own data demands. This is not to mention the untold and damaging psychological effects which permeated all social relationships as a consequence, and which still exist today.

5. See 'Pollution Watchdog Criticised in Report' *The Financial Times* 21 August, 1991.

6. See Napier 'Putting a Price on Pollution' *The Financial Times* 28 February, 1991.

7. A surprise visit by inspectors to Holloway Prison for women in London resulted in the team withdrawing from the assignment because conditions were so poor. See 'Shocked Team of Inspectors Walks out of Holloway' *The Times* 19 December, 1995.

8. The EU environmental audit regulation requires that external verifiers do not provide other services to the audited site, although this requirement has been the subject of considerable negotiation.

9. In his review of Power (1994*b*), Hatherly (1995*a*) argues that I place too much emphasis on audit's potential to displace trust and that I draw too swift conclusions from the immediate aftermath of the audit explosion. It is fair to say that short term problems may not hold in the long run.

10. Armstrong (1991), like Perrow, suggests that the 'visualization of organizations as systems of contracts' is central to the cogency of agency theories of organization. However, contracts never substitute entirely for trust but only displace it. Armstrong argues that this displacement of trust is primarily responsible for the rise of the monitor at the expense of operational management in British industry. Once set in motion, 'An accounting managerial culture creates both a supply and a demand for additional accounting functions which therefore tend to expand' (Armstrong, 1991:19). This crisis of the foreman is being replicated in other contexts as a crisis of professional judgement and even, ironically of the judgement of auditors themselves.

11. It has been suggested that this regress to the $(n + 1)$th auditor can only be avoided where 'everyone becomes a guardian of everyone else' within tripartite structures which introduce community and where audit is embedded in institutional structures for dialogue (Braithwaite and Makkai, 1994:9–10).

12. Ewald is speaking of insurance in this context but the point can be applied to auditing, which can anyway be modelled as a kind of insurance even though practitioners deny that this is what they do.

13. See Beck (1992:20).

14. For example, there are similar stylistic shifts in criminal control: 'a move from the individual offender to opportunity structures and the control of whole populations' (Cohen, 1985:85).

15. In the case of factory inspectors this is the risk to reputation and credibility if prosecutions are undertaken which subsequently fail. Furthermore, legal burdens of proof on questions of causality generate a preference for clear cut, prosecutable breaches (Hawkins, 1992).

16. There are exceptions to this principle that the law will not intrude on the body of knowledge as such. What has passed for best practice in the past may be vulnerable to legal challenge.

17. Stone (1991:1338) suggests that environmental audit must be conducted at the 'nation' level.

18. Tax inspection provides an example of a practice which mixes formal and oppor-tunistic data gathering.
19. Similarly, warning signals for the North American Savings and Loan industry had existed for years but, given the career worries of regulators, led to a form of 'regulatory gambling' in an effort to preserve reputations (Kane, 1993:185).

BIBLIOGRAPHY

AAA (1966), *A Statement of Basic Accounting Theory* (Sarasota, Fl.: American Accounting Association).

AAA (1973), *A Statement of Basic Auditing Concepts* (Sarasota, Fl.: American Accounting Association).

AAA (1993), *The Auditor's Report* (Sarasota, Fl.: American Accounting Association) 16(2).

Aalders, M. (1993), 'Regulation and In-Company Environmental Management in the Netherlands', *Law & Policy* 15(2):75–94.

Abbott, A. (1988), *The System of Professions: An Essay on the Division of Expert Labour* (Chicago: Chicago University Press).

AICPA (1995), *Exposure Draft: Proposed Statement of Position, Environmental Remediation Liabilities* (New York: American Institute of Certified Public Accountants).

Alborn, T. L. (1995a), 'A Plague upon Your House: Commercial Crisis and Epidemic Disease in Victorian England', in Maasen *et al.* (eds.) (1995), 281–310.

Alborn, T. L. (1995b), 'The Moral of the Failed Bank: Professional Plots in the Victorian Money Market', *Victorian Studies* 199–225.

Aldersley, S. J. (1988), 'Discussant's Response to "Using and Evaluating Audit Decision Aids"', in Srivasta and Rebele (1988), 26–31.

APB (1993), *SAS 600, Auditors' Reports on Financial Statements* (London: Auditing Practices Board).

APB (1994), *The Audit Agenda* (London: Audit Practices Board).

APB (1995a), *Internal Financial Control Effectiveness—A Discussion Paper* (London: Auditing Practices Board).

APB (1995b), *SAS 520—Using the Work of an Expert* (London: Auditing Practices Board).

APC (1986), *Reliance on Other Specialists* (London: Auditing Practices Committee).

APC (1989a), *Auditing Guideline, Building Societies in the United Kingdom* (London: Auditing Practices Committee).

APC (1989b), *Auditing Guideline, Banks in the United Kingdom* (London: Auditing Practices Board).

APC (1990a), *Auditing Guideline, The Auditor's Responsibility in Relation to Fraud, Other Irregularities and Error* (London: Auditing Practices Committee).

APC (1990b), *Auditing Guideline, Communications between Auditors and Regulators under Sections 109 and 180(1)(q) of the Financial Services Act 1986* (London: Auditing Practices Committee).

APC (1990c), *Exposure Draft of an Auditing Guideline, the Auditor's Responsibility in Relation to Illegal Acts* (London: Auditing Practices Committee).

APC (1990d), *Practice Note 2: Accounting for Pension Costs under SSAP 24, Liaison between the Actuary and the Auditor* (London: Auditing Practices Committee).

APC (1991), *Practice Note 3, Client Assets: Guidance for Auditors of Investment Businesses* (London: Auditing Practices Committee).

Armstrong, P. (1991), 'Contradiction and Social Dynamics in the Capitalist Agency Relationship', *Accounting, Organizations and Society* 16(1):1–26.

ASB (1996), *Financial Reporting Standard 8, Accounting for Related Parties* (London: Accounting Standards Board).

ASC (1990a), *Technical Release 780, Accounting for Intangible Fixed Assets* (London: Accounting Standards Committee).

ASC (1990b), *Exposure Draft 52, Accounting for Intangible Fixed Assets* (London: Accounting Standards Committee).

Ashton, R. H. and Willingham, J. J. (1988), 'Using and Evaluating Audit Decision Aids', in Srivasta and Rebele (1988), 1–25.

Ashworth, W. J. (1996), *Memory, Foresight and Production*, Ph.D., University of Cambridge.

Ayres, I. and Braithwaite, J. (1992), *Responsive Regulation: Transcending the Deregulation Debate* (New York: Oxford University Press).

Baggott, R. (1989), 'Regulatory Reform in Britain: The Changing Face of Self-Regulation', *Public Administration* 67:435–54.

Baier, A. (1994), *Moral Prejudices: Essays on Ethics* (Cambridge, MA: Harvard University Press).

Baldwin, R. (1990), 'Why Rules Don't Work', *The Modern Law Review* 53:321–37.

Barwise, P., Higson, C., Likierman, A., and Marsh, P. (1989), *Accounting for Brands* (London: London Business School/ICAEW).

Beck, U. (1992), *Risk Society* (London: Sage).

Beck, U. (1995), *Ecological Politics in an Age of Risk* (Cambridge: Polity Press).

Beeton, D. (ed.) (1988), *Performance Measurement: Getting the Concepts Right* (London: Public Finance Foundation).

Beneviste, G. (1973), *The Politics of Expertise* (London: Croom Helm).

Beninger, R. (1986) *The Control Revolution: Technological and Economic Origins of the Information Society* (Cambridge MA: Harvard University Press).

Bijker, W. E., Hughes, T. P., and Pinch, T. (eds.) (1987), *The Social Construction of Technological Systems: New Directions in the Sociology and History of Technology* (Cambridge, MA: MIT Press).

Black, N. and Thompson, E. (1993), 'Obstacles to Medical Audit', *Social Science and Medicine* 36(7):849–56.

Boden, R. and Froud, J. (1996), 'Obeying the Rules: Accounting for Regulatory Compliance Costs in the United Kingdom', *Accounting, Organizations and Society* 21(6):529–47.

Bogdanor, V. (1994), *Can Government be run like a Business?* (London: Chartered Institute of Public Finance and Accountancy).

Boland, R. (1982), 'Myth and Technology in the American Accounting Profession', *Journal of Management Studies* 19(1):109–27.

Bourdieu, P. (1990a), 'Codification', in Bourdieu (1990b), 76–86.

Bourdieu, P. (1990b), *In Other Words: Essays towards a Reflexive Sociology* translated by M. Adamson (Cambridge: Polity Press).

Bowbrick, P. (1992), *The Economics of Quality, Grades and Brands* (London: Routledge).

Bowerman, M. (1994a), 'The National Audit Office and the Audit Commission in Areas where their VFM Responsibilities Interface', *Financial Accountability and Management* 10(1):47–64.

Bowerman, M. (1994*b*), 'Watching the Watchdogs', *Managerial Auditing Journal* 9(5):i–ii.

Bowerman, M. (1995), 'Auditing Performance Indicators: The Role of the Audit Commission in the Citizen's Charter Initiative', *Financial Accountability and Management* 11(2):173–85.

Braithwaite, J. (1984), *Corporate Crime in the Pharmaceutical Industry* (London: Routledge and Kegan Paul).

Braithwaite, J. and Fisse, B. (1987), 'Self-regulation and the Control of Corporate Crime', in Shearing and Stenning (eds.) (1987), 221–46.

Braithwaite, J. and Makkai, T. (1994), 'Trust and Compliance', *Policing & Society* 4(1):1–12.

Bregman, E. and Jacobson, A. (1994), 'Environmental Performance Review: Self-Regulation in Environmental Law', in Teubner, G. *et al.* (1994), 207–36.

Brewer, P. C. and Mills, T. Y. (1994), 'ISO 9000 Standards: An Emerging CPA Service Area', *Journal of Accountancy* (February), 63–7.

Brittan, S. (1996), 'The Snares of Stakeholding', *The Financial Times* 1 January.

Broadbent, J., Laughlin, R., and Shearn, D. (1992), 'Recent Financial and Administrative Changes in General Practice: An Unhealthy Intrusion into Medical Autonomy', *Financial Accountability and Management* 8(2):129–48.

Broadbent, J., Laughlin, R., Shearn, D., and Dandy, N. (1993), 'Implementing Local Management of Schools: A Theoretical and Empirical Analysis', *Research Papers in Education* 8(2):149–76.

Broadfoot, P. M. (1996), *Education, Assessment and Society* (Buckingham: Open University Press).

Brophy, M., Netherwood, A., and Starkey, R. (1995), 'The Voluntary Approach: An Effective Means of Achieving Sustainable Development?', *Eco-Management and Auditing* 2(3):127–32.

Brown, R. E. (1962), 'Changing Audit Objectives and Techniques', *The Accounting Review* 37:696–703.

BSI (1992), *Environmental Management Systems* (London: British Standards Institute).

BSI (1993), *Draft for Public Comment: Draft British Standard Revision of BS 7750: 1992 Specification for Environmental Management Systems (DC 93/400220)* (Linford Wood, Milton Keynes: British Standards Institute).

Burchell, G., Gordon, C., and Miller, P. (eds.) (1991), *The Foucault Effect: Studies in Governmentality* (London: Harvester Wheatsheaf).

Cadbury Committee (1992), *The Financial Aspects of Corporate Governance* (London: Institute of Chartered Accountants in England and Wales).

Carpenter, B. and Dirsmith, M. (1993), 'Sampling and the Abstraction of Knowledge in the Auditing Profession: An Extended Institutional Theory Perspective', *Accounting, Organizations and Society* 18(1):41–63.

CEC (1993), 'Council Regulation (EEC) No 1836/93 of 29th June 1993 allowing Voluntary Participation by Companies in the Industrial Sector in a Community Eco-Management and Audit Scheme', *Official Journal* (10 June) L 168, Vol. 36.

Chambers, A. (1996), 'Directors' Reports on Internal Financial Control', in Skerratt and Tonkin (eds.) (1996), 105–29.

Chandler, R. A., Edwards, J. R., and Anderson, M. (1993), 'Changing Perceptions of the Role of the Company Auditor, 1840–1940', *Accounting and Business Research* 23(92):443–59.

Chatfield, M. (1977), *A History of Accounting Thought* (New York: Robert E Krieger).

Chelimsky, E. (1985), 'Comparing and Contrasting Auditing and Evaluation: Some Notes on their Relationship', *Evaluation Review* 9(4):483–503.

Chelimsky, E. (1995), 'Politics, Policy and Research Synthesis', *Evaluation* 1(1):97–104.

Chelimsky, E. and Shadish, W. (eds.) (1997), *Evaluation for the 21st Century* (Newbury Park, Ca.: Sage).

Chua, W. F. (1995), 'Experts, Networks and Inscriptions in the Fabrication of Accounting Images: A Story of the Representation of Three Public Hospitals', *Accounting, Organizations and Society* 20(2/3):111–45.

CICA (1992), *Environmental Auditing and the Role of the Accounting Profession* (Toronto: Canadian Institute of Chartered Accountants).

CIPFA (1994a), *Corporate Governance in the Public Sector* (London: The Chartered Institute of Public Finance and Accountancy).

CIPFA (1994b), *Auditing the Public Services: A Contribution to the Debate on the Future of Auditing* (London: The Chartered Institute of Public Finance and Accountancy).

Clarke, M. (1986), *Regulating the City: Competition, Scandal and Reform* (Milton Keynes: Open University Press).

Coffey, A. (1994), 'Timing is Everything: Graduate Accountants, Time and Organisational Commitment', *Sociology* 28(4):943–56.

Cohen, S. (1985), *Visions of Social Control* (Cambridge: Polity Press).

Cooper, D., Radcliffe, V., and Robson, K. (1994), 'The Management of Professional Enterprises and Regulatory Change: British Accountancy and the Financial Services Act, 1986', *Accounting, Organizations and Society* 19(7):601–28.

Coopers & Lybrand (1993), *Research Accountability* (London: Coopers & Lybrand).

Cousins, J., Mitchell, A., and Sikka, P. (1993), 'Secret Government and Privileged Interests', *The Political Quarterly* 64(3):306–15.

Cushing, B. E. and Loebbecke, J. K. (1984a), 'Analytical Approaches to Audit Risk: A Survey and Analysis', *Auditing: A Journal of Practice and Theory* 3(1):23–41.

Cushing, B. E. and Loebbecke, J. K. (1984b), 'The Implications of Structured Audit Methodologies', *The Auditors Report* 8(2):10–11.

Cushing, B. E. and Loebbecke, J. K. (1986), *Comparison of Audit Methodologies of Large Accounting Firms: Accounting Research Study No. 26* (Sarasota: American Accounting Association).

Dandeker, C. (1990), *Surveillance, Power and Modernity* (Cambridge: Polity Press).

Day, P. and Klein, R. (1987), *Accountabilities: Five Public Services* (London: Tavistock).

Day, P. and Klein, R. (1990), *Inspecting the Inspectorates* (London: Joseph Rowntree Foundation).

Dent, M. (1993), 'Professionalism, Educated Labour and the State: Hospital Medicine and the New Managerialism', *The Sociological Review* 41(2):244–73.

Dewar, D. (1991), 'The Audit of Central Government', in Sherer and Turley (1991), 248–59.

Dezalay, Y. (1995a), 'Introduction: Professional Competition and the Social Construction of Transnational Markets', in Dezalay and Sugarman, D. (eds.) (1995), 1–21.

Dezalay, Y. (1995b), ' "Turf Battles" or "Class Struggles": The Internationalization of the Market for Expertise in the "Professional Society" ', *Accounting, Organizations and Society* 20(5):331–44.

Dezalay, Y. and Sugarman, D. (eds.) (1995), *Professional Competition and Professional Power: Lawyers, Accountants and the Social Construction of Markets* (London: Routledge).

Dicksee, L. R. (1892, 1895, 1898, 1900, 1902, 1904, 1905, 1907, 1912, 1915, 1919, 1922, 1924, 1928, 1933, 1940, 1951, 1969), *Auditing: A Practical Manual for Auditors* (London: Gee).

DiMaggio, P. J. and Powell, W. W. (1991), 'Introduction', in Powell and DiMaggio (eds.) (1991), 1–38.

Douglas, M. (1992a), 'The Normative Debate and the Origins of Culture', in Douglas (ed.) (1992b), 125–48.

Douglas, M. (ed.) (1992b), *Risk and Blame: Essays in Cultural Theory* (London: Routledge).

Dunsire, A. (1990), 'Holistic Governance', *Public Policy and Administration* 5(1):4–19.

Dunsire, A. (1993), 'Modes of Governance', in Kooiman (ed.) (1993), 21–34.

Dwyer, J. P. (1990), 'The Pathology of Symbolic Legislation', *Ecology Law Quarterly* 17(2):233–316.

Elkington, J. (1988), 'The Environmental Audit: Holy Grail or Essential Management Tool', in UNEP (1988), 17–20.

Elliott, R. K. (1983), 'Unique Audit Methods: Peat Marwick International', *Auditing: A Journal of Theory and Practice* 2(1):1–12.

Elliott, R. K. (1995), 'The Future of Assurance Services: Implications for Academia', *Accounting Horizons* 9(4):118–27.

EPA (1986), 'Environmental Auditing Policy Statement', *US Federal Register* 51 (131) 9 July.

Ewald, F. (1990), 'Norms, Discipline and the Law', in Post (ed.) (1990), 138–61.

Ewald, F. (1991), 'Insurance and Risk', in Burchell *et al.* (eds.) (1991), 197–210.

Exworthy, M. (1995), *Purchasing Clinical Audit: A Study in the South and West Region* (University of Southampton: Institute for Health Policy Studies).

Ezzamel, M. and Willmott, H. (1993), 'Corporate Governance and Financial Accountability: Recent Reforms in the UK Public Sector', *Accounting, Auditing and Accountability Journal* 6(3):109–32.

Farmer, L. and Teubner, G. (1994), 'Ecological Self-Organization', in Teubner *et al.* (1994), 3–13.

Fearnley, S. and Willett, C. (1995), 'The Audit Register: An Interpretive Muddle', *Accountancy* (October), 130–1.

Fielden, J. (1984), 'Pressures for Change in Public Sector Audit', in Hopwood and Tomkins (eds.) (1984), 212–28.

Finklestein, M. O. (1966), 'The Application of Statistical Decision Theory to Jury Discrimination Cases', *The Harvard Law Review* 80(2):338–76.

Fischer, K. and Schot, J. (eds.) (1992), *Environmental Strategies for Industry* (Washington D.C.: Island Press).

Fischer, M. J. (1996), ' "Real-izing" the Benefits of New Technologies as a Source of Audit Evidence: An Interpretive Field Study', *Accounting, Organizations and Society* 21(2/3):219–42.

Flint, D. (1988), *Philosophy and Principles of Auditing* (London: Macmillan).

Fogarty, T. (1996), 'The Imagery and Reality of Peer Review in the US: Insights from Institutional Theory', *Accounting, Organizations and Society* 21(2/3):243–67.

Francis, J. (1994), 'Auditing, Hermeneutics and Subjectivity', *Accounting, Organizations and Society* 19(3):235–69.

Freedman, J. (1993), 'Accountants and Corporate Governance', *The Political Quarterly* 64(3):285–97.

Friedman, F. B. (1991), 'Environmental Management for the Future: Environmental Auditing is Not Enough', *Cardozo Law Review* 12(5):1315–32.

Fuller, S. (1996), 'Toward a Philosophy of Science Accounting: A Critical Rendering of Instrumental Rationality', in Power, M. (ed.) (1996), 247–80.

Funnell, W. (1994), 'Independence and the State Auditor in Britain: A Constitutional Keystone or a Case of Reified Imagery', *Abacus* 30(2):175–95.

Gain, A. and Rosenhead, J. (1993), 'Problem Structuring for Medical Quality Assurance', Operational Research Working Paper No. LSEOR.93.8. (London: London School of Economics and Political Science).

Gambetta, D. (1988*a*), 'Can We Trust Trust?' in Gambetta (ed.) (1988*b*), 213–37.

Gambetta, D. (ed.) (1988*b*), *Trust: Making and Breaking Cooperative Relations* (Oxford: Basil Blackwell).

Gambetta, D. (1994), 'Godfather's Gossip', *Archive of European Sociology* XXXV:199–223.

Garrett, J. (1986), 'Developing State Audit in Britain', *Public Administration* 64(4):421–33.

Geis, G. and Stotland, E. (eds.) (1980), *White Collar Crime: Theory and Research* (Beverly Hills: Sage).

Gelber, M. (1995), 'Eco-Balance: An Environmental Management Tool Used In Germany', *Social and Environmental Accounting* 15(2):7–9.

Gibbins, R. (1984), 'The Psychology of Professional Judgement', *Journal of Accounting Research* 22(1):103–25.

Gibbins, R. (1992), 'Deception: A Tricky Issue for Behavioural Research in Accounting', *Auditing: A Journal of Practice and Theory* 11(2):113–26.

Giddens, A. (1990), *The Consequences of Modernity* (Cambridge: Polity Press).

Glynn, J. J. (1985*a*), *Value for Money Auditing in the Public Sector* (London: Prentice Hall/ICAEW).

Glynn, J. J. (1985*b*), 'Value for Money Auditing: An International Review and Comparison', *Financial Accountability and Management* 1(2):113–18.

Grabosky, P. N. (1990), 'Professional Advisers and White Collar Illegality: Towards Explaining and Excusing Professional Failure', *UNSW Law Journal* 13(1):73–96.

Grabosky, P. N. (1994*a*), 'Green Markets: Environmental Regulation in the Private Sector', *Law & Policy* 16(4):419–48.

Grabosky, P. N. (1994*b*), 'Organisational Leverage and the Technologies of Regulatory Compliance', Working Paper 24, Administration, Compliance and Governability Program (Canberra: Australian National University).

Grabosky, P. N. (1995a), 'Counterproductive Regulation', *International Journal of the Sociology of Law* 23:347–69.

Grabosky, P. N. (1995b), 'Using Non-Governmental Resources to Foster Regulatory Compliance', *Governance: An International Journal of Policy and Administration* 8(4):527–50.

Gray, R. (1993), *Accounting for the Environment* (London: Paul Chapman Ltd).

Greenough, J. (1991), 'The Audit Commission', in Sherer and Turley (eds.) (1991), 240–7.

Grobstein, M. and Craig, P. W. (1984), 'A Risk Analysis Approach to Auditing', *Auditing: A Journal of Theory and Practice* 3(2):1–16.

Gunningham, N. and Prest, J. (1993), 'Environmental Audit as a Regulatory Strategy: Prospects and Reform', *Sydney Law Review* 15(4):492–526.

Gwilliam, D. (1987), *A Survey of Auditing Research* (Prentice-Hall International/ICAEW).

Hacking, I. (1975), *The Emergence of Probability* (Cambridge: Cambridge University Press).

Hacking, I. (1983), *Representing and Intervening* (Cambridge: Cambridge University Press).

Hacking, I. (1990), *The Taming of Chance* (Cambridge: Cambridge University Press).

Hajer, M. (1994), "Verinnerlijking": The Limits to a Positive Management Approach', in Teubner *et al.* (eds.) (1994), 167–84.

Halliday, S. (1993), 'Quality Uncontrolled', *Accountancy* (September), 48–9.

Hancher, L. and Moran, M. (1989a), 'Organising Regulatory Space', in Hancher and Moran (eds.) (1989b), 271–99.

Hancher, L. and Moran, L. (eds.) (1989b), *Capitalism, Culture and Economic Regulation* (Oxford: Clarendon).

Hanlon, G. (1994), *The Commercialization of Accountancy: Flexible Accumulation and the Transformation of the Service Class* (London: St Martin's Press).

Hansen, M. H. and Madow, W. E. (1976), 'Some Important Events in the Historical Development of Sample Surveys', in Owen (ed.) (1976), 75–102.

Harden, I. (1993), 'Money and the Constitution: Financial Control, Reporting and Audit', *Legal Studies* 13(1):16–37.

Harden, I., White, F., and Donnelly, K. (1995), 'The Court of Auditors and Financial Control and Accountability in the European Community', Working Paper, University of Sheffield.

Harper, R. (1988), 'Not Any Old Numbers: An Examination of Practical Reasoning in an Accountancy Environment', *The Journal of Interdisciplinary Economics* 2:297–306.

Hatherly, D. (1995a), 'Review of *The Audit Explosion* by M. Power', *Accounting and Business Research* 24(96):350–1.

Hatherly, D. (1995b), 'The Audit Research Agenda: The Drive for Quality and its Dependence on Professional Judgement', University of Edinburgh.

Hawkins, K. (1984), *Environment and Enforcement: The Social Definition of Pollution* (Oxford: Oxford University Press).

Hawkins, K. (1992), ' "FATCATS" and Prosecution in a Regulatory Agency: A Footnote on the Social Construction of Risk', in Short and Clarke (eds.) (1992), 275–96.

Hawkins, K. and Thomas, J. (1984*a*), 'The Enforcement Process in Regulatory Bureaucracies', in Hawkins and Thomas (eds.) (1984*b*), 1–22.

Hawkins, K. and Thomas, J. (eds.) (1984*b*), *Enforcing Regulation* (Dordrecht: Kluwer-Nijhoff).

Hay, D. (1993), 'Internal Control: How it Evolved in Four English Speaking Countries', *The Accounting Historians' Journal* 20(1):79–102.

HEFC (1993), *Accountability for Research Funds* (Higher Education Funding Council).

Hemming, C. (1993), 'The EC Eco-Management and Audit Regulation: Experiences from the Pilot Exercise', *Eco-Management and Audit* 1(1):3–6.

Henkel, M. (1991), *Government, Evaluation and Change* (London: Jessica Kingsley).

Henley, D. (1989), 'External Audit', in Henley *et al.* (eds.) (1989), 247–78.

Henley, D., Holtham, C., Likierman, A., and Perrin, J. (eds.) (1989), *Public Sector Accounting and Financial Control* (London: Van Nostrand Reinhold International).

Hepworth, N. P. (1995), 'The Role of Performance Audit', Perfomance Audit Symposium, 7 June, Paris.

Herz, M. (1991), 'Environmental Auditing and Environmental Management: The Implicit and Explicit Federal Mandate', *Cardozo Law Review* 12(5):1241–63.

Hillary, R. (1993), *The Eco-Management and Audit Scheme: A Practical Guide* (Letchworth, UK: Technical Communications (Publishing) Ltd).

Holden, J. (1995), 'Quality Reviews', *Accountancy Age* 5 October, 21.

Holstrum, G. L. and Kirtland, J. L. (1983), 'Audit Risk Model: A Framework for Current Practice and Future Research', in Schultz and Brown (eds.) (1983), 267–309.

Hood, C. (1991), 'A Public Management for all Seasons?' *Public Administration* 69(1):3–19.

Hood, C. (1995), 'The "New Public Management" in the 1980s: Variations on a Theme', *Accounting, Organizations and Society* 20(2/3):93–109.

Hopwood, A. G. (1984), 'Accounting and the Pursuit of Efficiency', in Hopwood and Tomkins (eds.) (1984), 167–87.

Hopwood, A. G. and Miller, P. (eds.) (1994), *Accounting as Social and Institutional Practice* (Cambridge: Cambridge University Press).

Hopwood, A. G. and Tomkins, C. (eds.) (1984), *Issues in Public Sector Accounting* (Oxford: Phillip Allen).

Howarth, I. (1995), 'Prescription for Progress', *Times Higher Education Supplement* 3 November.

Huizing, A. and Dekker, H. C. (1992), 'The Environmental Issue on the Dutch Political Market', *Accounting, Organizations and Society* 17(5):427–48.

Humphrey, C. (1991), 'Audit Expectations', in Sherer and Turley (eds.) (1991), 3–21.

Humphrey, C. and Moizer, P. (1990), 'From Techniques to Ideologies: An Alternative Perspective on the Audit Function', *Critical Perspectives on Accounting* 1(3):217–38.

Humphrey, C., Moizer, P., and Turley, S. (1992), *The Audit Expectations Gap in the United Kingdom* (London: Institute of Chartered Accountants in England and Wales).

Husbands, C. (1992), 'A Black Look at the Books', *Times Higher Education Supplement* 4 December.

ICAEW (1992), *Business, Accountancy and the Environment: A Policy and Research Agenda* (London: Institute of Chartered Accountants in England and Wales).

ICAEW (1994), *Internal Control and Financial Reporting—Guidance for Directors of Listed Companies Registered in the UK* (London: Institute of Chartered Accountants in England and Wales).

ICAEW (1995), *Financial Reporting of Environmental Liabilities: A Discussion Paper* (London: Institute of Chartered Accountants in England and Wales).

ICAS/ICAEW (1989), *Auditing and the Future* (Edinburgh: Institute of Chartered Accountants of Scotland/Institute of Chartered Accountants in England and Wales).

ICC (1991), *Effective Environmental Auditing* (Paris: International Chamber of Commerce).

Ijiri, Y. and Jaedicke, R. K. (1966), 'Reliability and Objectivity of Accounting Measurement', *The Accounting Review* 41(3):474–83.

Jacobsen, A. J. (1991), 'Environmental Accountability Beyond Compliance: Externalities and Accounting', *Cardozo Law Review* 12(5):1333–6.

Jensen, M. C. and Meckling, W. H. (1976), 'Theory of the Firm: Managerial Behaviour, Agency Costs and Ownership Structure', *Journal of Financial Economics* 3:305–60.

Jones, C. (1993), 'Auditing Criminal Justice', *British Journal of Criminology* 33(2):187–202.

Kagan, R. A. (1984), 'On Regulatory Inspectorates and Police', in Hawkins and Thomas (eds.) (1984b), 37–64.

Kagan, R. A. and Scholz, J. T. (1984), 'The "Criminology of the Corporation" and Regulatory Enforcement Strategies', in Hawkins and Thomas (eds.) (1984b), 67–95.

Kane, E. J. (1993), 'Reflexive Adaptation of Business to Regulation and Regulation to Business', *Law & Policy* 15(3):179–89.

Katz, L. (1975), 'Presentation of a Confidence Interval Estimate as Evidence in a Legal Proceeding', *The American Statistician* (November), 138–42.

Keasey, K. and Wright, M. (1993), 'Issues in Corporate Accountability and Governance: An Editorial', *Accounting and Business Research* 23:291–303.

Kelly, K. (1995), *Out of Control* (New York: Addison-Wesley).

Kettl, D. F. (1993), *Sharing Power: Public Governance and Private Markets* (Washington D.C.: The Brookings Institution).

Kimmance, P. (1984), 'The Widening Scope of Local Government Audit and Private Sector Participation', in Hopwood and Tomkins (eds.) (1984), 229–47.

Kindleberger, C. P. (1978), *Manias, Panics and Crashes: A History of Financial Crises* (London: Macmillan).

Kirkham, E. J. and Gaa, C. J. (1939), 'Is there a Theory Basis of Audit Procedure?', *The Accounting Review* (June), 139–46.

Klein, R. and Carter, N. (1988), 'Performance Measurement: A Review of Concepts and Issues', in Beeton (ed.) (1988), 5–20.

Kooiman, J. (ed.) (1993), *Modern Governance: New Government-Society Interactions* (London: Sage).

KPMG Peat Marwick McLintock (1990), *Audit and Auditors: What the Public Thinks* (London: KPMG Peat Marwick McLintock).

Kraakman, R. H. (1986), 'Gatekeepers: The Anatomy of a Third Party Enforcement Strategy', *Journal of Law, Economics and Organization* 2:53–104.

Kramer, R. (1996), 'Divergent Realities and Convergent Disappointments in the Hierarchic Relation: Trust and the Intuitive Auditor at Work', in Kramer and Tyler (eds.) (1996), 216–45.

Kramer, R. and Tyler, T. (eds.) (1996), *Trust in Organizations* (Thousand Oaks, CA: Sage).

Kruskal, W. and Mosteller, F. (1979), 'Representative Sampling I: Non-Scientific Literature', *International Statistical Review* 47:13–24.

Kruskal, W. and Mosteller, F. (1980), 'Representative Sampling IV: The History of the Concept in Statistics 1895–1939', *International Statistical Review* 48:169–95.

Ladeur, K.-H. (1994), 'Coping with Uncertainty: Ecological Risks and the Proceduralization of Environmental Law', in Teubner *et al.* (eds.) (1994), 299–336.

La Follett, M. (1992), *Stealing into Print: Fraud, Plagiarism, and Misconduct in Scientific Publishing* (Berkeley and Los Angeles: University of California Press).

Latour, B. (1987), *Science in Action* (Milton Keynes: Open University Press).

Laughlin, R. C. (1991), 'Environmental Disturbances and Organizational Transitions and Transformations: Some Alternative Models', *Organization Studies* 12(2):209.

Laughlin, R. C. and Broadbent, J. (1995), 'Evaluating the "New Public Management" in the UK: A Constitutional Possibility', Sheffield University Management School.

Laughlin, R. C., Broadbent, J., and Willig-Atherton, H. (1994), 'Recent Financial and Accountability Changes in GP Practices in the UK: Initial Experiences and Effects', *Accounting, Auditing and Accountability Journal* 7(3):96–124.

Law, J. and Akrich, M. (1994), 'On Customers and Costs: A Story from Public Sector Science', *Science in Context* 7(3):539–61.

Lee, T. A. (1986), *Company Auditing* (London: Gee).

Lee, T. A. (1993), *Corporate Audit Theory* (London: Chapman & Hall).

Lewis, N. (1993), 'The Citizen's Charter and Next Steps: A New Way of Governing?', *The Political Quarterly* 64(3):316–26.

Lorenz, E. H. (1988), 'Neither Friends nor Strangers: Informal Networks of Sub-Contracting in French Industry', in Gambetta (ed.) (1988b), 194–210.

Lyon, D. (1994), *The Electronic Eye: The Rise of Surveillance Society* (Cambridge: Polity Press).

McBarnet, D. and Whelan, C. (1991), 'The Elusive Spirit of the Law: Formalism and the Struggle for Legal Control', *The Modern Law Review* 54(6):874–88.

McCahery, J., Picciotto, S., and Scott, C. (eds.) (1993), *Corporate Control and Accountability* (Oxford: Oxford University Press).

McInnes, W. (ed.) (1993), *Auditing into the Twenty First Century* (Edinburgh: Institute of Chartered Accountants in Scotland).

McNair, C. J. (1991), 'Proper Compromises: The Management Control Dilemma in Public Accounting and its Impact on Auditor Behaviour', *Accounting, Organizations and Society* 16(7): 635–53.

McRae, T. W. (1982), *A Study of the Application of Statistical Sampling to External Auditing* (London: Institute of Chartered Accountants in England and Wales).

McSweeney, B. (1988), 'Accounting for the Audit Commission', *The Political Quarterly* 59(1):28–43.

Maasen, S., Mendelsohn, E., and Weingart, P. (eds.) (1995), *Biology as Society, Society as Biology: Metaphors* (Dordrecht: Kluwer).

Manning, P. (1987), 'Ironies of Compliance', in Shearing and Stenning (eds.) (1987*b*), 293–316.

Manning, P. K. (1992), 'Managing Risk: Managing Uncertainty in the British Nuclear Installations Inspectorate', in Short and Clarke (eds.) (1992), 255–73.

Martens, S. C. and McEnroe, J. E. (1991), 'Interprofessional Struggles over Definition: Lawyers, Accountants and Illegal Acts', *Critical Perspectives on Accounting* 2:375–84.

Marx, G. T. (1981), 'Ironies of Social Control: Authorities as Contributors to Deviance Through Escalation, Nonenforcement and Covert Facilitation', *Social Problems* 28(3):221–46.

Marx, G. T. (1984), 'Notes on the Discovery, Collection, and Assessment of Hidden and Dirty Data', in Schneider and Kitsuse (eds.) (1984), 78–113.

Marx, G. (1990), 'The Case of the Omniscient Organization', *Harvard Business Review* (March–April), 4–12.

Mayntz, R. (1993), 'Governing Failures and the Problem of Governability: Some Comments on the Theoretical Paradigm', in Kooiman (ed.) (1993), 9–20.

Meyer, J. and Rowan, B. (1991), 'Institutionalized Organizations: Formal Structure as Myth and Ceremony', in Powell and DiMaggio (eds.) (1991), 41–62.

Meyer, J. and Rowan, B. (1992), 'The Structure of Educational Organizations', in Meyer and Scott (eds.) (1992), 71–97.

Meyer, J. and Scott, W. R. (eds.) (1992), *Institutional Environments and Organizations* (Thousand Oaks, Ca: Sage).

Meyerson, D., Weick, K., and Kramer, R. (1996), 'Swift Trust and Temporary Groups', in Kramer and Tyler (eds.) (1996), 166–95.

Middelhoek, A. J. (1995), 'Performance Audits and Compliance Audits', *De Accountant* December, 264–7.

Miller, P. (1990), 'On the Interrelations between Accounting and the State', *Accounting, Organizations and Society* 15(4):315–38.

Miller, P. (1994), 'Accounting as Social and Institutional Practice: an Introduction', in Hopwood and Miller (eds.) (1994), 1–39.

Miller, P. and O'Leary, T. (1987), 'Accounting and the Construction of the Governable Person', *Accounting, Organizations and Society* 12(3):235–65.

Miller, P. and O'Leary, T. (1993), 'Accounting Expertise and the Politics of the Product: Economic Citizenship and Modes of Corporate Governance', *Accounting, Organizations and Society* 18(2/3):187–206.

Miller, P. and O'Leary, T. (1994), 'The Factory as Laboratory', *Science in Context* 7(3):469–96.

Miller, P. and Rose, N. (1990), 'Governing Economic Life', *Economy and Society* 19(1):1–31.

Mills, P. A. (1987), 'The Probative Capacity of Accounts in Early-Modern Spain', *The Accounting Historian's Journal* 14(1):95–108.

Minow, N. and Deal, M. (1991), 'Corporations, Shareholders and the Environmental Agenda', *Cardozo Law Review* 12(5):1359–70.

Miranti, P. (1986), 'Associationalism, Statistics and Professional Regulation: Public Accountants and the Reform of the Financial Markets 1896–1940', *Business History Review* 60:438–68.

Miranti, P. (1988), 'Professionalism and Nativism: The Competition in Securing Public Accountancy Legislation in New York during the 1890s', *Social Science Quarterly* 69(2):361–80.

Mitchell, A., Puxty, A., Sikka, P., and Willmott, H. (1991), *Accounting for Change: A Proposal for the Reform of Audit and Accounting* (London: Fabian Society).

Montgomery, R. H. (1905, 1912, 1921, 1927, 1934, 1940, 1949, 1957), *Auditing Theory and Practice* (New York: Ronald Press Company).

Moran, M. (1986), *The Politics of Banking* (London: Macmillan).

Moran, M. (1991), *The Politics of the Financial Services Revolution: The USA, UK and Japan* (London: Macmillan).

Mosher, F. (1979), *The GAO: The Quest for Accountability in American Government* (Boulder, Co.: Westview Press).

Moyer, C. A. (1951), 'Early Developments in American Auditing', *The Accounting Review* 26(1):3–8.

Mullarkey, J. (1984), 'The Case for the Structured Audit', in Stettler and Ford (eds.) (1984), 73–84.

Munro, R. and Hatherley, D. J. (1993), 'Accountability and the Commercial Agenda', *Critical Perspectives on Accounting* 4:369–95.

Myers, J. H. (1985), 'Spiralling Upward: Auditing Methods as Described by Montgomery and His Successors', *The Accounting Historian's Journal* 12(1):53–7.

Napier, C. (forthcoming), 'The Antecedents of Unlimited Auditor Liability in the United Kingdom: A Study in Corporate Governance', *Accounting, Organizations and Society*.

Napier, C. and Power, M. (1992), 'Professional Research, Lobbying and Intangibles: A Review Essay', *Accounting and Business Research* 23(89):85–95.

Neave, G. (1988), 'On the Cultivation of Quality, Efficiency and Enterprise: An Overview of Recent Trends in Higher Education in Western Europe, 1986–1988', *European Journal of Education* 23(1/2):7–23.

Nichols, D. R. and Stettler, H. (eds.) (1982), *Auditing Symposium VI, Proceedings of the 1982 Touche Ross/University of Kansas Symposium on Auditing* (Kansas: University of Kansas).

Noke, C. (1981), 'Accounting for Bailiffship in Thirteenth Century England', *Accounting and Business Research* 12 (Spring):137–51.

Nolan, M. and Scott, G. (1993), 'Audit: an Exploration of Some Tensions and Paradoxical Expectations', *Journal of Advanced Nursing* 18:759–66.

Normanton, E. L. (1966), *The Accountability and Audit of Government* (Manchester: Manchester University Press).

Olson, S. K. and Wootton, C. W. (1991), 'Substance and Semantics in the Auditor's Standard Report', *The Accounting Historian's Journal* 18(2):85–111.

O'Riordan, T. and Weale, A. (1989), 'Administrative Reorganization and Policy Change: The Case of Her Majesty's Inspectorate of Pollution', *Public Administration* 67:277–94.

Orts, E. W. (1995), 'Reflexive Environmental Law', *Northwestern University Law Review* 89(4):1227–340.

Osborne, D. and Gaebler, T. (1992), *Reinventing Government* (Reading, MA: Addison Wesley).

Owen, D. B. (ed.) (1976), *On the History of Statistics and Probability* (New York: Dekker).

Packwood, T., Kerrison, S., and Buxton, M. (1994), 'The Implementation of Medical Audit', *Social Policy and Administration* 28(4):299–316.

Parker, L. and Guthrie, J. (1993), 'The Australian Public Sector in the 1990s: New Accountability Regimes in Motion', *Journal of International Accounting, Auditing and Taxation* 2(1):59–81.

Parker, M. and Jary, D. (1995), 'The McUniversity: Organizations, Management and Academic Subjectivity', *Organization* 2(2):319–38.

Parker, R. H. (1990), 'Regulating British Corporate Financial Reporting in the Late Nineteenth Century', *Accounting, Business and Financial History* 1(1):51–71.

Pendelbury, M. and Sherim, O. S. (1990), 'Auditors' Attitudes to Effectiveness Auditing', *Financial Accountability and Management* 6(3):177–89.

Pendelbury, M. and Sherim, O. S. (1991), 'Attitudes to Effectiveness Auditing: Some Further Evidence', *Financial Accountability and Management* 7(1):57–63.

Pentland, B. (1993), 'Getting Comfortable with the Numbers: Auditing and the Micro-Production of Macro-Order', *Accounting, Organizations and Society* 18(7/8):605–20.

Pentland, B. and Carlile, P. (1996), 'Audit the Taxpayer, Not the Return: Tax Auditing as an Expression Game', *Accounting, Organizations and Society* 21(2/3):269–87.

Perrow, C. (1990), 'Economic Theories of Organization', in Zukin and DiMaggio (eds.) (1990).

Pildes, R. H. and Sunstein, C. R. (1995), 'Reinventing the Regulatory State', *The University of Chicago Law Review* 62(1):1–129.

Pinch, T. and Bijker, W. E. (1987), 'The Social Construction of Facts and Artifacts: Or How the Sociology of Science and the Sociology of Knowledge Might Benefit Each Other', in Bijker *et al.* (eds.) (1987), 17–50.

Piper, A. and Jones, R. (1995), 'Auditors' Review of Cadbury Compliance Statements', in Tonkin and Skerratt (eds.) (1995), 29–53.

Pollitt, C. (1990), 'Doing Business in the Temple? Managers and Quality Assurance in the Public Services', *Public Administration* 68:435–52.

Pollitt, C. (1993a), 'The Struggle for Quality: The Case of the National Health Service', *Politics and Policy* 21(3):161–70.

Pollitt, C. (1993b), 'Audit and Accountability: The Missing Dimension?', *Journal of the Royal Society of Medicine* 86(April):209–11.

Pollitt, C. (1995), 'Justification by Works or by Faith? Evaluating the New Public Management', *Evaluation* 1(2):133–54.

Pollitt, C. and Summa, H. (1997), 'Performance Audit: Travellers' Tales', in Chelimsky and Shadish (eds.) (1997), 86–108.

Porter, T. (1986) *The Rise of Statistical Thinking 1820–1900* (Princeton: Princeton University Press).

Porter, T. (1994), 'Making Things Quantitative', *Science in Context* 7(3):389–407.

Post, R. (ed.) (1990), *Law and the Order of Culture* (University of California Press).

Powell, W. W. and DiMaggio, P. J. (eds.) (1991), *The New Institutionalism in Organizational Analysis* (Chicago: Chicago University Press).

Power, M. (ed.) (1990), *Brand and Goodwill Accounting Strategies* (Cambridge: Woodhead Faulkner).

Power, M. (1991), 'Auditing and Environmental Expertise: Between Protest and Professionalisation', *Accounting, Auditing and Accountability Journal* 4(3):37–62.

Power, M. (1992*a*), 'From Common Sense to Expertise: the Pre-history of Audit Sampling', *Accounting, Organizations and Society* 17:37–62.

Power, M. (1992*b*), 'The Politics of Brand Accounting in the United Kingdom', *European Accounting Review* 1(1):39–68.

Power, M. (1993*a*), 'Auditing and the Politics of Regulatory Control in the UK Financial Services Sector', in McCahery *et al.* (eds.) (1993), 187–202.

Power, M. (1993*b*), 'The Politics of Financial Auditing', *The Political Quarterly* 64(3):272–84.

Power, M. (1994*a*), 'The Audit Society', in Hopwood and Miller (eds.) (1994), 299–316.

Power, M. (1994*b*), *The Audit Explosion* (London: Demos).

Power, M. (1994*c*), 'From the Science of Accounts to the Financial Accountability of Science', *Science in Context* 7(3):355–87.

Power, M. (1994*d*), 'Constructing the Responsible Organization: Accounting and Environmental Representation', in Teubner *et al.* (eds.) (1994), 369–92.

Power, M. (1995*a*), *Auditing and the Decline of Inspection* (London: CIPFA).

Power, M. (1995*b*), 'Auditing, Expertise and the Sociology of Technique', *Critical Perspectives on Accounting* 6:317–39.

Power, M. (ed.) (1996*a*), *Accounting and Science: Natural Inquiry and Commercial Reason* (Cambridge: Cambridge University Press).

Power, M. (1996*b*), 'Making Things Auditable', *Accounting, Organizations and Society* 21(2/3):289–315.

Power, M. (forthcoming), 'Expertise and the Construction of Relevance: Accountants and Environmental Audit', *Accounting, Organizations and Society*.

Pratley, A. (1995), 'Auditing, Financial Management and Evaluation: An Interview with Alan Pratley', *Evaluation* 1(2):251–63.

Preston, A. M., Cooper, D. J., and Scarborough, P. (1995), 'Transformations in the Code of Ethics of the US Accounting Profession, 1917 and 1988: Changing Narratives of Legitimation', *Accounting, Organizations and Society* 20(6):507–46.

Pritchard, C. and Willmott, H. (forthcoming), 'Just How Managed is the McUniversity?' *Organization Studies*.

Prytherch, R. H. (1942), 'How Much Test-Checking is Enough?', *The Journal of Accountancy* 74(6):525–30.

Puxty, A., Sikka, P., and Willmott, H. (1994), 'Systems of Surveillance and the Silencing of Academic Labour', *British Accounting Review* 26:137–71.

Radcliffe, V. (1995), Knowing Efficiency: The Development and Operationalisation of Efficiency Auditing in Alberta, Ph.D., University of Alberta.

Randall, B. and Frishkoff, P. (1976), 'An Examination of the Status of Probability Sampling in the Courts', in Stettler (ed.) (1976), 93–102.

Rehbinder, E. (1992), 'Reflexive Law and Practice: The Corporate Officer for Environmental Protection as an Example', in Teubner and Febbrajo (eds.) (1992), 579–608.

Reiss, A. (1984), 'Selecting Strategies of Social Control over Organizational Life', in Hawkins and Thomas (eds.) (1984*b*), 23–35.

Rhodes, R. A. W. (1981), *Inspectorates in British Government* (London: George Allen and Unwin).

Rhodes, R. A. W. (1994), 'The Hollowing out of the State: the Changing Nature of the Public Service in Britain', *The Political Quarterly* 65(2):138–51.

Roberts, J. (1991), 'The Possibilities of Accountability', *Accounting, Organizations and Society* 16(4):355–68.

Roberts, S. and Pollitt, C. (1994), 'Audit or Evaluation? A National Audit Office VFM Study', *Public Administration* 72:527–49.

Rose, N. (1991), 'Governing by Numbers: Figuring out Democracy', *Accounting, Organizations and Society* 16(7):673–97.

Rose, N. (1996), 'The Death of the Social: Re-figuring the Territory of Government', *Economy and Society* 25(3):327–56.

Rose, N. and Miller, P. (1992), 'Political Power beyond the State: Problematics of Government', *British Journal of Sociology* 43(2):173–205.

Roslender, R. (1992), *Sociological Perspectives on Modern Accountancy* (London: Routledge).

Rousseau, M. (1988), 'France's Experience with Self-Monitoring to Combat Industrial Pollution', in UNEP (1988), 22–5.

Russell, P. (1991), 'Department of Trade and Industry Investigations', in Sherer and Turley (eds.) (1991), 76–98.

Russell, P. (1996), 'Exercising Self-Control', *Accountancy* (March), 126–7.

Sammalisto, K. (1995), 'Quality Auditors and Environmental Auditors: Can These Two Roles be Combined?', *Eco-Management and Auditing* 2(2):57–64.

Schneider, J. W. and Kitsuse, J. I. (eds.) (1984), *Studies in the Sociology of Social Problems* (Norwood, NJ: Ablex Publishing).

Schultz, J. J. and Brown, C. E. (eds.) (1983), *Symposium on Auditing Research V* (University of Illinois).

Self, P. (1993), *Government by the Market? The Politics of Public Choice* (London: Macmillan Press).

Selznick, P. (1994), 'Self-Regulation and the Theory of Institutions', in Teubner *et al.* (eds.) (1994), 395–402.

Shapiro, M. (1992), 'Data Audit by a Regulatory Agency: Its Effect and Implication for Others', *Accountability in Research* 2:219–29.

Shapiro, S. (1987a), 'Policing Trust', in Shearing and Stenning (eds.) (1987b), 194–220.

Shapiro, S. (1987b), 'The Social Control of Impersonal Trust', *American Journal of Sociology* 93(3):623–58.

Shaylor, M., Welford, R., and Shaylor, G. (1994), 'BS7750: Panacea or Palliative?', *Eco-Management and Auditing* 1(Part 2):26–30.

Shearing, C. and Stenning, P. (1987a), 'Reframing Policing', in Shearing and Stenning (eds.) (1987b), 9–18.

Shearing, C. D. and Stenning, P. C. (eds.) (1987b), *Private Policing* (Newbury Park, CA: Sage).

Shearn, D., Laughlin, R. C., Broadbent, J., and Willig-Atherton, H. (1995), 'The Changing Face of School Governor Responsibilities: A Mismatch between Government Intention and Actuality?' *School Organisation* 15(2):175–88.

Sherer, M. and Turley, S. (eds.) (1991), *Current Issues In Auditing* (London: Paul Chapman Ltd., 2nd edition).

Sherman, B. (1994), 'Governing Science: Patents and Public Sector Research', *Science in Context* 7(3):515–37.

Sherwood, K. (1990), 'An Auditor's Approach to Brands', in Power (ed.) (1990), 78–86.

Short, J. F. and Clarke, L. (eds.) (1992), *Organizations, Uncertainties and Risk* (Boulder: Westview Press).

Sieber, S. D. (1981), *Fatal Remedies: The Ironies of Social Intervention* (New York: Plenum Press).

Sikka, P. and Willmott, H. (1995), 'The Power of Independence: Defending and Extending the Jurisdiction of Accounting in the UK', *Accounting, Organizations and Society* 20(6):547–81.

Simmons, P. and Wynne, B. (1992), 'Responsible Care: Trust, Credibility and Environmental Management', in Fischer and Schot (eds.) (1992), 201–26.

Simmons, P. and Wynne, B. (1994), 'State, Market and Mutual Regulation? Socio-Economic Dimensions of the Environmental Regulation of Business', Lancaster University.

Sinclair, A. (1995), 'The Chameleon of Accountability: Forms and Discourses', *Accounting, Organizations and Society* 20(2/3):219–37.

Sitkin, S. and Stickel, D. (1996), 'The Road to Hell: The Dynamics of Distrust in an Era of Quality', in Kramer and Tyler (eds.) (1996), 196–215.

Sitkin, S. B. and Bies, R. J. (eds.) (1994), *The Legalistic Organization* (Thousand Oaks, CA: Sage).

Skerratt, L. and Tonkin, D. (eds.) (1996), *Financial Reporting 1995–6: A Survey of UK Reporting Practice* (Milton Keynes: Accountancy Books).

Smith, T. (1992), *Accounting for Growth* (London: Century Business).

Solomons, D. (1986), *Making Accounting Policy* (New York: Oxford University Press).

Sorensen, J. E., Grove, H. D., and Sorensen, T. L. (1980), 'Detecting Management Fraud: The Role of the Independent Auditor', in Geis and Stotland (eds.) (1980), 221–51.

Srivasta, R. P. and Rebele, J. E. (eds.) (1988), *Auditing Symposium IX: Proceedings of the 1988 Touche Ross/University of Kansas Symposium* (Kansas: University of Kansas).

Staub, W. A. (1904), 'Mode of Conducting an Audit', *The Accountant* 22 October, 453–8.

Staub, W. A. (1942), *Auditing Developments During the Present Century* (Cambridge Ma.: Harvard University Press).

Stempf, V. H. (1936), 'Influence of Internal Control Upon Audit Procedure', *Journal of Accountancy* 62(3):170–85.

Stephan, F. F. (1948), 'History of the Uses of Modern Sampling Procedures', *Journal of the American Statistical Association* 43:12–39.

Stettler, H. (ed.) (1976), *Auditing Symposium III: Proceedings of the 1976 Touche Ross/University of Kansas Symposium on Auditing Problems* (Kansas: University of Kansas).

Stettler, H. and Ford, N. (eds.) (1984), *Auditing Symposium VII: Proceedings of the 1984 Touche Ross/University of Kansas Symposium on Auditing Problems* (Kansas: University of Kansas).

Stevens, M. (1981), *The Big Eight* (New York: Macmillan Publishing).

Stigler, S. M. (1977), 'Eight Centuries of Sampling Inspection: the Trial of the Pyx', *Journal of the American Statistical Association* 72:493–500.

Stone, C. D. (1991), 'Beyond the Transactional Audit', *Cardozo Law Review* 12(5):1337–42.

Streeck, W. and Schmitter, P. (1985a), 'Community, Market, State—and Associations? The Prospective Contribution of Interest Governance to Social Order', in Streeck and Schmitter (eds.) (1985b), 1–29.

Streeck, W. and Schmitter, P. (eds.) (1985b), *Private Interest Government* (Beverly Hills, CA: Sage).

Sugarman, D. and Teubner, G. (eds.) (1990), *Regulating Corporate Groups* (Baden-Baden: Nomos).

Sullivan, J. D. (1984), 'The Case for the Unstructured Audit Approach', in Stettler and Ford (eds.) (1984), 61–8.

Sunstein, C. R. (1990), 'Paradoxes of the Regulatory State', *The University of Chicago Law Review* 57:407–41.

Tattersall, J. (1991), 'Auditing in the Financial Services Sector', in Sherer and Turley (eds.) (1991), 201–10.

Taylor, I. R. (1955), 'A Statistical Approach to Auditing', *Accounting Research* 6(1):49–57.

Taylor, E. M. and Perry, C. E. (1931), *Principles of Auditing* (London: Textbooks Limited).

Taylor, P. and Turley, S. (1986), *The Regulation of Accounting* (Oxford: Basil Blackwell).

Teubner, G., Farmer, L., and Murphy, D. (eds.) (1994), *Environmental Law and Ecological Responsibility: The Concept and Practice of Ecological Self-Organization* (Chichester: John Wiley).

Teubner, G. (1990), 'Unitas Multiplex: Corporate Governance in Group Enterprises', in Sugarman and Teubner (eds.) (1990), 67–104.

Teubner, G. and Febbrajo, A. (eds.) (1992), *State Law and Economy as Autopoietic Systems* (Milan: Giuffre).

Thomson, R. and Barton, A. (1994), 'Is Audit Running out of Steam?', *Quality in Health Care* 3:225–9.

Tomkins, C. (1986), 'Local Authority Audit under the Audit Commission and What it Means to one Private Sector Professional Firm', *Financial Accountability and Management* 2(1):35–51.

Tonkin, D. and Skerratt, L. (eds.) (1995), *Financial Reporting 1994–5: A Survey of UK Reporting Practice* (Milton Keynes: Accountancy Books).

Touche Ross (1994), *Risk Management and Control of Derivatives* (London: Touche Ross & Co).

Trow, M. (1993), 'Managerialism and the Academic Profession'. Paper presented at the 'Quality Debate' Conference, Milton Keynes, 24 September. Partly reprinted as 'The Business of Learning', *Times Higher Education Supplement* 8 October, 1993.

Trueblood, R. M. and Cyert, R. M. (1957), *Sampling Techniques in Accounting* (Engelwood Cliffs, NJ: Prentice Hall).

Tuckman, A. (1995), 'Ideology, Quality and TQM', in Wilkinson and Willmott (eds.) (1995b), 54–81.

Turley, S. (1989), 'Concepts and Values in the Audit Methodologies of Large Accounting Firms', in ICAS/ICAEW (1989).

Tyler, T. and Kramer, R. (1996), 'Whither Trust?' in Kramer and Tyler (eds.) (1996), 1–15.

Upson, A. (1995), 'Users Missing Out in the Internal Control Debate', *Accountancy Age* 26 October.

UNEP (1988), *Industry and Environment: Environmental Auditing* (Paris, United Nations Environmental Programme).

Van Cleve, G. (1991), 'The Changing Intersection of Environmental Auditing, Environmental Law and Environmental Policy', *Cardozo Law Review* 12(5):1215–40.

Vance, L. L. (1950), *Scientific Method for Auditing* (Berkeley and Los Angeles: University of California Press).

Vance, L. L. and Neter, J. (1956), *Statistical Sampling for Auditors and Accountants* (John Wiley).

Van Gunsterten, H. R. (1976), *The Quest for Control: A Critique of the Rational–Central–Rule Approach in Public Affairs* (Chichester: John Wiley).

Van Maanen, J. and Pentland, B. (1994), 'Cops and Auditors: the Rhetoric of Records', in Sitkin and Bies (eds.) (1994), 53–90.

Van Matre, J. G. and Clark, W. N. (1976), 'The Statistician as Expert Witness', *The American Statistician* February, 2–5.

Vinten, G. (ed.) (1995), *Whistleblowing: Subversion or Corporate Citizenship?* (London: Paul Chapman Publishing).

Vogel, D. (1986), *National Styles of Regulation: Environmental Policy in Britain and the United States* (Ithaca: Cornell University Press).

Walsh, K. (1995), 'Quality through Markets: The New Public Service Management', in Wilkinson and Willmott (eds.) (1995b), 82–104.

Watts, R. L. and Zimmerman, J. L. (1979), 'The Demand for and Supply of Accounting Theories: The Market for Excuses', *The Accounting Review* 54:273–304.

Weait, M. (1993), 'Icing on the Cake? The Contribution of the Compliance Function to Effective Financial Services Regulation', *The Journal of Asset Protection and Financial Crime* 1(1):83–90.

Welford, R. (1992), *European Environment, Special Supplement: The Eco-Audit Scheme and the British Standard on. Environmental Management Systems* (Bradford: European Research Press Ltd.).

Westergaard, M. (1932), *Contributions to the History of Statistics* (London: King).

White, F., Harden, I., and Donnelly, K. (1994), 'Audit and Government Accountability—A Framework for Comparative Analysis', Political Economy Research Centre, Working Paper 2, Sheffield University.

White Paper (1989), *Working for Patients* (London: HMSO Cmd 555).

White Paper (1993), *Realizing Our Potential: A Strategy for Science, Engineering and Technology* (London: HMSO Cm 2250).

Wilensky, H. (1967), *Organizational Intelligence* (New York: Basic Books).

Wilkinson, A. and Willmott, H. (1995a), 'Introduction', in Wilkinson and Willmott (1995b), 1–32.

Wilkinson, A. and Willmott, H. (eds.) (1995b), *Making Quality Critical* (London: Routledge).

Willmott, H. (1995), 'Managing the Academics: Commodification and Control in the Development of University Education in the UK', *Human Relations* 48(9):993–1027.

Wilson, G. K. (1984), 'Social Regulation and Explanations of Regulatory Failure', *Political Studies* XXXII:203–25.

Wolnizer, P. W. (1987), *Auditing as Independent Authentication* (Sydney: Sydney University Press).

Woolston, H. (1993), *Environmental Auditing: an Introduction and Practical Guide* (London: British Library).

Yates, F. (1946), 'A Review of Recent Statistical Developments in Sampling and Sampling Surveys', *Journal of the Royal Statistical Society* 109:12–30.

Zukin, S. and DiMaggio, P. (eds.) (1990), *Structures of Capital: The Social Organization of the Economy* (Cambridge: Cambridge University Press).

INDEX

Page numbers in the form '148 n.' refer to Notes.